CORPORATIONS AND TRANSNATIONAL HUMAN RIGHTS LITIGATION

Since the mid-1980s, beginning with the unsuccessful Union Carbide litigation in the USA, litigants have been exploring ways of holding multinational corporations [MNCs] liable for offshore human rights abuses in the courts of the company's home States. The highest profile cases have been the human rights claims brought against MNCs (such as Unocal, Shell, Rio Tinto, Coca Cola, and Talisman) under the Alien Tort Claims Act in the United States. Such claims also raise issues under customary international law (which may be directly applicable in US federal law) and the Racketeer Influenced and Corrupt Organizations [RICO] statute. Another legal front is found in the USA, England and Australia, where courts have become more willing to exercise jurisdiction over transnational common law tort claims against home corporations. Furthermore, a corporation's human rights practices were indirectly targeted under trade practices law in groundbreaking litigation in California against sportsgoods manufacturer Nike. This new study examines these developments and the procedural arguments (eg regarding personal jurisdiction and especially *forum non conveniens*) which have been used to block litigation, as well as the principles that can be gleaned from cases which have settled. The analysis is important for human rights victims in order to know the boundaries of possible available legal redress. It is also important for MNCs, which must now take human rights into account in managing the legal risks (as well as moral and reputation risks) associated with offshore projects.

Volume 4 in the series Human Rights Law in Perspective

Human Rights Law in Perspective
General Editor: Colin Harvey

The language of human rights figures prominently in legal and political debates at the national, regional and international levels. In the UK the Human Rights Act 1998 has generated considerable interest in the law of human rights. It will continue to provoke much debate in the legal community and the search for original insights and new materials will intensify.

The aim of this series is to provide a forum for scholarly reflection on all aspects of the law of human rights. The series will encourage work which engages with the theoretical, comparative and international dimensions of human rights law. The primary aim is to publish over time books which offer an insight into human rights law in its contextual setting. The objective is to promote an understanding of the nature and impact of human rights law. The series is inclusive, in the sense that all perspectives in legal scholarship are welcome. It will incorporate the work of new and established scholars.

Human Rights Law in Perspective is not confined to consideration of the UK. It will strive to reflect comparative, regional and international perspectives. Work which focuses on human rights law in other states will therefore be included in this series. The intention is to offer an inclusive intellectual home for significant scholarly contributions to human rights law.

Volume 1 Importing the Law in Post-Communist Transitions

Catherine Dupré

Volume 2 The Development of the Positive Obligations Under the European Convention on Human Rights by the European Court of Human Rights

Alastair Mowbray

Volume 3 Human Rights Brought Home: Socio-Legal Studies of Human Rights in the National Context

Edited by Simon Halliday and Patrick Schmidt

Corporations and Transnational Human Rights Litigation

SARAH JOSEPH
Monash University, Melbourne

·HART·
PUBLISHING
OXFORD – PORTLAND OREGON
2004

Hart Publishing
Oxford and Portland, Oregon

Published in North America (US and Canada) by
Hart Publishing c/o
International Specialized Book Services
5804 NE Hassalo Street
Portland, Oregon
97213-3644
USA

Distributed in the Netherlands, Belgium and Luxembourg by
Intersentia, Churchillaan 108
B2900 Schoten
Antwerpen
Belgium

© Sarah Joseph 2004

Sarah Joseph has asserted her right under the Copyright, Designs and
Patents Act 1988, to be identified as the authors of this work

Hart Publishing is a specialist legal publisher based in Oxford, England.
To order further copies of this book or to request a list of other
publications please write to:

Hart Publishing, Salter's Boatyard, Folly Bridge,
Abingdon Road, Oxford OX1 4LB
Telephone: +44 (0)1865 245533 or Fax: +44 (0)1865 794882
e-mail: mail@hartpub.co.uk
WEBSITE: http//www.hartpub.co.uk

British Library Cataloguing in Publication Data
Data Available
ISBN 1-84113-457-0 (hardback)

Typeset by Hope Services (Abingdon) Ltd
Printed and bound in Great Britain on acid-free paper by
TJ International, Padstow, Cornwall

Contents

Series Editor's Preface	ix
Preface	xi

1 Introduction — 1
- Informal Accountability — 6
- Self Regulation — 7
- Legal Accountability — 8
  - International Human Rights Law — 8
  - National Laws — 11
  - Extraterritorial Laws — 12
- Transnational Human Rights Litigation against Corporations — 13
  - Criminal Liability — 13
  - Civil Liability — 14
  - Common Law and Civil Law — 15
  - Litigation in the United States of America — 16
  - Litigation in non-US forums — 19
- Conclusion — 20

2 The Alien Tort Claims Act — 21
- Historical Development of the ATCA — 21
- Human Rights Norms within 'the Law of Nations' — 22
- Requirement of State Action — 33
  - Abstention Issues Associated with State Action Doctrine — 39
  - Act of State — 40
    - Political Question — 44
    - Comity — 46
- Private Actor Abuses — 48
- A Summary of Corporate Complicity under ATCA — 50
- The International Treaty Limb of ATCA — 53
- Choice of Law under ATCA — 54
- The Future for ATCA — 55
  - Rolling back *Filartiga*: Attacks upon the ATCA in Litigation — 55
  - Potential Legislative Amendments — 60
  - Consequences of Defusing the ATCA — 61
- The Torture Victim Protection Act — 61
- Conclusion — 63

3 Other Jurisdictional Bases in the US — 65

Tort Jurisdiction — 65
  A Brief Overview of Relevant Tort Principles — 67
  Doe v Unocal — 68
  Other Examples of Transitory Tort Cases — 72
  Choice of Law — 74
  Do Tort Cases against Private Sector Parties Raise Human Rights Issues? — 76
Jurisdiction under § 1331 — 77
Liability under RICO — 78
Conclusion — 81

4 Procedural Obstacles in the US — 83

Personal Jurisdiction — 83
Forum non Conveniens — 87
  Deference to Plaintiff's Choice — 88
  Adequate Alternative Forum — 89
  Public Interests Considerations — 92
  Weighing Respective Private Interests — 94
  Retaliatory Legislation: Trumping *Forum non Conveniens*? — 96
  Conditional FNC Dismissals — 97
  Conclusion on FNC in the US — 98

5 A New Front: The *Nike* Case — 101

The Case of *Kasky v Nike* — 101
Assessment of the *Nike* Case — 106
  Corporate Rights of Freedom of Expression — 107
  Corporate Silence: An Undesirable Consequence of the *Nike* Case — 109
  Improving the Quality of the Debate regarding Corporations and Human Rights — 111

6 Transnational Human Rights Litigation in Other Countries — 113

England — 113
  Extraterritorial Jurisdiction over Corporations — 113
  Subject Matter Jurisdiction — 115
  Forum non Conveniens in England — 115
  Choice of Law — 119
  Advantages and Disadvantages of Litigation in England — 120
Australia — 122
Canada — 125
Conclusion — 128

7	**Parent Corporation Liability in Transnational Human Rights Cases**	129
	The Corporate Veil	129
	Joint Liability	132
	Direct Parent Liability	134
	Multinational Group Liability	138
	Multinational Economic Networks	142
	Conclusion	143
8	**Conclusion**	145
	Summary of Current Litigation	145
	Is Transnational Human Rights Litigation against TNCs 'a Good Thing'?	148
	Litigation Pressure will Increase	151
	The Limits of Transnational Human Rights Litigation against Companies	153
	An International Approach?	153
Appendix: Table of Selected Cases		155
Index		171

Series Editor's Preface

This book examines the role of human rights litigation in challenging the actions of transnational corporations. The starting point for the study is that these corporations commit human rights abuses; and on occasions their actions amount to serious criminal behaviour. It offers useful guidance on the nature, scope and limitations of this form of transnational legal action. The study will be of interest not just to individuals seeking redress, but also to corporations wishing to manage risk. The work puts the debate in context by highlighting just how powerful these corporations are and the difficulties facing any individual or group taking the path of transnational litigation. Dr Sarah Joseph explores the different methods (formal and informal) for holding corporations to account. There is a particular focus on the US, but other jurisdictions are included (Australia, Canada and the UK). Dr Joseph outlines developments so far, the main procedural obstacles and includes her thoughts on possible future directions. This book is an impressive and balanced assessment of the law and practice which recognises the potential and limits of this litigation. She asks whether the trend is a 'good thing', and advances arguments in support of it, but notes that whatever view is taken it is unlikely to disappear. It seems that if old avenues are closed down new ones will be discovered in the search to make transnational corporations accountable for the consequences of their actions.

Colin Harvey
July 2004

Preface

This book is the product of an Australian Research Council Linkage grant on 'Multinational Corporations and Human Rights', awarded to myself and other members of the Castan Centre for Human Rights Law at the Monash Law Faculty in 2001. Our industry partners for this grant are Premier Oil (UK) and Futureye.

The book analyses the phenomenon of transnational human rights litigation against companies in a number of jurisdictions. The majority of the salient cases have been brought in the United States under the *Alien Tort Claims Act* [ATCA], as detailed in Chapter 2. Just as I completed the substantive manuscript in early December 2003, word came through of a pending challenge to the constitutionality of ATCA, and, in the alternative, the prevailing broad interpretation of that statute, in the US Supreme Court in *Sosa v Alvarez*. That case is expected to be decided in June or July of 2004. Thus, I faced the nightmare of any academic legal author: a sudden significant change in the law! I am grateful to my publisher, Richard Hart, for his willingness to proceed with the book as scheduled, rather than wait six months for the decision in that case. An update regarding the decision in *Sosa v Alvarez* and its impact on the issues raised in this book will be available via the publisher's website at www.hartpub.co.uk/updates.html. In any case, the demise of ATCA, if it should occur in the *Sosa* decision, will not signal the end of transnational human rights litigation against companies. As is discussed in Chapters 2, 3 and 5, alternative causes of action, which may provide wholesale replacements for ATCA, are available or potentially available in the US. The existing bases of transnational human rights litigation in non-US jurisdictions, as detailed in chapter 6, will be unaffected by any major change in the law regarding ATCA.

Most of this book was written during a sabbatical spent at the University of Minnesota Law School in late 2002. I am grateful to that faculty for their hospitality, especially David Weissbrodt (and family!), Kristi Rudelius-Palmer, Mary Thacker, and Kevin Washburn (and family!). The balance of the book was written during a period of teaching relief funded by the ARC in late 2003.

I must also thank the following people, in alphabetical order, who provided invaluable information in the writing of this book: Irene Bahgoomanians, Judith Chomsky, Terry Collingsworth, Jenny Green, Rick Herz, Richard Jones, Justine Nolan, Beth Stephens, and Halina Ward. David Weissbrodt, Adam McBeth, Robert McCorquodale, Christian Witting, David Kinley and Mark Davison provided much-appreciated feedback on earlier drafts of the manuscript or individual chapters. Jenny Schultz did a sterling job of proofreading, while Tori Elliot and Anne McCasland-Pexton assisted in the preparation of footnotes. Adam McBeth and Tori Elliott are largely responsible for the Appendix which provides brief details of the salient cases. I must of course add thanks to Colin Harvey for his faith in commissioning the book in the first place! Finally, I must thank the staff at the Castan Centre for Human Rights Law, the Monash Law Faculty, and especially my family and friends for their support.

Dr Sarah Joseph
Castan Centre for Human Rights Law
Monash University

May 2004

1
Introduction

TRANSNATIONAL CORPORATIONS (TNCs)[1] are very powerful entities in the current world order. Indeed, it is trite to note that the power of some TNCs outstrips the power of certain nation-states.[2] In 2000, the Institute for Policy Studies reported that corporations made up 51 of the top 100 'economies' in the world.[3] The same report recorded that the top 200 TNCs had a combined revenue in 2000 greater than the combined GDPs of all States excluding those of the top ten countries.[4] Given the enormous economic and consequent de facto political power exercised by TNCs, which is aided by the increased rate of globalised economic interdependence and freer international markets, it is not surprising that TNCs can and do influence the enjoyment of internationally recognised human rights by a wide range of people, including employees, consumers, people who live in the area of their operations, and other stakeholders.[5]

---

[1] In the UN document Norms on the Responsibilities of Transnational Corporations and other Business Enterprises with regard to Human Rights' (2003) UN doc E/CN/.4/Sub.2/2003/12/Rev.2 (2003), a TNC is defined in paragraph 20 therein as 'an economic entity operating in more than one country or a cluster of economic entities operating in two or more countries—whatever their legal form, whether in their home country or country of activity, and whether taken individually or collectively.' A TNC may also be defined as 'a cluster of corporations of diverse nationality joined together by ties of common ownership and responsive to a common management strategy'; this definition has been adapted from D Vagts, 'The Multinational Enterprise: A New Challenge for Transnational Law' (1970) 83 *Harvard Law Review* 739, 740, quoting Vernon, 'Economic Sovereignty at Bay' (1968) 47 *Foreign Affairs* 110, 114. It is conceded that numerous definitions for TNCs, or alternatively, 'multinational corporations' or 'multinational enterprises' have been put forward by economists and international organisations; see generally P Muchlinski, *Multinational Enterprises and the Law* (Oxford, Blackwell, 1995) 12–15.

[2] See C Grossman and D Bradlow, 'Are We Being Propelled Towards a People-Centered Transnational Legal Order?' (1993) 9 *American University Journal of International Law and Policy* 1, 8–9; D Cassel, 'International Security in the Post Cold-War Era': Can International Law Truly Affect Global Political and Economic Stability? Corporate Initiatives: A Second Human Rights Revolution?' (1996) 19 *Fordham International Law Journal* 1963, 1963 and 1979; F Johns, 'The Invisibility of the Transnational Corporation: An Analysis of International Law and Legal Theory' (1994) 19 *Melbourne University Law Review* 893, 904; Muchlinski, *ibid* at 6–7.

[3] Sarah Anderson and John Cavanagh, 'Top 200: The Rise of Global Corporate Power' *Institute for Policy Studies*, 4 December 2000 <http://www.ips-dc.org/reports/top200.htm> (12 August 2003). The list of the 'top 100 economies in 1999' in Table 2 therein was compiled by comparing the GDPs of States from the World Bank's World Development Report of 2000, and the sales figures of the top corporations as reported in *Fortune* magazine.

[4] *Ibid*. Again, the data was calculated using figures from the World Bank's World Development Report of 2000.

[5] See S Joseph, 'Taming the Leviathans: Multinational Enterprises and Human Rights' (1999) 46 *Netherlands International Law Review* 171, 173–74. The following paragraph also comes largely from this source.

2   *Introduction*

Of course, corporate activity can facilitate the increased enjoyment of human rights worldwide.[6] For example, TNCs may promote economic development, which enhances a population's enjoyment of most human rights.[7] Nevertheless, there is no doubt that TNCs can and do perpetrate human rights abuses. For example, TNCs can mistreat and exploit their workforces, thereby breaching labour rights.[8] TNCs may have lax rules regarding worker safety, which threaten workers' rights to health and at worst, their rights to life.[9] Lax safety regulations can also threaten the lives of people in the vicinity of manufacturing plants, evinced catastrophically in 1984 in Bhopal, India when toxic gas leaked out of a Union Carbide Plant, killing 2000 people and injuring over 200,000. TNC activity can cause extensive environmental damage, which can impact on numerous rights, including the rights to health, minority rights, and the right to self-determination.[10] For example, Shell's oil extractions in Ogoniland in Nigeria caused grave environmental harm, with consequent impacts on the rights to food and an adequate standard of living.[11] Irresponsible marketing policies can hide the dangers of hazardous products, and pose an unacceptable threat to the life and health of consumers; relevant products might include unsafe drugs or consumables,[12] automobiles with minimal safety features, and

---

[6] See, eg, WH Meyer, 'Human Rights and TNCs: Theory Versus Quantitative Analysis' (1996) *Human Rights Quarterly* 368, 391–97.

[7] *Ibid* at 368, quoting K Pritchard, 'Human Rights and Development: Theory and Data' in DP Forsythe *Human Rights and Development* (Basingstoke, Macmillan, 1989) 329; see also Cassel, above n 2, at 1980.

[8] See generally, 'Human Rights: Ethical Shopping' *The Economist* (London, United Kingdom, 3 June 1995) 58. Labour rights are recognised under a variety of international treaty provisions, such as numerous International Labor Organisation [ILO] Conventions.

[9] One's right to health is recognised under the International Covenant on Economic Social and Cultural Rights [ICESCR], article 12; the right to life is recognised under International Covenant on Civil and Political Rights [ICCPR], article 6. As an example of such an occurrence, the British company Thor made an 'explicit decision' to export its hazardous mercury business to South Africa, after facing criticism and regulation of the same practices in the UK; see M Anderson, 'Transnational Corporations and Environmental Damage: Is Tort Law the Answer?' (2002) 41 *Washburn Law Journal* 399, 403, n 12. See also *Ngcobo v Thor and Sithole v Thor*, unreported decisions of the Queen's Bench, discussed in R Meeran, 'Liability of Multinational Corporations: A critical stage in the UK' in M Kamminga and S Zia-Zarifi (eds), *Liability of Multinational Corporations under International Law* (The Hague, Kluwer, 2000) 251, 255–56.

[10] Minority rights are recognised under the ICCPR, article 27, and self-determination is recognised under article 1 of both Covenants. See, on TNCs and self-determination, Johns, above n 2, at 907–8.

[11] The rights to food and an adequate standard of living are recognised in ICESCR, article 11. See generally J Eaton, 'The Nigerian Tragedy, Environmental Regulation of Transnational Corporations, and the Human Right to a Healthy Environment' (1997) 15 *Boston University International Law Journal* 261, 264–71, and S Skogly, 'Complexities in Human Rights Protection: Actors and Rights Involved in the Ogoni Conflict in Nigeria' (1997) 15 *Netherlands Quarterly of Human Rights* 47.

[12] An example of inappropriate marketing of consumables was the marketing by Nestlé of unsuitable baby-milk products in Africa, which ultimately led to the adoption by the World Health Organisation ['WHO'] of an International Code of Marketing of Breast-Milk Substitutes 1981; see Muchlinski, above n 1, at 7, n 19.

cigarettes.[13] TNCs may also abuse their power and pervert the political processes within a State, undermining democratic rights.[14] A most dramatic example of this was the attempted overthrow of the Allende government in 1970 in Chile, which was engineered in large part by ITT, an American TNC.[15] Less spectacular, but nevertheless anti-democratic, is the use of bribery to influence governments to adopt policies that are beneficial to a TNC.

As TNCs have expanded their operations across the world, they have increasingly found themselves operating in countries with serious civil unrest, and/or very bad human rights records. Commercial operations in such countries, particularly the large scale projects of mining and energy corporations, often face opposition which is occasionally violent, and their personnel and infrastructure can be endangered in these volatile situations.[16] A growing number of companies have consequently employed local army divisions or unofficial paramilitary forces to provide security for their installations, a situation aptly described by Professor Forcese as 'militarised commerce'.[17] Some TNCs in such situations have been accused of colluding with these military units in perpetrating egregious human rights abuses, including torture and killings,[18] and even genocide, war crimes and crimes against humanity,[19] against opponents of their foreign ventures. For example, such allegations have been levelled at Shell[20] and Chevron[21] regarding their respective operations in Nigeria, the Canadian energy company Talisman in Sudan,[22] Exxon in Aceh in Indonesia,[23] Freeport

---

[13] See generally on human rights and tobacco marketing, J Wike, 'The Marlboro Man in Asia: US Tobacco and Human Rights' (1996) 29 *Vanderbilt Journal of Transnational Law* 330.

[14] Democratic rights, in the form of the right to equal participation in public affairs, are recognised under article 25 ICCPR. See generally, T Franck, 'The Emerging Right to Democratic Governance' (1992) 86 *American Journal of International Law* 52.

[15] See 53 UN ESCOR (1822nd mtg) 19, 22, UN Doc E/SR, 1822 (1972). A successful coup was mounted against the Allende government in 1973.

[16] C Forcese, 'Deterring 'Militarized Commerce': The Prospect of Liability for 'Privatized' Human Rights Abuses' (2000) 31 *Ottawa Law Review* 171, 173.

[17] *Ibid*.

[18] Torture is prohibited by article 7 ICCPR and the Convention Against Torture and Other Cruel Inhuman or Degrading Treatment or Punishment [CAT]. Security of the person is protected by article 9 ICCPR.

[19] Genocide, war crimes, and crimes against humanity are prohibited by treaties such as the Genocide Convention, the Geneva Conventions, and the treaties establishing the International Criminal Court, as well as the ad hoc international courts for Yugoslavia and Rwanda. It is generally accepted that these crimes are prohibited by customary international law and even *jus cogens*. See, eg, *Restatement (Third) of the Foreign Relations Law of the United States* § 702 (1987).

[20] *Wiwa v Royal Dutch Petroleum* 96 Civ 8386, 2002 US Dist LEXIS 3293 (SDNY 2002). See also Cassel, above n 2, at 1965–66.

[21] *Bowoto v Chevron Texaco Corp* No 99-2506 SI, 2004 US Dist LEXIS 4603 (ND, Cal 2004). See also Forcese, above n 16, at 179–80. The role of oil companies in human rights abuses in Nigeria, including discussion of the allegations against Chevron and especially Shell, are discussed in Human Rights Watch, *The Price of Oil: Corporate Responsibility and Human Rights Violations in Nigeria's Oil Producing Communities* (New York, Human Rights Watch, 1999).

[22] *Presbyterian Church of Sudan v Talisman Energy* 244 F Supp 2d 289 (SDNY 2003).

[23] See also T Collingsworth, 'Boundaries in the Field of Human Rights: The Key Human Rights Challenge: Developing Enforcement Mechanisms' (2002) *Harvard Human Rights Journal* 183, 190–91, on the Exxon litigation, where no interim decisions had been made at the time of writing.

4   *Introduction*

McMoran in Irian Jaya in Indonesia,[24] Rio Tinto in Bougainville in Papua New Guinea,[25] and BP in Colombia.[26] The energy companies Unocal and Total have been accused of colluding with the government of Myanmar to coerce local people into forced labour to work on the construction of an oil pipeline in that country.[27] Coca Cola has been accused of involvement in the killing of a trade union leader and intimidation of other union members at a bottling plant in Colombia.[28] Similar allegations have been directed at Del Monte with regard to the detention and torture of trade union leaders involved in a dispute with its business partners in Guatemala.[29] As a final example, Enron has been accused of complicity in suppressing opposition to its energy operations in India.[30]

TNCs are capable of abusing human rights, like probably all entities. The effects of TNC abuse are however amplified by the inherent power of TNCs. A key question therefore arises: how may TNCs be held *accountable* for the perpetration of human rights violations?

The most obvious source of accountability is regulation by the State in which the abuses occur. The types of human rights abuses highlighted above, barring the extraordinary 'militarised commerce' examples, can occur anywhere in the world. However, most of the recent criticisms of corporate human rights practices have focused on their behavior in developing nations,[31] where the accelerated process of economic globalisation has generated a marked increase in multinational activity and foreign direct investment.[32] TNCs are often more economically powerful than the developing States in which they operate, many of which perceive that they need to attract TNC investment in order to develop their economies. Vulnerable and/or corruptible governments may lack the political will to enact or enforce corporate human rights liability laws,[33] fearing that

[24] *Beanal v Freeport-McMoran Inc* 197 F 3d 161 (5th Cir 1999). See Forcese, above n 16, at 182–3.
[25] *Sarei v Rio Tinto Plc* 221 F Supp 2d 1116 (CD Cal 2002).
[26] See Forcese, above n 16, at 176–7; see also 'BP hands "tarred" in Pipeline Dirty War', *Guardian* (London, United Kingdom, 17 October 1998) 20.
[27] *Doe v Unocal* 2002 US App LEXIS 19263 (9th Cir 2002) and *Doe v Unocal* 27 F Supp 2d 1174 (CD Cal 1998). See also Collingsworth, above n 23, at 188–90 and Forcese, above n 16, at 178–9.
[28] See Collingsworth, *ibid* at 191–3. A court has recently found that Coca Cola was not responsible for the acts of its Colombian business partners, in *Sinaltrainal v Coca-Cola Co* 256 F Supp 2d 1345 (SD Fla 2003). Rights of association are recognised under article 22 of the ICCPR, while trade union rights of association are also recognised under article 8 of the ICESCR, and a number of ILO treaties.
[29] Collingsworth, above n 23, at 193–195.
[30] See Human Rights Watch, *The Enron Corporation: Corporate Complicity in Human Rights Violations* (New York, Human Rights Watch, 1999), and Forcese, above n 16, at 181–2.
[31] See however Joseph, above n 5, at 199–201 on the potential for TNCs to impact detrimentally on human rights in developed countries.
[32] Note that most foreign direct investment continues to take place in developed States; see Muchlinski, above n 1, at 30–1.
[33] See S Zia-Zarifi, 'Suing Multinational Corporations in the US for Violating International Law' (1999) 4 *University of California at Los Angeles Journal of International Law and Foreign Affairs* 81, 86–7; J Cassels, 'Outlaws: Multinational Corporations and Catastrophic Law' (2000) 31 *Cumberland Law Review* 311, 313, 317–19; B Stephens, 'Corporate Liability: Enforcing Human Rights Law through Domestic Litigation' (2001) 24 *Hastings International and Comparative Law Review* 401, 402. An extraordinary example of a country actually enacting legislation to protect a

greater regulation and accountability, for example in the environmental or labour arenas, may provoke TNCs to withdraw their investments.[34] Furthermore, developing nations may have underdeveloped legal systems, and therefore may lack the legal and technical expertise to properly regulate TNC operations.[35] For example, developing nations may lack the legal machinery, such as resources to undergo complex discovery of documents, to unravel the corporate veil which may shield an asset-rich parent company behind an asset-poor local subsidiary.[36] Even if the veil is lifted to expose the parent, the judgment may not be enforceable in the jurisdiction where the parent's assets are located.[37] Alternatively, it may be practically impossible for many plaintiffs to seek redress in developing nations, as legal aid is rarely available.[38] The consequent result can be that the TNC operates in a developing host State with effective impunity.[39] The danger of TNC impunity within a host State is particularly high with regard to examples of militarised commerce, where the TNC is accused of colluding with host governments in the perpetration of human rights violations and even atrocities. In such situations, it is often futile and even dangerous for the victims of militarised commerce to seek legal redress in the State where the violations occur.

Of course, legal accountability is not completely absent in the developing world.[40] Nevertheless, it is presently unsatisfactory and unrealistic to expect

company was in Papua New Guinea regarding BHP's possible liability for environmental damage in its operations on the Ok Tedi river basin; PNG enacted the *Compensation (Prohibition of Foreign Legal Proceedings) Act* 1995 (PNG), which rendered the seeking of compensation in a foreign court a criminal offence. 'BHP's lawyers apparently drafted the legislation': M Whincop and M Keyes, *Policy and Pragmatism in the Conflict of Laws* (Aldershot, Ashgate, 2001) 116–17. See ch 6, p 124, on the litigation regarding the Ok Tedi mine in Australia.

[34] S Joseph, 'An Overview of the Human Rights Accountability of Multinational Enterprises' in M Kamminga and S Zia-Zarifi, above n 9, at 78. See also Muchlinski, above n 1, at 44–45 and 228–33, describing the phenomenon of Export Processing Zones in developing States, where pro-business regulatory regimes operate within 'policy enclaves'.

[35] See, eg, Cassels, above n 33, at 317, describing the inadequacy of Indian safety standards for regulating operations such as that of Union Carbide in Bhopal in the early 1980s; Cassels states that India's standards were 'based on a paradigm of labor-intensive low-tech industry'; see also H Ward, 'Securing Transnational Corporate Accountability through National Courts: Implications and Policy Options' (2001) 24 *Hastings International and Comparative Law Review* 451, 463–64. See also Anderson, above n 9, at 417–18.

[36] Joseph, above n 5, at 177; World Development Movement, *A Law unto Themselves—Holding Multinationals to Account: Discussion Paper* (September 1998) 4.

[37] For example, a recent judgment against Shell, Dow Chemicals, and Standard Fruit by a Nicaraguan court was found to be unenforceable by a Californian court. 'Nicaragua: Pesticide Claim Dismissed' *New York Times* (New York 25 October 2003). See also ch 8, text at and in n 13.

[38] See, *Lubbe v Cape plc* [2000] 4 All ER 268 (HL) and *Connelly v RTZ Corporation plc* [1998] AC 854 (HL).

[39] See also GGA Tzeutschler, 'Corporate Violator: The Alien Tort Liability of Transnational Corporations for Human Rights Abuses Abroad' (1999) 30 *Columbia Human Rights Law Review* 359, 361–62, 382.

[40] See H Ward, 'Legal Issues in Corporate Citizenship', Swedish Partnership for Global Responsibility, February 2003 <http://www.iied.org/docs/cred/legalissues_corporate.pdf> (29 December 2003) 25, detailing a new initiative by the Thai Department of Labour Protection and Social Welfare aimed at addressing 'the lack of enforcement on labour issues and to promote compliance with voluntary labour standards'.

6 *Introduction*

TNC human rights accountability with regard to a certain operation to emanate exclusively from the host State in which that operation exists.[41] Therefore, it is necessary to examine alternative sources and forms of accountability.

INFORMAL ACCOUNTABILITY

The most visible form of TNC accountability regarding human rights abuses has arisen in the informal, non-governmental arena.[42] Most noticeable to the public at large have been the protests and disruptions, aimed at economic globalisation in general rather than TNCs in particular, at major intergovernmental and economic world meetings since the 'Battle of Seattle' in 1999. Non-governmental organisations (NGOs) have become highly adept at mobilising public opinion against unethical corporations.[43] Numerous prominent corporations have suffered the wrath of high profile negative NGO campaigns, including Nestlé, Shell, McDonalds, Coca Cola, and Nike.[44] Negative publicity about a corporation's ethics can lead to consumer boycotts, as well as difficulties in attracting or retaining quality staff. Consumer outrage can inspire regulatory action by governments[45] or shareholder revolts.[46] Furthermore, non-governmental activism has had tangible results in making TNCs change their behaviour. For example, such pressure has encouraged many TNCs to disengage from States which commit gross and pervasive violations of human rights.[47] Finally, grassroots criticism has encouraged many corporations to adopt internal codes of conduct, an increasingly common form of self-regulation which is discussed directly below.[48]

---

[41] See Joseph, above n 34, at 78.

[42] See PJ Spiro, 'New Global Potentates: Nongovernmental Organisations and the 'Unregulated' Marketplace' (1996) 18 *Cardozo Law Review* 957, 959–60; 'Human Rights: Ethical Shopping', *The Economist* (London, United Kingdom, 3 June 1995) 58; 'The Fun of Being a Multinational' *The Economist* (New York, United States, 20 July 1996) 51.

[43] See Spiro, above n 42, at 959–60; R McCorquodale, 'Human Rights and Global Business' in S Bottomley and D Kinley (eds), *Commercial Law and Human Rights* (Aldershot, Ashgate, 2002) 111–13.

[44] Non-governmental activism can also exist at a level short of confrontation and campaigns against corporate bad behaviour. Instances of NGO/corporate dialogue in the arena of ethics and human rights are increasingly common. NGO/corporate engagement is important, as businesspeople are unlikely to be human rights experts, so they need assistance in addressing and even recognising human rights issues.

[45] See, eg, Mass Gen Laws ch 7, §§ 22G–22M (West Supp 1998), a Massachusetts law that prohibited the state from contracting with companies that did business with Myanmar (Burma). This statute was ultimately ruled unconstitutional in *Crosby v National Foreign Trade Council* 530 US 363 (SCt, 2000).

[46] Spiro, above n 42, at 960.

[47] See Spiro, above n 42, at 959; 'The Fun of Being a Multinational' *The Economist* (London, United Kingdom, 20 July 1996) 51.

[48] S Webley (IBE), 'The Nature and Value of Internal Codes of Conduct in M Addo (ed), *Human Rights Standards and the Responsibility of Transnational Corporations* (The Hague, Kluwer Law International, 2000) 107–13. This paragraph has been largely dapted from Joseph, above n 34, at 81.

Grassroots activism may currently be the best known mechanism for encouraging TNC respect for human rights. However, there are limits to the effectiveness of NGO campaigns. Professor McCorquodale has noted that such pressure, and 'therefore the resultant impact', has been 'piecemeal and inconsistent'.[49] True accountability can only arise if these unofficial watchdogs are supplemented by formal, *legal* mechanisms for holding TNCs liable for human rights abuse.[50]

Alongside activism designed to mobilise consumers, there are also initiatives designed to harness the power of investors to catalyse socially responsible conduct on the part of companies within investment portfolios. 'Socially responsible investment' [SRI] products, where companies are included or excluded on the basis of their social and/or environmental records, are widely available from many investment institutions.[51] Various reporting criteria have been formulated, such as those in the Global Reporting Initiative,[52] which assist companies in producing social and environmental reports to market their ethical credentials to SRI funds and/or directly to investors. At present, SRI has had only a small impact on investor behaviour. For example, there is no clear evidence that the share price of delinquent companies drops as a result of negative publicity.[53] Therefore, one may doubt the present-day efficacy of SRI per se as a brake on irresponsible corporate behaviour.

SELF-REGULATION

There has been a recent trend of corporations adopting their own voluntary codes of conduct, which address the need for respect for human rights.[54] These codes can set minimum standards for the company's own behaviour, as well as standards for the types of countries the company will be willing to invest in, and

---

[49] McCorquodale, above n 43, at 112.
[50] See also Anderson, above n 9, at 404
[51] There is a wide variation in the criteria used to identify a 'socially responsible' company for the purpose of SRI products. For example, corporate social responsibility may be evinced by improvement in one's practices, adherence to a certain set of global standards, or by representing the 'best practice' in a certain sector. See A McBeth, 'The Role and Responsibilities of the Finance Industry in Relation to Human Rights: A Legal Analysis' (unpublished paper, on file with the author) 3–5. Note, for example, that the Dow Jones Sustainability Index, which may be used by investors and SRI managers to evaluate companies, generally uses a 'best in class' approach, and includes British American Tobacco [BAT] as the 'best' tobacco company (see www.sustainability-index.com). On the other hand, the FTSE4Good index, the parallel evaluation mechanism in the UK, automatically excludes any company involved in tobacco; see <http://www.ftse.com/ftse4good/FTSE4GoodCriteria.pdf> (5 January 2003).
[52] See <http://www.globalreporting.org> (5 January 2003).
[53] S Zadek and M Forstater (New Economics Foundation), 'Making Civil Regulation Work' in Addo, above n 48, at 70. On the other hand, adverse judicial decisions have influenced share prices; see Ward, above n 35, at 464.
[54] Joseph, above n 34, at 82–83.

standards for the behaviour of acceptable business partners.[55] Furthermore, industry-wide codes have been adopted by groups of like companies, such as the Apparel Industry Partnership Initiative in the United States[56] and the Fairwear campaign in Australia,[57] as well as cross-industry codes such as the Ethical Trading Initiative in the United Kingdom.[58] The growing number of codes may indicate that corporations, including TNCs, are now taking issues of human rights and other ethical matters seriously.

It may be premature to assess the real impact of corporate codes of conduct on corporate behaviour. However, there are reasons for reservations about their efficacy. Codes only bind those corporations that adopt them, which are by no means all corporations. Moreover, there are concerns that the adoption and publication of such codes are often public relations exercises.[59] Codes will not be effective unless there is vigorous enforcement and independent monitoring of their implementation. It is doubtful that most codes are policed to a satisfactory extent. It seems too easy for a TNC to flout the requirements of its own code when serious profits are at stake.[60] Self-regulation cannot be relied upon as a primary means of ensuring respect for human rights by TNCs. Such voluntary measures must be supplemented by legally binding standards.[61]

LEGAL ACCOUNTABILITY

International Human Rights Law

TNCs have been accused of, and have indeed perpetrated, acts that breach internationally recognised human rights. Therefore, it is instructive to examine the extent to which TNCs are liable in international human rights law for the abuses that they commit.

A starting point for the liability of TNCs under international human rights law is the Universal Declaration of Human Rights (UDHR), where the preamble

---

[55] See, generally, K Gordon and M Miyake, 'Deciphering Codes of Corporate Conduct: A Review of their Contents', (OECD Working Papers on International Investment, Number 1999/2, 29 November 1999); RJ Liubicic, 'Corporate Codes of Conduct and Product Labelling Schemes: The Limits and Possibilities of Promoting International Labor Rights' (1998) 30 *Law and Policy in International Business* 111.

[56] See J Johnson, 'Public-Private-Public Convergence: How the Private Actor can shape Public International Labour Standards' (1998) 24 *Brooklyn Journal of International Law* 291, 299–302.

[57] See D Kinley, 'Human Rights as Legally Binding or Merely Relevant' in S Bottomley and D Kinley (eds), above n 43, at 33–36.

[58] See <www.ethicaltrade.org> (18 August 2003).

[59] See JC Anderson, 'Respecting Human Rights: Multinational Corporations Strike Out' (2000) 2 *University of Pennsylvania Journal of Labor and Employment Law* 463, 489. See also Liubicic, above n 54, at 140–50.

[60] S Skogly, 'Economic and Social Human Rights, Private Actors, and International Obligations' in Addo, above, note 48, at 249–51.

[61] See also 'Private Initiatives for Corporate Responsibility: An Analysis' (OECD Working Papers on International Investment, Number 2001/1, 14 February 2001) 18.

states that 'every organ of society' is bound to abide by its substantive human rights provisions. However, international human rights law is not well adapted to hold TNCs accountable for the human rights abuses that they perpetrate. In international human rights law, only the State is generally charged with duties to secure human rights for individuals within jurisdiction. This is symptomatic of the State-centric focus of public international law.[62]

Nevertheless, international human rights law has made some progress towards imposing human rights duties in the non-government sphere. Human rights duties are recognised as having a tripartite character: States are required to respect, protect and ensure the enjoyment of human rights by persons within jurisdiction.[63] In order to properly fulfil their duties to protect and ensure enjoyment of human rights, States must control private entities within jurisdiction. These duties are expressly enunciated in certain treaties, such as article 2(e) on the Convention on the Elimination of all Forms of Discrimination against Women, and can be inferred from the general obligatory provisions of the International Covenants.[64] The 'horizontal' application of international human rights, ie the duty of States to give effect to human rights between private parties, has also been confirmed in international human rights jurisprudence.[65] In this way, non-government bodies like TNCs are targeted indirectly under international law. Direct responsibility, including the obligation to enforce those indirect duties, continues however to reside with national governments.

Exceptionally, some duties are imposed directly on non-governmental bodies in international law. For example, non-governmental bodies are prohibited under customary international law and under certain treaties from committing universal crimes, such as piracy, genocide, war crimes, and crimes against humanity. The extent of the liability of non-governmental bodies under customary international law is highly uncertain. The international criminal tribunals for Rwanda and Yugoslavia, and the International Criminal Court [ICC], have jurisdiction to try individuals for war crimes, crimes against humanity, and genocide.[66] However, this does not mean that those crimes are the *only* ones for which non-governmental liability may attach; it simply means

---

[62] Joseph, above n 5, at 175.

[63] See 'Maastricht Guidelines on Violations of Economic, Social And Cultural Rights' (1998) 20 *Human Rights Quarterly* 691, [6], see also H Shue, *Basic Rights: Subsistence, Affluence and United States Foreign Policy* (New Jersey, Princeton University Press, 1980) 57.

[64] For example, the Human Rights Committee has confirmed that the duty to 'respect' and 'ensure' Covenant rights in article 2(1) of ICCPR requires States parties to protect people from abuses of their rights by other people; see generally S Joseph, J Schultz, and M Castan, *The International Covenant on Civil and Political Rights: Cases, Commentary and Materials* 2nd edn, (Oxford University Press, 2004), 36–37.

[65] *Ibid.* See also *Awas Tingni Community v Nicaragua*, case no 79, Inter-Am CHR (Judgment of the Inter-American Court of Human Rights of 31 Aug 2001); and *Social and Economic Rights Action Center v Nigeria*, Comm 155/96, Ref: ACHPR/COMM/A044/1 (African Commission on Human and People's Rights, 27 May 2002). In both decisions, violations of rights were entailed inter alia, in a state's failure to prevent human rights abuses by corporations.

[66] The ICC has no jurisdiction over artificial bodies like corporations. Under Article 25, it has jurisdiction only over 'natural persons'.

that they are the only 'non-governmental international crimes' for which an international tribunal has subject matter jurisdiction.[67] Given the lack of relevant international tribunals, it is not surprising that the most comprehensive judicial discussion of non-governmental liability under customary international law has arisen in national courts, particularly in human rights litigation against corporations under the *Alien Tort Claims Act* in the US.[68]

There do exist 'soft', non-binding international law instruments which act as guides for the appropriate behaviour of TNCs,[69] such as the Draft United Nations Code of Conduct on Transnational Corporations,[70] the OECD Guidelines for Multinational Enterprises, June 2000,[71] the ILO Tripartite Declaration of Principles Concerning Multinational Enterprises and Social Policy (1977),[72] and the UN Global Compact.[73] Of course, the fact of non-enforceability does not render these documents worthless; the standards therein can be useful points of reference for national governments that wish to impose binding domestic duties on TNCs, for NGOs seeking ammunition for campaigns against certain TNCs, and for corporations adopting and implementing internal codes of conduct.

The most comprehensive proposed outline of human rights duties for TNCs is the 'United Nations Norms on Responsibilities of Transnational Corporations and Other Business Enterprises with Regard to Human Rights',[74] which was adopted by the UN Sub-Commission on the Promotion and Protection of Human Rights in its 2003 session. The current document envisages enforceability of the norms by 'national courts and/or international tribunals, pursuant to national and international law'.[75] Therefore, the Norms could usher in a level of direct international enforceability of human rights responsibilities against TNCs.

In April 2004, the document was considered by the UN Comission on Human Rights. The Commission, by consensus, noted the importance of the issue of corporate human rights responsibility, and recommended that its parent body,

---

[67] For example, there is no doubt that piracy by non-governmental entities is prohibited in international law, even though no international tribunal currently has jurisdiction over this crime.
[68] See ch 2, pp 48–49.
[69] See generally Kinley, above n 57.
[70] See Annex to UN doc E/1990/94.
[71] Organisation for Economic Co-operation and Development (OECD), *OECD Guidelines for Multinational Enterprises: Revision 2002*, (Paris, OECD Publications 2000) <http://www.oecd.org/dataoecd/56/36/1922428.pdf> (23 December 2003).
[72] Reprinted in 17 *International Legal Materials* 422 (1978) [hereafter, ILO Declaration].
[73] The UN Global Compact is a promotional rather than a quasi-regulatory instrument. Businesses are encouraged to sign up to the Compact and commit to adhere to its nine core principles, which relate to the protection and promotion of human rights, labour standards, and environmental standards. See, generally, <http://www.unglobalcompact.org> (5 January 2003). See also B King, 'The UN Global Compact: Responsibility for Human Rights, Labor, and the Environment in Developing Nations' (2001) 34 *Cornell International Law Journal* 481, and WH Meyer, 'Human Rights, the UN Global Compact, and Global Governance' (2001) 34 *Cornell International Law Journal* 501.
[74] United Nations, *United Nations Norms on the Responsibilities of Transnational Corporations and Other Enterprises with Regard to Human Rights*, UN doc E/CN/.4/Sub.2/2003/12/Rev.2 (2003).
[75] *Ibid*, para 18.

Legal Accountability 11

the Economic and Social Council, request of the High Commissioner for Human Rights to Compile a comprehensive report on the topic, to be considered by the Commission in 2005. No specific action was taken on the Norms, though there is clearly scope for future action.[76]

In any case, it is likely that any future international enforceability will be confined to the small category of universal crimes, rather than the norms in toto. It is difficult to imagine the creation of an international tribunal with the capacity to deal with all potential human rights abuses by TNCs, given the range of duties outlined in the Norms and the vast number of TNCs in the world. Therefore, in the short to medium term at least, human rights responsibilities for TNCs will be largely enforced by national rather than international bodies, even if the Norms are transformed into binding international law.

Presently, in the absence of internationally binding comprehensive human rights duties for TNCs, one must look to national laws to uncover the extent of the current legal accountability of TNCs for human rights abuses.

National Laws

Of course, relevant municipal laws have existed for many years in many countries which impose domestic human rights responsibilities on corporations, such as laws regarding anti-discrimination, sexual harassment, workplace relations, environmental standards, occupational health and safety, and consumer welfare.[77] Bills of rights will be particularly relevant if they are applied as between private parties, as is arguably the case in the UK.[78] Criminal laws will apply in some States to punish certain types of egregious corporate behaviour.[79]

Such corporate accountability laws tend to exist in developed nations. As noted above, greater standards of behaviour from TNCs are often demanded by developed countries compared to developing nations.[80] Developing countries often lack appropriate legal mechanisms and/or the political will to enforce relevant mechanisms. A question therefore arises regarding the extent to which accountability for corporate operations in developing host countries can be imposed extraterritorially. As it is generally recognised in international law that States can exercise extraterritorial jurisdiction over wrongs committed abroad by their own nationals,[81] perhaps greater regulation of TNCs should

---

[76] See Decision 2004/116 in UN doc E/CN.4/2004/L.11/Add.7, p 82.
[77] See, for a list of relevant cases involving both legislation and common law in the US, JJ Paust, 'Human Rights Responsibilities of Private Corporations' (2002) 35 *Vanderbilt Journal of Transnational Law* 801, 808–9, especially n 23.
[78] See, eg, *Venables v News Group Newspapers* [2001] 1 All ER 98; *Re A (Children) (Conjoined Twins)* [2000] 4 All ER 961 (CA). In these cases, the *Human Rights Act* assisted the Court in resolving a clash of rights between two private parties. However, it is arguable that the pre-existing law would have sufficed to resolve the cases in a similar way.
[79] See, eg, Crimes Amendment (Corporate Manslaughter) Bill 2003 (NSW).
[80] See also Eaton, above n 11, at 274.
[81] Muchlinski, above n 1, at 124.

12 *Introduction*

come from the home States of TNCs, their States of incorporation,[82] which are usually developed countries.[83] For example, the developed home State is more likely to possess the requisite technical expertise to impose adequate safety standards, and to have a legal system more able to cope with the proper attribution of responsibility within complex corporate arrangements.[84]

Extraterritorial Laws

International human rights law has not yet evolved so as to hold States responsible for the actions of their non-government citizens, including corporate nationals, abroad.[85] Home States are not currently liable in international human rights law for failing to prevent, punish, or otherwise regulate the delinquencies of their TNCs' overseas operations. In the absence of such a legal obligation, home States have been reluctant to regulate the extraterritorial activities of their TNCs; they may perceive that such regulation puts their corporations at a competitive disadvantage with other countries' corporations.[86] Nevertheless, in the last few years, creative litigants have forged potential new paths for holding TNCs liable in the courts of their developed home countries for their allegedly egregious activities in developing host countries. That is, TNCs are being sued at home for their alleged extraterritorial human rights abuses.

Of course, the extraterritorial application of a State's law to regulate actions which occur in another State can be very controversial. Instances of the extraterritorial regulation of TNCs will likely emanate from developed States. Given that reality, the extraterritorial application of laws arguably impinges on the sovereignty of the territorial State, and perhaps amounts to a form of 'judicial imperialism' by developed countries over their former colonies. A less symbolic concern is that the extraterritorial application of laws can result in the imposition of protectionist laws, which strip other countries of legitimate competitive

---

[82] See *Barcelona Traction Light and Power Co Ltd Case* [1970] ICJ Rep 3 (ICJ) para 70.
[83] See Eaton, above n 11, at 274, n 76, citing R Fowler, 'International Environmental Standards for Transnational Corporations' (1995) 25 *Environmental Law* 1, 2, in stating that ninety per cent of the world's TNCs originate in developed nations. See also Muchlinski, above n 1, at 31.
[84] See, eg, Eaton, above n 11, at 278, n 88. Note however that complex jurisdictional issues are likely to arise with regard to home State jurisdiction over foreign subsidiaries or affiliates; States have very different rules regarding the existence of jurisdiction in such situations; see generally Muchlinski, above n 1, at 126–71. See also generally, ch 7.
[85] Johns, above n 2, at 895–96; Joseph, above n 5, at 178. See however, arguing that such a duty might exist, M Sornarajah, 'Linking State Responsibility for Certain Harms caused by Corporate Nationals Abroad to Civil Recourse in the Legal Systems of Home States' in C Scott (ed) *Torture as Tort* (Oxford, Hart Publishing, 2001) 491, especially at 507–11. The Convention on Combating Bribery of Public Officials in International Business Transactions 1997 (available via <http://www.oecd.org>), Arts 2 and 4, is a rare example of a treaty that explicitly obliges States to regulate their citizens' extraterritorial behaviour. See also *OECD Guidelines For Multinational Enterprises*, above n 71, at para 1.2. The UN Norms, on the other hand, are silent on this issue.
[86] See Cassel, above n 2, at 1975; Eaton above n 11, at 276; P Spiro, 'New Players on the International Scene' (1997) 2 *Hofstra Law and Policy Symposium* 19, 30.

advantages, disguised as human rights enforcement.[87] On the other hand, arguments may be raised that it is unjust and immoral to permit corporations to escape liability for violations of human rights simply because the victim is from a developing country, when an analogous victim in a developed country could expect redress.

This book is largely concerned with an analysis of the phenomenon and mechanics of transnational human rights litigation, rather than the desirability of such. However, the latter is raised throughout the book, particularly in Chapter 8.

TRANSNATIONAL HUMAN RIGHTS LITIGATION AGAINST CORPORATIONS

Criminal Liability

The most egregious examples of TNC human rights abuse are not only human rights violations; they amount to serious criminal behaviour. For example, if one assumes that the allegations cited above regarding militarised commerce are true, corporations have been guilty either directly of or as an accessory to crimes of torture, murder, genocide, and enslavement. Is it possible for a home State to hold its corporations criminally liable for such egregious acts if committed in another jurisdiction?

In most States, criminal laws generally only apply to acts committed or at least partially committed within the territory and jurisdiction of the State applying the criminal law.[88] Therefore, a TNC's overseas act could perhaps be subjected to prosecution at home if the impugned actions were planned, and in some way partially executed, in the boardrooms at headquarters.[89] Exceptionally, States may apply criminal laws to their own citizens for acts committed in another jurisdiction.[90] Even rarer are instances of a State exercising universal jurisdiction to prosecute non-nationals who have committed universal crimes, such as war crimes, genocide, and crimes against humanity, under the principal of universal jurisdiction. Until recently, Belgium had a controversial law enabling the prosecutions in that country of perpetrators of extreme human rights violations anywhere in the world, regardless of the nationality of the perpetrators or the victims. Under this law, the French energy company Totalfinaelf was being

---

[87] Joseph, above n 34, at 86.
[88] See Forcese, above n 16, at 186–87. See also J Clough, 'Not-so Innocents Abroad: Corporate Criminal Liability For Human Rights Abuses' (unpublished, manuscript on file with the author, 2003).
[89] See Forcese, above n 16, at 190.
[90] See Clough, above n 88, and Forcese, above n 16, at 190–92 (for Canadian examples). See eg, the *Foreign Corrupt Practices Act* 5 USC §§ 78dd–1, 781, 78o (1994), providing for civil and criminal enforcement against individuals and corporations in respect of bribery of foreign officials, whether at home or abroad; see also *Criminal Code Act* (Cth), s 270(3), which makes it a criminal offence to have engaged in the slave trade inside or outside Australia.

investigated over allegations of complicity in forced labour in Myanmar, which could have opened the way to criminal prosecution of the company.[91] Belgium however recently amended the relevant law so that it now only applies to Belgian citizens and long-term residents, or where the victims are Belgian, presumably forestalling any criminal action against Totalfinaelf.[92]

A comprehensive discussion of the potential for criminal prosecutions of companies for overseas human rights abuses is beyond the scope of this book. It will suffice to note that no TNC has recently been prosecuted for transnational human rights abuses.[93] All of the instances thus far of transnational human rights litigation against corporations are civil rather than criminal.

Civil Liability

It may seem that civil suits trivialise human rights abuses, and that criminal prosecutions would be more appropriate tools of human rights accountability.[94] Nevertheless, civil suits can potentially result in huge damages awards, directly harming TNCs' financial bottom line, a 'language TNCs can understand and follow'.[95] Civil suits may also encourage out-of-court settlements that deliver a measure of redress to aggrieved plaintiffs.[96] They can lead to a thorough investigation and airing of salient facts,[97] which may have critical consequences for a

---

[91] See, generally, <http://www.birmanie.net/birma/frame11.html> (15 November 2002) and S Smis and K Van der Borght, 'Legislation, Belgium: Act Concerning the Punishment of Grave Breaches of International Humanitarian Law' (1999) 38 *International Legal Materials* 918.

[92] These legislative changes were prompted by US pressure after prosecutions were launched against various US political and military leaders, including President George W Bush, Donald Rumsfeld, Colin Powell, and General Tommy Franks, as well as British Prime Minister Tony Blair, with regard to their alleged actions during the invasion of Iraq in 2003. See 'Universal Incompetence' *The Economist* (New York, United States, 28 June 2003) 54.

[93] However, TotalFinaElf is currently being investigated in France with a view to the laying of possible criminal charges regarding its alleged actions in Myanmar; see Ward, above n 40, at 17.

[94] B Stephens, 'Translating Filartiga: A Comparative and International Law Analysis of Domestic Remedies for International Human Rights Violations' (2002) 27 *Yale Journal of International Law* 1, 26–27, 31–32. See also Anderson, above n 9, at 423.

[95] Zia-Zarifi, above n 33, at 146.

[96] For example, litigation against a number of garment companies regarding their work practices in *Doe v The Gap* No CV–01–0031, 2001 WL 1842389 (DN Mar I Nov 6, CD Cal 2001) was recently settled. The settlement provides for monetary compensation as well as the implementation and independent monitoring of better work practices; see International Restructuring Education Network Europe (IRENE), *Lawsuits against Multinational Corporations for Labor Rights Violations* (Amsterdam, September 2002) 42 (copy on file with the author). Litigation against Chentex Garments regarding the firing of 700 unionised workers in Nicaragua was settled in 2001, with the reinstatement and payment of double back pay to those union leaders and members, as well as the dropping of criminal charges against the relevant union members; see IRENE, at 47. *Lubbe v Cape Plc* [2000] 4 All ER 268 (HL) was settled in 2001 with the proposed payment by Cape of £21 million into a trust fund for persons suffering asbestos-related diseases as a result of Cape's former operations in South Africa; see IRENE, at 52. See also ch 2, n 196, on the settlement of the 'Holocaust' litigation against various companies.

[97] Stephens, above n 94, at 14.

corporation's reputation even in the absence of a finding of legal liability, as 'embarrassing mismatches' between corporate rhetoric and their actions on the ground may be exposed.[98] They can have a significant adverse effect on a corporation's share price.[99] Litigation can also raise the profile of relevant concurrent NGO campaigns, giving campaigners much-needed publicity and leverage.[100] Furthermore, civil suits can be instigated by victims themselves, whereas criminal laws normally must be activated by a State official, such as a District Attorney or an Attorney-General,[101] who may not always have the political will to take action against a home corporation in order to vindicate the grievances of offshore victims. Finally, from a pragmatic point of view, civil suits are offering a means of rendering corporations legally responsible for their human rights abuses, thus deterring human rights abusive conduct and providing remedies or at least vindication to victims[102] in the current absence of criminal prosecutions.[103]

Common Law and Civil Law

So far, transnational human rights litigation against corporations has arisen, almost exclusively, in common law countries.[104] Courts in common law countries may exercise civil jurisdiction over foreigners and foreign companies regarding their extraterritorial actions; this is not generally the case in civil law countries.[105] However, the lenient common law rules regarding the exercise of personal jurisdiction over non-resident aliens cannot be the main reason for the effective confinement of such cases to common law countries, as most of the

---

[98] Ward, above n 35, at 465.
[99] Ward, *ibid* 464, notes that Cape plc's shares dropped 27% on the day that a procedural decision of the House of Lords went against it in *Lubbe v Cape Plc* [2000] 4 All ER 268 (HL). *Lubbe* is discussed below in ch 6, p 117–18.
[100] See Collingsworth, above n 23, at 193, describing how litigation against Coca Cola has focused attention on a union campaign against Coke regarding its allegedly antipathetic practices towards trade unions. For more information, see www.cokewatch.com.
[101] J Terry, 'Taking Filartiga on the Road: Why Courts outside the United States should accept Jurisdiction over Actions involving Torture Committed Abroad' in Scott, above n 85, at 116–17. See also Anderson, above n 9, at 409.
[102] See Tzeutschler, above note 39, at 377–78, noting how plaintiffs are often motivated by a desire for vindication and a change in TNC policies rather than monetary damages. See also, generally, Terry, *ibid* at 111–18.
[103] Anderson, above n 9, at 424.
[104] The only cases in civil law jurisdictions have arisen under Louisiana state jurisdiction, and in Quebec. Both Louisiana and Quebec are constituent parts of nations that generally operate under a common law system.
[105] European civil law States generally only exercise jurisdiction in tort claims when the tort occurs within jurisdiction, or where the alleged tortfeasor is domiciled in the State, jurisdictional bases which are enshrined in the Brussels Convention on Jurisdiction and the Enforcement of Judgments in Civil and Commercial Matters. See Stephens, above n 94, at 24. In contrast, common law States are able to exercise jurisdiction over foreign persons for their overseas actions; see below, pp 83–87 and 113–14.

salient cases have been pursued against corporate nationals.[106] A more likely reason for the lack of relevant cases in civil law countries is that civil law countries rely far less than common law countries on litigation and the consequent generation of judicial precedent to develop the law.[107] The common law system therefore allows for judges to be more creative and influential in solving the legal problems before them, which enhances the chances of success for plaintiffs who are bringing novel legal arguments.[108]

In fact, the great majority of the salient cases have arisen in one jurisdiction, the United States, due to the existence of a number of unique causes of action available in that country, as well as the distinctive plaintiff-friendly nature of the US legal system. Therefore, Chapters 2–5 focus on developments in the US. However, there have been a few cases in the United Kingdom, Australia, and Canada, which are discussed in Chapter 6.

Litigation in the United States of America

The US is the site of most of the litigation discussed in this book. The predominant role of US courts is explained by a number of factors. To begin with, the US has a number of laws, such as the *Alien Tort Claims Act*, the *Torture Victim Protection Act*, and the *Racketeer Influenced and Corrupt Organisations* statute, which provide plaintiffs with unique substantive causes of action against TNCs that have breached their human rights.

Notwithstanding these unique laws, the US is in any case an especially desirable forum for plaintiffs asserting civil claims against TNCs for breaches of human rights due to a number of important procedural advantages. First, unsuccessful litigants are not required to pay opponents' costs, unless the claim is deemed utterly vexatious. This is particularly important in these corporate human rights cases, where the legal arguments raised are novel and therefore especially risky.[109] Second, a plaintiff's lawyer often acts on a contingency basis, significantly lowering a plaintiff's own legal costs in case of a loss. The lucrative potential rewards for a successful law firm encourage lawyers to run such cases.[110] There is also a substantial public interest legal sector in the US willing to take on such cases for minimal fees.[111] Third, comparative studies have

---

[106] Indeed, the lenient Anglo-American approach to personal jurisdiction is offset by the ability of common law courts to dismiss cases due to the existence of a more convenient forum. This doctrine of *forum non conveniens* [FNC], which has proven to be a stumbling block for many human rights litigants, does not generally exist in civil law countries. See below, ch 4 on FNC in the US, and ch 6 for a discussion of FNC in other countries.

[107] Ward, above n 40, at 16.

[108] See James G Apple and Robert P Deyling, *A Primer on the Civil Law System*, Federal Judicial Center, <http://www.fjc.gov/public/pdf.nsf/lookup/CivilLaw.pdf/$file/CivilLaw.pdf> (7 January 2003) 37.

[109] Stephens, above n 94, at 29.

[110] *Ibid* at 30.

[111] *Ibid* at 30.

shown that US damages awards tend to be higher than in other States.[112] For example, 'punitive' damages, which are not designed to compensate plaintiffs but to punish defendants, and express 'society's revulsion for [the impugned] conduct', are more commonly awarded in the US.[113] Fourth, US rules regarding discovery are comparatively lenient to plaintiffs, which is of great importance when much evidence is likely to lie in the corporate defendant's control.[114] It is certainly true that 'the US legal system offers a uniquely supportive framework for civil lawsuits seeking damages for international human rights abuses',[115] which is important when (as is often the case) redress is simply unavailable in the country where the alleged abuse takes place.

Criticisms may fairly be raised about the litigious nature of US society, and the prospect of corporations being unduly harassed by human rights suits. The early transnational human rights cases were generally brought by public interest litigators against foreign government officials, who were unlikely to satisfy any resultant damages award. Favourable judgments for plaintiff human rights victims provided an important measure of vindication for such plaintiffs, but rarely provided them with financial compensation. The same is not likely to be true of litigation against corporations, which have deeper pockets and are less able to flee the jurisdiction. The prospect of huge human rights claims against corporations could attract avaricious commercial lawyers bent on haranguing corporations to gain a lucrative slice of a class action settlement.[116] There are fears that this brand of litigation could mutate into a form of global 'ambulance-chasing'.[117] However, concerns about aggressive and unworthy lawsuits are hardly unique to human rights litigation in the US; they arise as a natural corollary to the plaintiff-friendly nature of the US legal system.

Transnational human rights cases in the US against TNCs have been brought on a number of bases. The most celebrated of these legal routes is the *Alien Tort Claims Act* (ATCA) of 1789, an ancient statute that permits aliens to sue in US courts for breaches of their rights under the law of nations. ATCA has been interpreted to permit aliens to sue persons for committing egregious breaches of their human rights. Since 1997, a number of ATCA cases have been brought against TNCs for alleged perpetration of severe human rights abuses in their offshore operations. ATCA plaintiffs against corporations have a number of

---

[112] *Ibid* at 31.
[113] *Ibid* at 15: 'A punitive damages claim thus transforms a civil 'action into one that shares certain attributes with a criminal prosecution'.
[114] *Ibid* at 15–16.
[115] *Ibid* at 16.
[116] See GC Hufbauer and NK Mitrokostas, *Awakening Monster: The Alien Tort Statute of 1789* (Washington DC, Institute of International Economics, 2003) 77–84, drawing parallels between human rights litigation against companies, and the history of US asbestos litigation, described by the authors at p 83 as 'a lavish welfare program for lawyers' (at p 83); see also pp 47–8. See also E Schrage, 'Judging Corporate Accountability in the Global Economy' (2003) 42 *Columbia Journal of Transnational Law* 153, 154.
[117] Schrage, *ibid* at 154.

18 *Introduction*

significant substantive legal hurdles to clear before they are successful. For example, in most instances, the plaintiff must confirm the existence of state action in order to ground an ATCA case, by establishing a sufficient link between the corporation's actions and those of a government.[118] Often corporations have been accused of aiding and abetting abuses committed by governments, so US courts have also had to grapple with concepts of accessory liability under the statute. Only in rare instances will an ATCA claim lie in the absence of state action, though such instances have arisen in the ATCA corporate cases. The state action requirement gives rise to the likely relevance of a number of principles upon which courts may abstain from exercising jurisdiction, due to the potential interference posed by the litigation to the foreign affairs powers of the US federal government. The complexities of the ATCA cases against corporations are analysed in Chapter 2.

The *Torture Victim Protection Act* (TVPA) was enacted by the US Congress in 1991 as an adjunct to *ATCA*. It explicitly provides for a civil cause of action for both aliens and US citizens against individuals who commit torture, or extrajudicial killings, under the 'apparent authority' of a foreign government. The TVPA has not been extensively explored in US case law, as it is almost completely blanketed by ATCA.[119] However, at the time of writing, there was a pending Supreme Court challenge to ATCA, which could result in that statute's emasculation or even a declaration of constitutional invalidity. In such a circumstance, the TVPA would provide a replacement cause of action in many of the pending ATCA cases against TNCs, especially those concerning 'militarised commerce'. The TVPA is discussed at the end of Chapter 2.

Most of the salient US cases have arisen under ATCA. A number of other litigation strategies, discussed in Chapters 3 and 5, are nevertheless available to prospective human rights litigants in the US. Two particular actions are often appended as alternative causes of action in ATCA cases against corporations. Under 28 USC § 1331, US federal courts have jurisdiction to hear cases arising under the US Constitution and US federal laws. Arguably, such laws include customary international law as a species of federal common law. Numerous ATCA cases have included claims that the human rights abuses at issue constituted violations of customary international law, thus giving rise to § 1331 jurisdiction.[120] The *Racketeer Influenced and Corrupt Organisations* statute (RICO) has also been invoked as an alternative basis of corporate liability in the relevant ATCA cases. Though RICO was originally enacted to tackle organised crime groups, the scope of the definition of 'racketeering' is so broad that it can, in some instances, encompass human rights abuses committed by corporations.[121]

---

[118] In transnational human rights cases, this government will normally be a foreign government. ATCA actions can however lie in circumstances where the relevant government is the US government; see, eg, *Alvarez-Machain v US* 331 F 3d 604 (9th Cir 2003).

[119] The TVPA does extend ATCA jurisdiction in one respect, by providing a cause of action to US citizens.

[120] See, eg, *Bodner v Banque Paribas* 114 F Supp 2d 117 (EDNY 2000).

[121] *Wiwa v Royal Dutch Petroleum* 96 Civ 8386, 2002 US Dist LEXIS 3293 (SDNY 2002).

US cases brought under ATCA, TVPA, § 1331, and RICO usually concern allegations of extreme human rights abuse. An alternative, if less dramatic, legal front is also available in such cases, and in cases regarding 'lesser' forms of human rights abuse, in the US. Such cases may be brought as ordinary tort claims.[122] Finally, groundbreaking litigation arose under Californian law against sporting goods giant Nike, which was sued under trade practices legislation for allegedly making false and misleading commercial statements regarding its overseas labour practices.[123] The Nike litigation is distinguishable in that the corporation was not sued directly over its alleged human rights abuses abroad. However, in targeting a corporation's attempts to defend its reputation by allegedly sanitising its human rights record, the *Nike* plaintiffs were indirectly seeking to improve corporate conduct abroad.

Litigants in the US must overcome a number of procedural hurdles, which are examined in Chapter 4, in order to successfully proceed with a transnational human rights suit against a corporation. If the defendant corporation is a foreigner, the plaintiff must establish that the relevant US court has personal jurisdiction over that defendant. Plaintiffs must also normally fend off applications by defendants to have the case dismissed on the ground of *forum non conveniens* (FNC). Under this doctrine, a US court may dismiss a suit on the grounds that a foreign forum is a more convenient site for the litigation. FNC has proven to be a particularly burdensome obstacle for transnational human rights plaintiffs.[124] However, recent decisions indicate that US courts may be becoming more amenable to exercising jurisdiction over transnational civil claims against home[125] and even foreign corporations.[126]

Litigation in non-US forums

A handful of salient cases have arisen outside the United States in the UK, Australia, and Canada. These cases have essentially been based on ordinary tort law, as these forums lack the extraordinary bases of claim, such as ATCA and TVPA, that exist in the US. There is however the possibility of claims in the UK and Canada being based on international law directly incorporated into domestic law. The procedural hurdles of personal jurisdiction and FNC also exist in these jurisdictions. Ironically, considering the reputation of the US for plaintiff

---

[122] See, eg, *In re Union Carbide Corp Gas Plant Disaster at Bhopal* 634 F Supp 842 (SDNY 1986) 867 and *Martinez v Dow Chemical Co* 219 F Supp 2d 719 (ED La 2002).

[123] *Kasky v Nike* 27 Cal 4th 939 (2002). The case settled in 2003. See generally, ch 5.

[124] P Blumberg, 'Asserting Human Rights Against Multinational Corporations under United States Law: Conceptual and Procedural Problems' (2002) 50 *American Journal of Comparative Law* 493, 505.

[125] *Martinez v Dow Chemical Co* 219 F Supp 2d 719 (ED La 2002) and *Bowoto v Chevron* Case no 99–2506 (NDC 1999).

[126] *Wiwa v Royal Dutch Petroleum* 226 F 3d 88 (2d Cir. 2000) and *Presbyterian Church of Sudan v Talisman Energy* 244 F Supp 2d 289 (SDNY 2003).

friendliness, these procedural obstacles are probably easier to overcome in these non-US jurisdictions. Litigation in non-US forums is discussed in Chapter 6.

CONCLUSION

None of the salient cases has yet been decided on the merits.[127] Therefore, a number of issues have not been comprehensively addressed in any of the cases in any of the jurisdictions. The most important outstanding issue relates to the circumstances in which a parent company will be held liable for the actions of its subsidiaries. This issue is crucial as most of the alleged human rights abuses in these cases have been perpetrated in a developing country by a subsidiary corporation in that country which may lack sufficient capital to provide adequate redress, and/or which may not be amenable to personal jurisdiction in the TNC's 'home' country. To what extent can a human rights litigant pierce the corporate veil, or, alternatively, directly target the parent company for its actions or omissions regarding supervision of its subsidiary? This issue is addressed in Chapter 7. Chapter 8 concludes the book, and contains some observations on the desirability of the phenomenon of transnational human rights litigation against companies.

This book details and analyses the developments in these recent civil cases, to serve as a guide to the new ways in which corporations may be liable in domestic courts for human rights abuses. Even though there are no final merits judgments, the interim decisions to date give important clues as to the possible extent of modern transnational corporate human rights liability. This analysis is thus important for transnational human rights victims in order to know the boundaries of possible available legal redress. It is also important for TNCs, which must now take human rights into account in managing the legal risks (as well as moral and reputation risks) associated with offshore projects.

---

[127] A number have been finally dismissed prior to a full merits hearing, or settled.

2
The Alien Tort Claims Act

MOST OF THE transnational human rights cases against corporations have arisen under the *Alien Tort Claims Act* [ATCA] in the US. At the time of writing, the constitutionality and interpretation of this statute were the subject of an appeal before the US Supreme Court, which has never previously considered such matters. An update on the decision, *Sosa v Alvarez-Machain*, and its effect on matters discussed in this chapter, will be available soon after publication of the decision, expected in June or July 2004, via the publisher's website: www.hartpub.co.uk/updates.html.

HISTORICAL DEVELOPMENT OF THE ATCA

The ATCA states:

> The district courts shall have original jurisdiction of any civil action by an alien for a tort only, committed in violation of the law of nations or a treaty of the United States.[1]

The ATCA was originally enacted as part of s 9 of the *Judiciary Act* in 1789, and lay largely dormant for nearly 200 years, before providing the basis for watershed litigation in 1980, when Dolly and Joel Filartiga successfully sued a former Paraguayan police inspector-general, Americo Norberto Peña-Irala, for torturing and killing a member of their family.[2] The case confirmed that ATCA provides aliens with a right to sue in tort over certain egregious breaches of human rights (such as torture and extra judicial killings), even when those acts take place abroad.[3] No other State has a statute comparable to ATCA.[4] The specific cause of action in *Filartiga v Peña-Irala* was reaffirmed and extended in the

---

[1] 28 USC § 1350.
[2] *Filartiga v Peña-Irala* 630 F 2d 876 (2d Cir 1980).
[3] Thus, the ordinary presumption against extraterritorial application for US statutes was rebutted. See generally, M Gibney and RD Emerick, 'The Extraterritorial Application of United States Law and the Protection of Human Rights: Holding Multinational Corporations to Domestic and International Standards' (1996) 10 *Temple International and Comparative Law Journal* 123.
[4] B Stephens, 'Translating Filartiga: A Comparative and International Law Analysis of Domestic Remedies for International Human Rights Violations' (2002) 27 *Yale Journal of International Law* 1, 32.

Torture Victim Protection Act 1991 [TVPA].[5] TVPA is discussed in greater detail below.[6]

At the time of writing the Supreme Court of the United States had made no decisions on the substantive meaning of ATCA. The *Filartiga* interpretation of the meaning of ATCA has been confirmed on numerous occasions in District and Circuit Courts,[7] and indeed has expanded. For example, accountability was extended beyond actual perpetrators to those in a position of command responsibility in *Xuncax v Gramajo*.[8] In *Kadic v Karadzic*, ATCA liability was extended to officials of de facto, yet unrecognised, governments.[9] More importantly for the purposes of this book, the Second Circuit in *Kadic* confirmed that ATCA could ground certain actions against individuals acting in a private rather than official capacity. And in 1997, in *Doe v Unocal [Unocal 1997]*,[10] it was held for the first time that ATCA actions could lie against private corporations.[11]

In *Unocal 1997*, Paez J of the Central California District Court permitted the plaintiffs, a group of Myanmar farmers, to proceed with an ATCA suit against Unocal, a Californian energy corporation, alleging that Unocal, acting through its partners in the Myanmar military and police forces, had committed a range of egregious human rights abuses, including forced labour, forced relocations, torture, rape, and murder, in conducting its Yadana gas pipelines project in southern Myanmar.[12] Since the *Unocal 1997* decision, human rights challenges under ATCA have been brought against numerous corporations including Shell, Rio Tinto, Freeport McMoran, Exxon-Mobil, Pfizer, and Coca Cola for the alleged perpetration of human rights abuses abroad.

HUMAN RIGHTS NORMS WITHIN 'THE LAW OF NATIONS'

The first limb of ATCA grants aliens rights to sue in tort for breaches of 'the law of nations'. This term logically refers to sources of international law beyond treaty law, as that is the subject matter of the second ATCA limb.[13] Non-treaty

---

[5] 28 USC § 1350 App.
[6] See below, text at nn 286–98.
[7] Only the DC Circuit has manifested opposition to *Filartiga*; see below, text at nn 272–73.
[8] 886 F Supp 162 (D Mass 1995) 185–89. See also B Stephens, 'Accountability: International Human Rights Violations Against Corporations in US Courts' in M Kamminga and S Zia-Zarifi (eds), *Liability of Multinational Corporations under International Law* (The Hague, Kluwer, 2000) 214.
[9] 70 F 3d 232 (2d Cir 1995). In that case, liability attached to Radovan Karadzic as the de facto head of the Bosnian Serb enclave of Srpska during the Bosnian war.
[10] *Doe I v Unocal Corp* 963 F Supp 880 (CD Cal 1997).
[11] The liability of corporations under the ATCA was comprehensively reviewed and reaffirmed in the recent decision in *Presbyterian Church of Sudan v Talisman Energy* 244 F Supp 2d 289 (SDNY 2003) 308–19.
[12] The facts surrounding the joint venture are examined in greater detail in ch 3, at p 69.
[13] This second limb is discussed below, text at nn 239–46.

sources of binding international norms are customary international law and *jus cogens* norms. Customary international laws are binding international norms arising from the 'general and consistent practice of states [state practice] followed by them from a sense of legal obligation [*'opinio juris'*]'.[14] Ordinary customary law binds all States except for those who have persistently objected to its application. *Jus cogens* is that inner core of customary laws that is not subject to the 'persistent objector' exception: *jus cogens* norms are non-derogable in all circumstances. Therefore, 'the corpus of [customary international law] is much larger than that of *jus cogens*'.[15]

Generally, it seems that US courts are satisfied that ATCA is activated if the human rights violation at issue breaches customary international law; the alleged violation need not amount to a breach of a *jus cogens* norm.[16] For example, *Filartiga* itself clearly adopted the customary law standard, and its reasoning evinces an assiduous investigation of whether the alleged violations therein fulfilled the 'state practice' and '*opinio juris*' tests.[17] The *Filartiga* view has not however been unanimously followed; a few courts have apparently adopted the higher *jus cogens* standard.[18]

The issue has been confused by the adoption by some US courts, particularly within the Ninth Circuit since *Forti v Suarez-Mason* in 1987, of a test that requires breaches of 'the law of nations' to be 'definable, obligatory, and universally condemned'.[19] This test does not emanate from international law. Rather, it is a product of domestic ATCA jurisprudence.[20] At face value, this test appears to prescribe a stricter standard than customary international

---

[14] *Restatement (Third) of the Foreign Relations Law of the US* § 102(2) (1987). The Restatement is one of the most influential secondary sources of international law for the purposes of findings in US courts.

[15] J Ratner, 'Back to the Future: Why a Return to the Approach of the Filartiga Court is essential to Preserve the Legitimacy and Potential of the Alien Tort Claims Act' (2002) 35 *Columbia Journal of Law and Social Problems* 83, 86.

[16] See *Presbyterian Church of Sudan v Talisman Energy* 244 F Supp 2d 289 (SDNY 2003) 306, n 18, *Alvarez-Machain v US* 331 F 3d 604 (9th Cir 2003) 614–15, and *Abdullahi v Pfizer* No 01 Civ 8118, 2002 US Dist LEXIS 17436 (SDNY 2002) 5. See also T Collingsworth, 'Boundaries in the Field of Human Rights: The Key Human Rights Challenge: Developing Enforcement Mechanisms' (2002) *Harvard Human Rights Journal* 183, 196–7; JJ Paust, 'Human Rights Responsibilities of Private Corporations' (2002) 35 *Vanderbilt Journal of Transnational Law* 801, 824; see also M Swan, 'International Human Rights Tort Claims and the Experience of United States Courts: An Introduction to the US Case Law, Key Statutes, and Doctrines' in C Scott (ed), *Torture as Tort* (Oxford, Hart Publishing, 2001) 91–92.

[17] See discussion in Ratner, above n 15, at 93–97.

[18] *Ibid* at 97–103. See, eg, *Xuncax v Gramajo* 886 F Supp 162 (D Mass 1995) 184. Given however the lack of international law expertise amongst some federal judges, it is possible that courts have not appreciated that the standards of customary international law and *jus cogens* are very different (Ratner, *ibid*, at 103).

[19] *Forti v Suarez-Mason* 672 F Supp 1531 (ND Cal 1987) 1539–40.

[20] The test was probably derived from a law review article, JM Blum and RG Steinhardt, 'Federal Jurisdiction over International Human Rights Claims: The Alien Tort Claims Act after Filartiga v Pena-Irala' (1981) 22 *Harvard International Law Journal* 53, 88. Edwards J used the test in *Tel-Oren v Libyan Arab Republic* 726 F 2d 774 (DC Cir 1984) 781, and was followed in *Forti v Suarez-Mason* 672 F Supp 1531 (ND Cal 1987).

law.[21] For example, due to the persistent objector rule, it is not necessary that a norm of custom be 'universally' followed. However, the 'universal' limb of the test is a misnomer, and should therefore be dropped. As stated at a later stage in the *Forti* litigation, 'to meet this burden plaintiffs need not establish unanimity among nations. Rather, they must show a general recognition among states that a specific practice is prohibited'.[22] So formulated, the *Forti* test conforms to the customary international law standard. 'Obligatory' means that the right is one which is considered mandatory, rather than hortatory or merely desirable. The 'obligatory' limb of the test is not controversial, and also conforms to the customary international law standard. 'Definable' means that 'sufficient criteria exist to determine what amounts to a violation of the norm'.[23] The requirement of definability, or specificity, arguably augments the standard test for identifying customary international law.[24] However, a satisfactory level of definability is a desirable and perhaps necessary precondition to municipal justiciability, and is therefore perhaps an essential adjunct for a domestic court seeking to enforce customary international law. The tripartite *Forti* test therefore does not eject customary international law as the ATCA standard: it is an attempt (albeit clumsy with the addition of the 'universal' limb) to translate the test for identifying customary international law test into a domestic context.

Certainly, adoption of the *Forti* test does not relieve a court of the necessity to undertake a *Filartiga*-style inquiry into 'the status of the international legal consensus' of a particular human right. Unfortunately, US courts have often failed to investigate the international legal status of a human right with the same impressive rigor as displayed in *Filartiga*, sometimes resorting to conclusory statements on the important issue of whether a right is or is not part of the law of nations.[25] In this respect, the rigorous analysis by the Second Circuit in its recent decision in *Flores v Southern Peru Copper* of whether certain behaviour violated customary international law is to be welcomed.[26]

Neither the state practice/*opinio juris* test nor the tripartite *Forti* test yield clear-cut answers for the identification of customary international law norms. The content of the list of human rights protected by customary international law is the subject of great academic debate, which will not be extensively dis-

---

[21] See WS Dodge, 'Which Torts are in Violation of the Law of Nations?' (2001) 24 *Hastings International and Comparative Law Review* 351, 355; see also Ratner, above n 15, at 104–5.

[22] *Forti v Suarez-Mason* 694 F Supp 707 (ND Cal 1988) 709. See also B Stephens and M Ratner, *International Human Rights Litigation in US Courts* (New York, Transnational Publishers Inc, 1996) 52.

[23] S Zia-Zarifi, 'Suing Multinational Corporations in the US for Violating International Law' (1999) 4 *University of California at Los Angeles Journal International Law and Foreign Affairs* 81, 91.

[24] Ratner, above n 15, at 104.

[25] See *ibid* at 102–3 and 108–9.

[26] 343 F 3d 140 (2d Cir 2003). The court conducted a thorough examination on the question of whether intra-national pollution breaches customary international law; it decided that it did not.

cussed here.[27] More relevant to the discussion at hand are the findings regarding the content of customary international law by courts in ATCA litigation.

Proof of 'the law of nations' is established from a variety of sources, such as international treaties and other primary international documents, international case law, and the works of jurists and respected international law academics.[28] For example, the presence of a widely ratified treaty in an area will help to establish a principle as part of the law of nations. In *Sarei v Rio Tinto*, the Court noted that the principles in the United Nations Convention on the Law of the Sea (UNCLOS) were likely to represent the law of nations, as UNCLOS had been ratified by 166 States.[29] Such reasoning bodes well for the ATCA relevance of rights within the most widely ratified human rights treaties, such as the Convention on the Rights of the Child (CRC).[30] However, a high rate of ratification of a treaty is not a decisive indicator of the content of customary international law. In *Rio Tinto*, other evidence was cited to bolster the view that UNCLOS reflected customary international law.

One of the most authoritative (and perhaps more conservative) lists of customary human rights[31] for the purposes of findings in US courts, is in the *Restatement (Third) of the Foreign Relations Law of the United States* at § 702: genocide, slavery or slave trade, murder, disappearance, torture or other cruel, inhuman and degrading treatment or punishment, prolonged arbitrary detention, systematic racial discrimination, and consistent patterns of gross violations of internationally recognised rights. 'Consistent patterns of gross violations of internationally recognised rights' is an avenue for holding perpetrators of multiple or

---

[27] See, generally, eg, T Meron, *Human Rights and Humanitarian Norms as Customary Law* (Oxford, Clarendon Press, 1989). It is possible that the 'state practice' limb is applied differently in customary human rights law, compared to other areas of customary international law. Many international law experts are more willing to accept State pronouncements (eg denunciations of the practice of torture) as 'state practice' rather than actual state actions (eg unacknowledged yet systemic acts of torture), for the purpose of identifying customary human rights norms. See *Restatement (Third) of the Foreign Relations Law of the US* § 701 (1987), Reporter's Note 2 on Practice creating customary human rights law; see also B Simma and P Alston, 'The Sources of Human Rights Law: Custom, *Jus Cogens*, and General Principles' (1992) 12 *Australian Year Book of International Law* 82; CA Bradley and JL Goldsmith, 'The Current Illegitimacy of International Human Rights Litigation' (1997) 66 *Fordham Law Review* 319, 327–28.

[28] Stephens and Ratner, above n 225, at 54–58; see also *Sarei v Rio Tinto* 221 F Supp 2d 1116 (CD Cal 2002).

[29] 221 F Supp 2d 1161 (CD Cal 2002) 1161. *Sarei* is discussed, below, text at n 81. Interestingly, the US is not one of those 166 States, though it has signed UNCLOS. Earlier in *Sarei v Rio Tinto* 221 F Supp 2d 1116 (CD Cal 2002) 1157–8, the failure of the US to ratify the American Convention on Human Rights was cited as 'relevant' in diminishing the value of a report of the Inter-American Commission on Human Rights for the purposes of identifying the law of nations. The US has signed the American Convention.

[30] As at January 2004, the US and Somalia are the only two States not to have ratified the CRC. The US has signed the CRC.

[31] The list is not expressed to be exhaustive. Indeed, note 11 thereto states that the same rights are *jus cogens* norms. Customary human rights norms extend beyond *jus cogens* violations.

at least mass abuses liable even when the individual abuses fall short of customary human rights violations.[32]

At the more radical end of the spectrum of arguments regarding the content of customary human rights law are contentions that the entire Universal Declaration of Human Rights (UDHR) represents custom.[33] Following from such arguments, any UDHR right can ground an ATCA claim.[34] However, the ATCA decisions to date indicate that some UDHR rights are excluded from the ambit of customary international law. Certainly, a number of UDHR rights do not satisfy the 'definable' limb of the *Forti* test.

So far, courts have decided that prohibitions on torture,[35] summary execution,[36] genocide,[37] war crimes,[38] sexual assault,[39] forced labour,[40] slavery,[41] forced relocation,[42] disappearance,[43] cruel, inhuman and degrading treatment[44] (including medical experimentation without informed consent),[45] forced exile,[46] forced displacement,[47] arbitrary detention,[48] arbitrary arrest,[49] crimes

---

[32] *Tachiona et al v Mugabe and ZANU-PF* 234 F Supp 2d 401 (SDNY 2002) 426–7; Stephens and Ratner, above n 22, at 86–87; GGA Tzeutschler, 'Corporate Violator: The Alien Tort Liability of Transnational Corporations for Human Rights Abuses Abroad' (1999) 30 *Columbia Human Rights Law Review* 359, 416–17; R Herz, 'Litigating Environmental Abuses Under the Alien Tort Claims Act: A Practical Assessment' (2000) 40 *Vanderbilt Journal of Transnational Law* 545, 580.

[33] See *Restatement (Third) of the Foreign Relations Law of the US* § 701 (1987), n 4; L Sohn, 'The New International Law: Protection of the Rights of Individuals rather than States' (1982) 32 *American University Law Review* 1, 17.

[34] Stephens and Ratner, above n 22, at 56.

[35] Eg *Filartiga v Peña-Irala* 630 F 2d 876 (2d Cir 1980) 884.

[36] *Ibid*.

[37] Eg *Kadic v Karadzic* 70 F 3d 232 (2d Cir 1995) 241–3; see also *Presbyterian Church of Sudan v Talisman Energy* 244 F Supp 2d 289 (SDNY 2003) 327, noting that 'non-Muslims' can constitute an ethnic group, the intentional elimination of which constitutes genocide.

[38] Eg *Sarei v Rio Tinto* 221 F Supp 2d 1116 (CD Cal 2002) 1139–42; *Bodner v Banque Paribas* 114 F Supp 2d 117 (EDNY 2000) 128.

[39] *Kadic v Karadzic* 70 F 3d 232 (2d Cir 1995) 242–43.

[40] Eg *John Doe I v Unocal Corp* 2002 US App LEXIS 19263 (9th Cir 2002) 14208 (*Unocal 2002*).

[41] Eg *ibid*.

[42] This is implicit in Paez J's decision in *Doe I v Unocal Corp* 963 F Supp 880 (CD Cal 1997).

[43] Eg *Xuncax v Gramajo* 886 F Supp 162 (D Mass 1995) 184–85.

[44] Eg *Xuncax v Gramajo* 886 F Supp 162 (D Mass 1995) 184–85. This view is not unanimous. See below, text at n 109.

[45] *Abdullahi v Pfizer* No 01 Civ 8118, 2002 US Dist LEXIS 17436 (SDNY September 16, 2002) 16–18.

[46] *Wiwa v Royal Dutch Petroleum Co* No 96 Civ 8386, 2002 US Dist LEXIS 3293 (SDNY Feb 22, 2002) 25. 'Forced exile' arises where a person flees due to credible threats to his/her own life and safety: *ibid* at 26.

[47] *Presbyterian Church of Sudan v Talisman Energy* 244 F Supp 2d 289 (SDNY 2003) 325; the defendant 'apparently concede[d] that displacement violates international law'.

[48] See Stephens and Ratner, above n 22, at 75–76 on how the cases do not appear to require that arbitrary detention be 'prolonged' in order to attract ATCA liability; see also *Alvarez-Machain v US* 331 F 3d 604 (9th Cir 2003) 621–22. See however the discussion in *Eastman Kodak Co v Kavlin* 978 F Supp 1078 (SD Fla 1997) 1092–94, appearing to require that arbitrary detention be prolonged.

[49] *Martinez v City of Los Angeles* 141 F 3d 1373 (9th Cir 1998) 1384.

against humanity,[50] racial discrimination,[51] aircraft hijacking,[52] and pollution contrary to UNCLOS,[53] as well as rights to associate and organise,[54] life, liberty and personal security,[55] peaceful assembly and association,[56] and freedoms of political belief, opinion, and expression,[57] qualify as norms which attract ATCA liability. The most expansive decision in this regard is in *Ralk v Lincoln County, Ga*, where the court stated that the plaintiff 'could bring a claim under the [ATCA] for violations of the [International Covenant on Civil and Political Rights]'.[58] This statement was not qualified, indicating that any violation of the ICCPR would suffice. In this respect, *Ralk* must be deemed exceptional, considering the number of individual ICCPR rights that have been found *not* to ground ATCA cases.

The following rights have been found by US courts not to activate ATCA because they are not breaches of the law of nations: the rights to life,[59] health,[60] sustainable development,[61] freedom from discrimination per se,[62] and freedom of speech,[63] as well as prohibitions on terrorism,[64] cultural genocide,[65]

---

[50] *Kadic v Karadzic* 70 F 3d 232 (2d Cir 1995) 236; *Wiwa v Royal Dutch Petroleum Co*, No 96 Civ 8386, 2002 US Dist LEXIS 3293 (SDNY Feb 22, 2002) 30–2, as defined in article 7 of the Statute of the ICC; *Sarei v Rio Tinto* 221 F Supp 2d 1116 (CD Cal 2002) 1149–51.

[51] *Sarei v Rio Tinto* 221 F Supp 2d 1116 (CD Cal 2002) 1151–55. Earlier cases focused on *systematic* racial discrimination as a breach of the law of nations: see *ibid* at 1152 (though Morrow J in *Rio Tinto* does not comment on the difference between racial discrimination and systematic racial discrimination) citing, eg *Kadic v Karadzic* 70 F 3d 232 (2d Cir 1995) 240; see also *Tachiona et al v Mugabe and ZANU-PF* 234 F Supp 2d 401 (SDNY 2002) 439–40.

[52] *Burnett v Al Baraka Investment and Development Corporation* 274 F Supp 3d 86 (DDC 2003) 99–100.

[53] *Sarei v Rio Tinto* 221 F Supp 2d 1116 (CD Cal 2002) 1162.

[54] *Estate of Rodriguez v Drummond* 256 F Supp 2d 1250 (WD Al 2003) 1264; the court was only willing to find that such rights activated ATCA for the purposes of preliminary proceedings in the litigation. Thus, the court indicated that the matter could be re-argued at the merits stage of the proceedings.

[55] *Wiwa v Royal Dutch Petroleum Co*, No 96 Civ 8386, 2002 US Dist LEXIS 3293 (SDNY Feb 22, 2002) 36. The right to life, as formulated in article 6 of the ICCPR, was also found to be part of customary international law, and therefore within the law of nations, in *Estate of Winston Cabello v Armando Fernandez-Larios* 157 F Supp 2d 1345 (SD Fla 2001) 1359. Cf however *Flores v Southern Peru Copper* 343 F 3d 140 (2d Cir 2003) 160–61 (see n 59 below).

[56] *Wiwa v Royal Dutch Petroleum Co*, No 96 Civ 8386, 2002 US Dist LEXIS 3293 (SDNY Feb 22, 2002) 36. See however below, text at and in n 99.

[57] *Tachiona et al v Mugabe and ZANU-PF* 234 F Supp 2d 401 (SDNY 2002) 434; see generally, 420–34.

[58] (2000) 81 F Supp 2d 1372 (SD Ga) 1380.

[59] *Flores v Southern Peru Copper* 343 F 3d 140 (2d Cir 2003) 160–61; cf *Estate of Winston Cabello v Armando Fernandez-Larios* 157 F Supp 2d 1345 (SD Fla 2001) 1359 (see n 55 above).

[60] *Flores v Southern Peru Copper* 343 F 3d 140 (2d Cir 2003) 160–61.

[61] *Sarei v Rio Tinto* 221 F Supp 2d 1116 (CD Cal 2002).

[62] *Doe v The Gap* No CV–01–0031, 2001 WL 1842389 (DN Mar I Nov 6, CD Cal 2001) 22.

[63] *Guinto v Marcos* 654 F Supp 276 (SD Cal 1986) 280.

[64] *Tel-Oren v Libyan Arab Republic* 726 F 2d 774 (DC Cir 1984) 795–96. Note that the status of terrorism as an internationally recognised wrong may have evolved since 1984, with important developments such as United Nations Security Council Resolution 1373, S/Res1373 (2001), 28 September 2001, under which new international obligations were imposed on States to combat terrorism.

[65] *Beanal v Freeport-McMoran Inc* 197 F 3d 161 (5th Cir 1999) 166–68.

28 The Alien Tort Claims Act

environmental abuses inside one State,[66] constructive exile,[67] expropriation by a State of its national's property,[68] forced prison labour,[69] forced conscript labour,[70] and transborder abduction.[71] Furthermore, claims relating to more commonplace tortious or criminal behaviour, such as fraud,[72] negligence,[73] commercial torts,[74] and conversion,[75] also fall outside the ATCA as they fail to raise international law claims.[76] The following analysis examines some of the more borderline decisions on the identification of human rights within the 'law of nations'.

In *Beanal v Freeport McMoran*, the plaintiffs alleged that the defendants caused egregious environmental damage within Indonesia in breach of the law of nations.[77] The plaintiffs cited numerous international declarations regarding the protection of the environment, such as the Rio Declaration of 1992,[78] to support this contention. However, the Fifth Circuit found that existing environmental law standards were 'devoid of articulable or discernible standards and regulations' and therefore did not fall within ATCA.[79] Furthermore:

> the argument to abstain from interfering in a sovereign's environmental practices carries persuasive force especially when the alleged environmental torts and abuses occur within the sovereign's borders and do not affect neighboring countries.[80]

In *Sarei v Rio Tinto*, a case concerning Rio Tinto's alleged involvement in human rights abuses on the island of Bougainville before and during a secessionist war with Papua New Guinea, another attempt was made to generate an

---

[66] Ibid; see also *Flores v Southern Peru Copper* 343 F 3d 140 (2d Cir 2003).

[67] *Xuncax v Gramajo* 886 F Supp 162 (D Mass 1995) 189. 'Constructive exile' arises where a person flees because of fear brought about by acts committed on others.

[68] *Guinto v Marcos* 654 F Supp 276 (SD Cal 1986) 280, n 1; *Nat'l Coalition Gov't of the Union of Myanmar v Unocal, Inc* 176 FRD 329 (CD Cal 1997) 345, *Tachiona et al v Mugabe and ZANU-PF* 234 F Supp 2d 401 (SDNY 2002) 440. See also *Presbyterian Church of Sudan v Talisman Energy* 244 F Supp 2d 289 (SDNY 2003) 324–5, where the court noted that 'confiscation of property without just compensation does not violate the law of nations'; the court did not qualify that finding by referring explicitly to the confiscation of the property of *nationals*.

[69] *Ge v Peng* 201 F Supp 2d 14 (DDC 2000) 18.

[70] *Roe v Unocal* 70 F Supp 2d 1073 (CD Cal 1999) 1080.

[71] *Alvarez-Machain v US* 331 F 3d 604 (9th Cir 2003) 618–20.

[72] *Hamid v Price Waterhouse* 51 F 3d 1411 (9th Cir 1995) 1418.

[73] *Jones v Petty Ray Geophysical Geosource* 722 F Supp 343 (SD Tex 1989) 348.

[74] *De Wit v KLM Royal Dutch Airlines* 570 F Supp 613 (SDNY 1983) 618.

[75] *Cohen v Hartman* 634 F 2d 318 (5th Cir 1981) 320.

[76] See generally, Lawyers Committee for Human Rights and the Rutherford Institute, Amicus Brief [LCHR brief], in *Sosa v Alvarez-Machain*, Petition for Writ of Certiorari in the US Supreme Court, No 03–339, <http://www.lchr.org/workers_rights/wr_other/ATCASosaamicusfinal100703.pdf> (5 January 2003) 8.

[77] 197 F 3d 161 (5th Cir 1999).

[78] Rio Declaration on Environment and Development, June 13 1992, UN Doc. A/CONF. 15 1/5 rev 1 (1992).

[79] 197 F 3d 161 (5th Cir 1999) 167. The Court came to similar findings regarding the rights to be free from cultural genocide and to sustainable development.

[80] Ibid; the Court also noted that Principle 2 of the Rio Declaration asserts that States have the sovereign right to exploit their own resources pursuant to their own environmental and developmental policies.

ATCA claim out of environmental abuses. Instead of basing their claim on a free-standing environmental right, the plaintiffs claimed that the environmental damage caused by the defendant's mining operations 'deprived Bougainvilleans of their right to life, health, and security of the person'.[81] Thus, the *Rio Tinto* plaintiffs attempted to base their claim on rights that are more clearly internationally recognised than the environmental right invoked in *Beanal*.[82] The Court concluded however that 'the plaintiffs have not demonstrated that violation of these rights *via environmental harm* is 'a specific, universal and obligatory' norm outlawed by international law'.[83] As in *Beanal*, the Court ultimately concluded that environmental harms within one country, regardless of the characterisation of their consequences (ie whether linked to other rights such as life, health, and security) do not fall within the scope of ATCA torts.[84] A similar decision was reached in *Flores v Southern Peru Copper*,[85] which concerned allegations of environmental abuse in Peru.

Therefore, it appears that ATCA does not currently provide an avenue for litigants to seek remedies for environmental harms inside a State, due to lack of the requisite specificity and an adequate level of international condemnation.[86] The situation may, however, be different for pollution that extends beyond a State's borders. In 1991 in *Amlon Metals v FMC Corp*, the Court denied that transboundary environmental harms activated ATCA.[87] *Aguinda v Texaco*[88] concerned environmental harm allegedly caused by Texaco's subsidiaries in Ecuador, which spread downriver to Peru. Rakoff J noted that environmental abuses were unlikely to fall within ATCA, and did not make any distinction between intra-territorial harm and transborder harm. However, Rakoff J did not undertake an extensive analysis, as the case was dismissed on other grounds.[89] In contrast to *Amlon* and *Aguinda*, the District Court in *Beanal* hinted that transborder harm could be part of the law of nations.[90] The Circuit Courts in *Beanal* and *Flores* explicitly drew attention to the localised nature of the impugned harm in dismissing the ATCA relevance of the environmental claims.[91] Finally,

---

[81] *Sarei v Rio Tinto* 221 F Supp 2d 1116 (CD Cal 2002).
[82] The right to a clean environment per se is not recognised in a treaty. On the other hand, the rights to life, liberty, and health are recognised, respectively, by article 6 of the International Covenant on Civil and Political Rights [ICCPR], article 9 ICCPR, and article 12 International Covenant on Economic Social and Cultural Rights [ICESCR]. Note however that the court in *Flores v Southern Peru Copper* 343 F 3d 140 (2d Cir 2003) decided that the rights to life and health are not in any case part of the law of nations.
[83] *Sarei v Rio Tinto* 221 F Supp 2d 1116 (CD Cal 2002) 1157, emphasis added.
[84] *Ibid* at 1160.
[85] *Flores v Southern Peru Copper* 343 F 3d 140 (2d Cir 2003).
[86] Zia-Zarifi, above n 23, at 114; cf, generally, Herz above n 32.
[87] *Amlon Metals v FMC Corp* 775 F Supp 668 (SDNY 1991) 671.
[88] 142 F Supp 2d 534 (SDNY 2001).
[89] The case was dismissed for forum non conveniens; see ch 4, pp 93–95 and 97.
[90] *Beanal v Freeport-McMoran, Inc* 969 F Supp 362 (E.D La 1997) 384; see also Herz, above n 32, at 634–8; and *Restatement (Third) of the Foreign Relations Law of the US* § 602 (1987).
[91] *Beanal v Freeport-McMoran Inc* 197 F 3d 161 (5th Cir 1999) 167; *Flores v Southern Peru Copper* 343 F 3d 140 (2d Cir 2003) 161 ff (focusing purely on 'intranational' pollution).

30 *The Alien Tort Claims Act*

Rio Tinto confirmed that pollution flowing into international waters contrary to UNCLOS is prohibited by the law of nations.[92] Thus, it is possible that transboundary environmental harms can be the subject of an ATCA suit.[93]

Three of the more controversial inclusions by US courts in the list of violations of the law of nations, due to their lack of definability, are the right to be free from cruel, inhuman and degrading treatment (eg in *Xuncax v Gramajo*),[94] the freedoms of assembly and association (*Wiwa v Royal Dutch Petroleum (Wiwa 2002)*),[95] and freedom of political beliefs, opinion, and expression (*Tachiona et al v Mugabe and ZANU-PF*).[96] In all of these cases, it seems that the Court has accepted that the *core* of the relevant right falls within ATCA, while the more controversial outer perimeters of the right may lie outside. For example, in *Xuncax*, Woodlock J stated:

> It is not necessary that *every aspect* of what might comprise a standard such as 'cruel, inhuman or degrading treatment' be fully defined and universally agreed upon before a given action meriting the label is clearly proscribed under international law, any more than it is necessary to define all acts that may constitute 'torture' or 'arbitrary detention' in order to recognise certain conduct as actionable misconduct under that rubric.[97]

In *Wiwa 2002*, certain allegations related to the use of force against the plaintiffs in the course of peaceful protest against Shell's operations in Nigeria.[98] While the rights of peaceful assembly and association per se are possibly not part of customary international law,[99] the right to be free from excessive force whilst one is engaging in peaceful assembly or association probably is.[100] The *Wiwa 2002* reasoning seems similar to the reasoning adopted in *Xuncax*.

In *Tachiona v Mugabe*, Marrero J found that the hounding by the governing party of 'political opponents through repeated acts of terror and violence'[101] violated 'an internationally recognised norm to a right to political beliefs, opinion and expression without arbitrary and unjustified interference by the

---

[92] *Sarei v Rio Tinto* 221 F Supp 2d 1116 (CD Cal 2002). Some of the ATCA claims in *Rio Tinto* related to environmental pollution in international waters, twelve miles off the coast of Papua New Guinea.

[93] Transborder pollution thus far seems to only relate to pollution that physically spreads across borders, rather than pollution caused in one country by the decisions (eg in corporate headquarters) made in another. See M Anderson, 'Transnational Corporations and Environmental Damage: Is Tort Law the Answer?' (2002) 41 *Washburn Law Journal* 399, 400, 403.

[94] 886 F Supp 162 (D Mass 1995) 187.

[95] No 96 Civ 8386, 2002 US Dist LEXIS 3293 (SDNY Feb 22, 2002) 36.

[96] 234 F Supp 2d 401 (SDNY 2002).

[97] *Xuncax v Gramajo* 886 F Supp 162 (D Mass 1995) 187. *Xuncax* is not a corporate case; the case concerned allegations of gross abuses against a Guatemalan defence minister.

[98] No 96 Civ 8386, 2002 US Dist LEXIS 3293 (SDNY Feb 22, 2002) 33–35. The *Wiwa* litigation is discussed further below in ch 3, text at nn 79–80.

[99] Indeed, 'the freedom to associate' per se was found to fall outside ATCA in *Doe v The Gap* No CV–01–0031, 2001 WL 1842389 (DN Mar I Nov 6, CD Cal 2001) 22.

[100] However, this particular alleged abuse, whereby the plaintiffs' lives were endangered, is more correctly classified as an allegation of the breach of the right to life or security of the person, rather than as a breach of the rights to peaceful assembly and association.

[101] *Tachiona et al v Mugabe and ZANU-PF* 234 F Supp 2d 401 (SDNY 2002) 423.

state'.[102] Similarly, regarding the ATCA actionability of the right to be free from cruel inhuman and degrading treatment, Marrero J stated that '[b]y any measure of decency, the public dragging of a dead body, especially in front of the victim's own home, for close kin and neighbours to behold the gruesome spectacle',[103] constitutes degrading treatment. Such behaviour undoubtedly breached the inner core of the respective rights, and therefore probably customary law, regardless of differing state interpretations of the customary status of the margins of the respective rights.[104]

Thus, it seems that some district courts are focusing more on whether the alleged concrete abuses activate ATCA, rather than on the customary status of the broader abstract right at issue. In other words, rights may be split into subsets of marginal and core violations, the latter generally falling within ATCA, regardless of the status of the designated abstract right at issue.[105] Such an approach appears to conform with the requirements of customary international law. Indeed, it may manifest a move away from an emphasis on 'definability' (under the tripartite *Forti* test) back to a more familiar test (for international lawyers) of customary international law.[106] While state practice and *opinio juris* is less likely to exist with regard to all elements of an abstract human right (regardless of its definability), it is likely to be present with regard to all 'blatant' violations of human rights, that is conduct that almost all States agree represents a violation of a recognised right.

The approach of separating out core and marginal human rights violations is certainly not uniform across US district courts. Regarding cruel, inhuman and degrading treatment, *Xuncax* was followed by district courts within the Second Circuit in *Jama v United States INS*,[107] *Wiwa 2002*, and *Tachiona v Mugabe*. However, *Xuncax* was not followed in *Sarei v Rio Tinto* within the Ninth Circuit. Rather, the *Rio Tinto* Court followed its fellow Californian court in the 1987 case of *Forti*[108] in deciding that the prohibition on cruel inhuman and degrading treatment was too vague a norm to fall within ATCA.[109]

---

[102] *Ibid* at 434.
[103] *Ibid* at 438.
[104] See *ibid* at 433, 438.
[105] See also eg, C Scott, 'Translating Torture into Transnational Tort: Conceptual Divides in the Debate on Corporate Accountability for Human Rights Norms' in Scott, above n 16, at 56.
[106] Indeed, Marrero J in *Tachiona et al v Mugabe and ZANU-PF* 234 F Supp 2d 401 (SDNY 2002) at 437 stated:

[U]niversally recognised norms ripen into settled law incrementally by the accretions of teachings informed by real events. Insofar as actual cases offer proper opportunities to resolve doubts and fill in gaps, the natural evolution of the law will be advanced by the authorised and principled exercise of judicial jurisdiction to decide them. Conversely, where uncertainty persists by dearth of precedent, declining to render decision that otherwise may help clarify or enlarge international practice, and thereby foster greater understanding and assent regarding the content of common behavioural rules, creates a self-fulfilling prophecy and retards the growth of customary international law.

[107] 22 F Supp 2d 353 (DNJ 1998).
[108] *Forti v Suarez-Mason* 694 F Supp 707 (ND Cal 1988) 712.
[109] *Sarei v Rio Tinto* 221 F Supp 2d 1116 (CD Cal 2002) 1162.

TNCs, as powerful economic creatures, are obviously capable of influencing, both beneficially and detrimentally, the enjoyment of economic social and cultural rights, such as the right to an adequate standard of living.[110] The most authoritative source of economic social and cultural rights is the International Covenant on Economic Social and Cultural Rights (ICESCR), article 2(1) of which states that such rights must be guaranteed 'progressively' by a State party 'to the maximum of [its] available resources'. The qualification of ICESCR rights by vague concepts such as progressiveness and the maximum available resources indicate that violations of economic social and cultural rights may fall outside ATCA,[111] because the boundary between violations and non-violations is too difficult to delineate. On the other hand, it is possible to delineate clear violations of the ICESCR,[112] just as it is possible to discern core violations of 'vague' civil and political rights. For example, mass evictions without justification, especially if inflicted with violence, would constitute a clear breach of the right to adequate shelter under article 11 of the ICESCR. Perhaps core violations of the rights in both of the International Covenants fall within ATCA. Furthermore, it may be noted that an important set of economic social and cultural rights, labour rights, are protected by alternative treaties established under the auspices of the International Labour Organization (ILO). The ILO treaties provide a 'definability' to labour rights that is missing from the text of the ICESCR. It may at least be arguable that the 'fundamental labour rights' identified by the ILO fall under the rubric of ATCA.[113]

US courts have confirmed that the definition of human rights protected by the 'law of nations' is a dynamic concept, which should be interpreted in a contemporary light.[114] It is probable that the scope of ATCA will expand further as customary international human rights law evolves.[115] Therefore, it is important for

---

[110] See C Scott, 'Multinational Enterprises and Emergent Jurisprudence on Violations of Economic Social and Cultural Rights' in A Eide, C Krause and A Rosas (eds), *Economic Social and Cultural Rights* 2nd edn (The Hague, Kluwer, 2001) 565.

[111] 'Developments in the Law—International Criminal Law: V. Corporate Liability for Violations of International Human Rights Law' (2001) 114 *Harvard Law Review* 2025, 2027–28, 2043; RE Robertson, 'Measuring State Compliance with the Obligation to Devote the 'Maximum Available Resources' to Realizing Economic, Social and Cultural Rights' (1994) 16 *Human Rights Quarterly* 693, 694.

[112] See 'Maastricht Guidelines on Violations of Economic, Social and Cultural Rights' (1998) 20 *Human Rights Quarterly* 691, 693–96.

[113] The 'fundamental labour rights' are identified in 'The ILO Declaration on the Fundamental Principles and Rights to Work', adopted June 1998 <http://www.ilo.org> (13 January 2003) at clause 1(2) as the rights to freedom of association and collective bargaining, freedom from forced or compulsory labour, freedom from child labour, and freedom from discrimination in employment.

[114] Only Bork J in *Tel-Oren v Libyan Arab Republic* 726 F 2d 774 (DC Cir 1984) 812–16 has explicitly contended that ATCA only grants jurisdiction in respect of violations recognised by the law of nations at the time of its enactment in 1789. However, tacit support for Bork J's originalist position may be discerned from Scalia J in *Sanchez-Espinoza v Reagan* 770 F 2d 202 (DC Cir 1985) 206 and Randolph J in *Al Odah v United States* 321 F 3d 1134 (DC Cir 2003) 1148. See below, text at n 266.

[115] Stephens and Ratner, above n 22, at 53–54.

TNCs to monitor the impact of their operations on all human rights found in the major human rights treaties. This is especially so given that the 'core' of all recognized human rights might fall within ATCA.

At the same time, US courts must ensure that their analysis of the meaning of 'the law of nations' conforms with the rigorous test for determining whether a norm falls inside or outside the rubric of customary international law. Conclusory statements in this regard are unhelpful, and serve to undermine the credibility of ATCA decisions. A rigorous analysis is also necessary to guard against the enforcement by US courts of human rights norms in an extraterritorial context that are simply *not* part of customary international law. In that situation, US courts are crossing the line between the legitimate protection of human rights endorsed by the large majority of nations, and judicial imperialism.

REQUIREMENT OF STATE ACTION

Most customary human rights norms apply only in the context of governmental action. Only a small number of human rights norms apply in customary international law in the absence of state action, and are discussed below.[116] Private actors can nonetheless be held liable for other human rights abuses if a sufficient connection exists between the private actor and abuses committed by a government or, alternatively, between a government and the private actor's abuses. Thus, in ATCA claims requiring state action against TNCs or other private bodies, some sort of joint responsibility of both the State and the private body for the impugned acts must be established in order for the case to proceed.[117] As noted in *Eastman Kodak v Kavlin*, 'it would be a strange tort system that imposed liability on state actors but not on those who conspired with them to perpetrate illegal acts through the coercive use of state power'.[118] In this respect, a domestic US counterpart can arguably be found in 42 USC § 1983, under which private actors can be held liable for civil rights violations (normally only enforceable against state actors) when committed 'under the colour' of governmental authority.[119] US courts have tended to use the tests adopted to determine 'state action' for domestic law purposes under § 1983 to determine whether 'state action' exists in an ATCA claim. Those tests are: public function, state compulsion, nexus, joint action, and proximate cause.

'Public function' liability arises if a private actor exercised powers 'traditionally the exclusive prerogative of the State'.[120] 'State compulsion' occurs when

---

[116] See below, text at nn 206–24.
[117] However, liability would rarely actually lie against a foreign government due to the doctrine of sovereign immunity (see below, text at nn 163–67).
[118] *Eastman Kodak Co v Kavlin* 978 F Supp 1078 (SD Fla 1997) 1091.
[119] SA Khalil, 'The Alien Tort Claims Act and Section 1983: The Improper Use of Domestic Law to 'Create' and 'Define' International Liability for Multinational Corporations' (2002) 31 *Hofstra Law Review* 207, 209.
[120] *Beanal v Freeport-McMoran, Inc* 969 F Supp 362 (ED La 1997) 379.

the private actor's actions are compelled by the State. These two tests can arise in an ATCA context when a plaintiff seeks to establish that a government is connected to a private party's impugned actions. The nexus test arises where there is such a connection between the private actor and the State that it is fair to treat the action of one as that of the other.[121] Joint action liability arises when private actors and governments are willful participants in a partnership, so that both are liable for abuses perpetrated by one party in performance of partnership tasks.[122] The main difference between 'nexus' and 'joint action' is that the former implies a continuing relationship, whereas the latter may relate to a single event.[123] Joint action and nexus may arise in circumstances where either the private party or the government is directly responsible for the alleged abuses, and the plaintiff seeks to establish the other party's joint responsibility, or where both the private actor and the government are directly liable. Proximate cause arises when a private actor exercises control over a State's perpetration of the abuse.[124] This final § 1983 test arises when a plaintiff seeks to hold a private party liable for the acts of a government. 'The distinctions among these approaches are not always clear'.[125] The Supreme Court has even mused that the tests are simply 'different ways of characterising the necessarily fact-bound inquiry that confronts the court'.[126] Unfortunately, the Supreme Court is also correct in its admission that § 1983 jurisprudence has 'not been a model of consistency'.[127] It is instructive to examine how the § 1983 tests have been applied in some of the salient cases.

Occasionally, an ATCA claim involves a complaint about the direct actions of a corporation, so a plaintiff will seek to establish a governmental connection for the purposes of establishing state action. For example, in *Beanal v Freeport McMoran*, Beanal alleged that the defendant company's control over a large tract of land (26,400 square kilometers) in Irian Jaya (Indonesia), which was policed by its own security personnel, amounted to exercise of a 'public function'. While the plaintiffs painted 'a picture . . . of Freeport's vast and draconian control over the Grasberg Mine area',[128] they nonetheless failed to establish state action, indicating that the public function test is very narrow.[129]

---

[121] Zia-Zarifi, above n 23, at 107. Another term for 'nexus' is 'symbiotic relationship': SM Hall, 'Multinational Corporations' Post-Unocal Liabilities for Violations of International Law' (2002) *George Washington International Law Review* 401, 410; Tzeutschler, above n 32, at 390–91.

[122] *Doe I v Unocal Corp* 963 F Supp 880 (CD Cal 1997) 890–91.

[123] Tzeutschler, above n 32, at 391; SJ Adams Lien, 'Employer Beware? Enforcing Transnational Labour Standards in the United States under the Alien Tort Claims Act' 6 (2002) *Journal of Small and Emerging Business Law* 311, 324–25.

[124] *Doe I v Unocal Corp* 110 F Supp 2d 1294 (CD Cal 2000) 1307 (*Unocal 2000*); see also *Sarei v Rio Tinto* 221 F Supp 2d 1116 (CD Cal 2002) 1145. Proximate cause is mainly a creature of Ninth Circuit jurisprudence; see C Forcese, 'ATCA's Achilles Heel: Corporate Complicity, International Law and the Alien Tort Claims Act' (2001) 26 *Yale Journal of International Law* 487, 507.

[125] Forcese, *ibid* at 502.

[126] *Lugar v Edmondson Oil Co* 457 US 922 (SCt 1982) 937.

[127] *Lebron v National R R Passenger Corp* 513 US 374 (SCt 1995) 378.

[128] *Beanal v Freeport-McMoran, Inc* 969 F Supp 362 (ED La 1997) 380.

[129] See also Zia-Zarifi, above n 23, at 113.

Abdullahi v Pfizer concerned an allegation of Pfizer's conduct of unsafe drug tests in Nigeria without the informed consent of those tested. The Court found that the plaintiffs sufficiently pleaded joint action between Pfizer and the Nigerian government, entailed in the latter's assignment of Nigerian physicians to work with Pfizer, its action to silence Nigerian doctors who were critical of the trials, its request to US authorities to export the relevant drug, and its backdating of a letter regarding the trials in order to feign compliance with relevant international protocols.[130]

ATCA corporate cases more often involve 'reverse state action', where a court is attempting to classify government behaviour as that of the private party.[131] For example, in *Eastman Kodak*, an Eastman Kodak employee was detained in Bolivia in appalling conditions on fabricated charges. The defendants, a corporation and one of its executive officers, were accused of conspiring with Bolivian State authorities to effect that detention. If true, the situation clearly amounted to one of joint action.[132]

In *Sarei v Rio Tinto*, the Court found that the complaint sufficiently asserted Rio Tinto's responsibility under the doctrines of joint action and/or proximate cause for certain human rights abuses committed by the Papua New Guinean government. For example, it was alleged that Rio Tinto threatened to 'reconsider' its considerable investments in PNG if the government failed to take action to stop local protests against Rio's mines in Bougainville, in full knowledge that this implicit threat of withdrawal would provoke military action against the protesters.[133] The Court accepted that the allegation, if proven, would render Rio Tinto liable for subsequent human rights abuses perpetrated by PNG forces in containing rebel activity in Bougainville.

The most extensive judicial discussion of the state action doctrine has arisen in the *Unocal* litigation. In *Doe v Unocal* (*Unocal 2000*), Lew J summarily dismissed the case, as he could not find a sufficient connection between Unocal and the abuses committed by the Myanmar military in the area of Unocal's pipeline project. Lew J held that joint action would only be established if there was evidence that Unocal 'participated in or influenced' the military's perpetration of the abuses.[134] Lew J added that proximate cause would only be established if Unocal exercised control over the military's decision to commit human rights abuses. Under these strict tests, which virtually required Unocal to command the perpetration of the abuses, or directly perpetrate them alongside the Myanmar military, Lew J found that Unocal could not be held liable for the military's abuses. Lew J's strict reading of proximate cause has been disputed by Professor Forcese, who has argued that the correct standard for proximate cause

---

[130] *Abdullahi v Pfizer* No 01 Civ 8118, 2002 US Dist LEXIS 17436 (SDNY 2002) 16–18.
[131] See *Sarei v Rio Tinto* 221 F Supp 2d 1116 (CD Cal 2002) 1144; see also Forcese, above n 124, at 498.
[132] See *Eastman Kodak Co v Kavlin* 978 F Supp 1078 (SD Fla 1997) 1091–92.
[133] *Sarei v Rio Tinto* 221 F Supp 2d 1116 (CD Cal 2002) 1148.
[134] *Unocal 2000*, above n 124, at 1306–7.

as evinced in § 1983 cases is whether the actions of a party lead to 'reasonably foreseeable' abuse by a third party.[135] Forcese's standard would have resulted in a different *Unocal 2000* summary decision, as Lew J conceded that evidence existed to show that Unocal either foresaw or should have foreseen that its actions would lead to government abuses.

Lew J's decision was overruled by the Ninth Circuit in *Doe v Unocal* (*Unocal 2002*).[136] This decision was in turn vacated on 14 February 2003, and the case is now being appealed to an eleven judge *en banc* panel within the Ninth Circuit.[137] Nevertheless, it is instructive to examine the reasoning in *Unocal 2002*. The Circuit majority classified all of the human rights allegations as lying within the limited category that may be activated purely by private abuse, so the majority judgment has little relevance to the issue of state action requirements. However, the majority did endorse Lew J's limited interpretation of 'proximate cause' for § 1983 purposes.[138]

Reinhardt J delivered a separate opinion in *Unocal 2002*. He decided that, as the question related to whether Unocal was somehow responsible for abuses committed by Myanmar military personnel, there was no need to decide whether the abuses could be activated in the absence of State action; the relevant State had clearly acted.[139] He then applied ordinary tort principles of joint liability, agency, and reckless disregard to the question of whether Unocal could be held liable for the actions of the Myanmar military,[140] without mentioning § 1983 as a basis for Unocal's liability.

Reinhardt J found that Unocal had a case to answer regarding joint liability for the alleged abuses, because the evidence indicated that it had 'freely elected to participate in a profit-making venture in conjunction with an oppressive military regime—a regime that had a lengthy record of instituting forced labour'.[141] Second, Unocal could potentially be liable under the 'agency' principle, because evidence suggested the military were in the relevant area essentially 'to support the pipeline project . . . at the request of and in close coordination with Unocal';[142] they were not present 'merely to maintain order, as was its function in other parts of the nation'.[143] Finally, Unocal could be held liable under the theory of 'reckless disregard'. Sufficient evidence had been adduced to

---

[135] Forcese, above n 124, at 505–7, 513.
[136] *Unocal 2002*, above n 40.
[137] Doe v Unocal Corp 2003 WL 359787, 14 February 2002.
[138] See *ibid* at note 29 therein. Lew J's interpretation of 'proximate cause' was also supported in *Sarei v Rio Tinto* 221 F Supp 2d 1116 (CD Cal 2002) 1145–46.
[139] *Unocal 2002*, above n 40, at 14246.
[140] *Ibid* at 14252. The majority conceded that Unocal's liability might also be established under tort principles, but declined to definitively answer this question (see p 14212, note 17).
[141] *Ibid* at 14259.
[142] *Ibid* at 14263.
[143] *Ibid* at 14263.

show that Unocal was both subjectively and objectively reckless[144] in engaging the Myanmar military to perform pipeline-related tasks, 'even though it had knowledge that the military engaged in widespread human rights abuses'.[145] Furthermore Unocal continued to engage the military even after it knew that the military was perpetrating abuses in carrying out their task of protecting the pipeline.

Tort principles regarding joint liability impose broader liability than the § 1983 principles, at least as interpreted by Lew J in *Unocal 2000*. For Lew J, Unocal could not be liable for the Myanmar military's abuses despite its apparent knowledge and acceptance of those abuses in the absence of affirmative participation in or control over the actual abuses.[146] Reinhardt J's tests for joint liability under ATCA cast a wider net by encompassing conduct (eg. directing the Myanmar military to protect the Yadana pipeline) that foreseeably facilitates the eventual perpetration of the abuses. Reinhardt J's test did not require as strong a nexus between Unocal and the actual abuses as that of Lew J. Adoption of Reinhardt J's tort approach would thus lower the threshold for the 'state action' requirement. Alternatively, adoption of Forcese's 'foreseeability' standard under the 'proximate cause' limb of § 1983 would probably yield the same result.[147]

It is questionable whether the complex § 1983 tests, which have evolved for the purpose of determining whether breaches of civil rights in the US have occurred, are appropriate tests in the ATCA context, which concerns *torts* arising from *international* rather than US law.[148] Perhaps § 1983 could be used to inform the issue, rather than as a straitjacket that constrains analysis within confusing, inconsistent parameters. It is at least arguable that § 1983 principles are inappropriate in the context of finding private actors liable for government actions, a scenario which is far less common under § 1983 jurisprudence than the reverse situation.[149]

Ordinary tort principles for identifying joint tortfeasors, as applied by Reinhardt J, provide one alternative template for ATCA 'state action' tests.[150] International law provides another: precedents from international criminal courts provide a growing body of law for determining the liability of

---

[144] Subjective recklessness arises when a party proceeds with a course of action despite knowing the substantial risks of harm in such a course of action. Objective recklessness arises when a party proceeds with a course of action when that party ought to have known that it entailed substantial risks of harm (*ibid* at 14264).

[145] *Ibid* at 14266. At 14265–66, Reinhardt J suggests that reckless disregard is also a basis for § 1983 liability, though he does not suggest that such liability is necessary in order to find Unocal liable for the Myanmar military's actions.

[146] See *Unocal 2000*, above n 124, at 1306–7; see also Forcese, above n 124, at 513.

[147] Forcese, above n 124, at 509.

[148] Collingsworth, above n 16, at 199; Forcese, *ibid* at 501–2.

[149] Forcese, *ibid* at 498.

[150] See also International Council on Human Rights Policy [ICHRP], *Beyond Voluntarism: Human Rights and Developing International Legal Obligations of Companies* (ICHRP, Versoix, 2002) 122–23 (also available via <http://www.ichrp.org/>) (5 January 2003).

co-perpetrators or accomplices in international law.[151] Indeed, as described below, the Circuit majority in *Unocal 2002* used 'aiding and abetting' principles from international law to find that the case against Unocal could proceed, though only in the context of abuses that do not require State action.[152]

In *Presbyterian Church of Sudan v Talisman Energy*, the court agreed that international criminal law was the appropriate source of law in determining whether the corporate defendant had aided and abetted the Sudanese government in committing war crimes and genocide.[153] While war crimes and genocide are two ATCA torts that can be committed in the absence of state action,[154] this fact was not explicitly relevant to the court's findings regarding the appropriate test for aiding and abetting. No mention was made of § 1983. The *Talisman* court did not adopt a specific test for aiding and abetting,[155] instead noting a myriad of formulations thereof from the jurisprudence of international courts such as the International Criminal Tribunal for the Former Yugoslavia (ICTY),[156] before concluding that the plaintiffs had 'properly allege[d] that Talisman aided and abetted or conspired with Sudan to commit various violations of the law of nations'.[157]

It has been suggested that accomplice liability for private actors in committing 'state action' human rights abuses is not prohibited by international law, and is therefore not a breach of the law of nations.[158] However, 'aiding and abetting' liability in international law for private actors has been confirmed with regard to the human rights abuses which come within the jurisdiction of the international criminal tribunals, such as the ICTY. Such abuses include crimes against humanity, which have not been accepted by US courts as being action-

---

[151] See generally, A Clapham and S Jerbi, 'Categories of Corporate Complicity in Human Rights Abuses' (2001) 24 *Hastings International and Comparative Law Review* 339, and A Ramasastry, 'Corporate Complicity: From Nuremberg to Rangoon: An Examination of Forced Labour Cases and their Impact on the Liability of Multinational Corporations' (2002) 20 *Berkeley Journal of International Law* 91.

[152] *Carmichael v United Tech Corp* 835 F 2d 109 (5th Cir 1988) 113 (in dicta) and *Cabello Barrueto v Fernandez Larios* 205 F Supp 2d 1325 (SD Fla 2002) 1332–33 (in the context of a state agent) support 'aiding and abetting' as a standard for imposing accomplice liability under ATCA. In *Cabello Barrueto*, an action against a Chilean general under ATCA, the court explicitly drew on international law in framing the applicable test for 'aiding and abetting'.

[153] *Presbyterian Church of Sudan v Talisman Energy* 244 F Supp 2d 289 (SDNY 2003) 320–24.

[154] See below, text at n 206.

[155] Compare the majority in *Unocal 2002*, where a more precise test was adopted; see below, text at n 218.

[156] *Presbyterian Church of Sudan v Talisman Energy* 244 F Supp 2d 289 (SDNY 2003) 323–24. For example, relevant assistance must be 'direct and substantial' (*Prosecutor v Tadic* Case no IT–94–1–T, 7 May 1997 (ICTY) [691–92]); 'all acts of assistance in the form of either physical or moral support [that] substantially contribute to the commission of the crime', which 'need not be indispensible': *Prosecutor v Furundzija* Case no. IT–95–17/1–T, Judgment, 10 December 1998 (ICTY) [209 and 235]); there must also be actual or constructive knowledge of the principal crime (*Tadic* at [659, 675–77]).

[157] *Presbyterian Church of Sudan v Talisman Energy* 244 F Supp 2d 289 (SDNY 2003) 324.

[158] See MD Ramsey, 'Multinational Corporate Liability under the Alien Tort Claims Act: Some Structural Concerns' (2001) *Hastings International and Comparative Law Review* 361, 364; see also Forcese, above n 124, at 497–98, and Khalil, above n 119, at 216–17.

able under ATCA without state action.[159] Therefore, 'aiding and abetting' liability for private actors in international law extends beyond the 'private actor' abuses (ie those that do not require state action) recognised thus far by US courts. Regarding customary human rights that fall outside the jurisdiction of the international criminal courts, the question of whether international law directly prohibits private actor complicity[160] in State breaches of customary human rights that require state action is obfuscated by the lack of international forums with jurisdiction over this issue. The absence of a forum does not necessarily imply the absence of substantive international legal liability.

So far, state action has only been established in cases where the relevant government has affirmatively participated in the relevant breach of human rights. Indeed, in most cases, it is the State that has actually perpetrated the abuse, and the plaintiff must establish a connection between the TNC and the abuse. Can state action be entailed in a State's acquiescence in a TNC's acts, or in its failure to control a TNC? Under human rights treaty law, States are required to control entities within jurisdiction; failure to do so breaches the relevant treaty.[161] However, it is uncertain the extent to which such a duty exists within customary international law, that is 'the law of nations'. If such a duty arises in customary law, it could be argued that a State's failure to adequately control a corporation amounts to 'state action' in international law for the purposes of activating ATCA. To the author's knowledge, such an argument has never been raised in an ATCA case. Of course, such an argument would significantly lessen the burden in establishing the state action element of the ATCA test in any case where a TNC has itself perpetrated a breach of the law of nations.

Abstention Issues Associated with State Action Doctrine

The state action requirement gives rise to the possibility of a number of jurisdictional blocks to litigation. First, one must note that foreign governments are largely immune from suit in the US under the *Foreign Sovereign Immunities Act* (FSIA).[162] ATCA does not remove sovereign immunity.[163] The FSIA extends to state agencies and instrumentalities,[164] but not individual servants except for

---

[159] See *Wiwa v Royal Dutch Petroleum Co*, No 96 Civ 8386, 2002 US Dist LEXIS 3293 (SDNY Feb 22, 2002) 37–39.

[160] Complicity in human rights abuses is indirectly prohibited under the doctrine of horizontality. States are directly obliged under international human rights law to protect and ensure against violations of the rights of people by other people within jurisdiction, including all private actors. In that situation however, the obligation is imposed directly on the State, and only indirectly on private actors. See also ch 1, p 9.

[161] See Ch 1, p 9, and Ch 3, pp 76–77.

[162] 28 USC, § 1330, 1602–11 (1988).

[163] *Argentine Republic v Amerada Hess Shipping Corp* 488 US 428 (SCt 1989); *Siderman de Blake v Republic of Argentina* 965 F 2d 699 (9th Cir 1992).

[164] See *Abrams v Societe Nationale Des Chemins de fer Francais* 175 F Supp 2d 423 (EDNY 2001), where a complaint against the French rail corporation for deportation of French Jews during World War II was dismissed as the company was a State agency or instrumentality. However, this decision

heads of State.[165] Sovereign immunity does not tend to arise in ATCA cases, as it is assumed that perpetrators of grave abuses are acting outside their official functions.[166] It seems unlikely that a private corporation, even when engaged in a corporate joint venture with a government, is in a position to benefit from the FSIA, as it would rarely be in such a subordinate position of government control.[167] Nonetheless, there are a number of other 'principles of abstention'[168] which a Court may invoke in order to deny jurisdiction in a case involving state action.

Act of State

US courts may abstain from exercising jurisdiction under the act of state doctrine, which applies when a US court is required to adjudicate claims relating to a foreign sovereign's official acts within its own territory.[169] The purpose of the doctrine is to maintain the constitutional separation of powers, so that the pre-eminence of the political branches of government over the judiciary is maintained in the realm of foreign relations.[170] Thus, the court evaluates a case's implications for the US's foreign relations: the greater the implications the greater the likelihood of a dismissal on the basis of 'act of state'.[171]

In *Banco Nacional de Cuba v Sabbatino*, the Supreme Court noted three factors in evaluating an 'act of state' argument.[172] First, the doctrine is less likely to apply when a State is accused of behavior that is condemned by international consensus. Considering that ATCA liability only lies for abuses that breach customary international law, the doctrine should rarely apply in ATCA cases.[173] Indeed, in *Sarei v Rio Tinto*, the court found that the alleged crimes against humanity and war crimes could not be classified as official state acts, so they fell outside the 'act of state' doctrine,[174] indicating that the most egregious

---

was vacated and remitted by the Second Circuit in *Abrams v Societe Nationale des Chemins de fer Francais* 332 F 3d 173 (2d Cir 2003) in order for the District Court to consider whether the Foreign Sovereign Immunities Act could constitutionally have a retroactive effect on the plaintiffs' rights.

[165] See *Republic of Philippines v Marcos* 665 F Supp 793 (ND Cal 1987) 797.
[166] Zia-Zarifi, above n 23, at 136; see also J Terry, 'Taking Filartiga on the Road: Why Courts outside the United States should accept Jurisdiction over Actions involving Torture Committed Abroad' in Scott, above n 16, at 126–27.
[167] See *Doe I v Unocal Corp* 963 F Supp 880 (CD Cal 1997) 886–89; Zia-Zarifi, above n 23, at 139–40; E Marcks, 'Avoiding Liability for Human Rights Violations in Project Finance' (2001) 22 *Energy Law Journal* 301, 304; Tzeutschler, above n 32, at 375.
[168] *Bigio v Coca Cola Co* 239 F 3d 440 (2d Cir 2000) 451.
[169] *Sarei v Rio Tinto* 221 F Supp 2d 1116 (CD Cal 2002) 1183.
[170] *Bigio v Coca Cola Co* 239 F 3d 440 (2d Cir 2000) 452.
[171] See *Banco Nacional de Cuba v Sabbatino* 376 US 398 (SCt 1964) 428.
[172] Ibid.
[173] See *Kadic v Karadzic* 70 F 3d 232 (2d Cir 1995) 250; *Unocal 2002*, above n 40, at 14233.
[174] *Sarei v Rio Tinto* 221 F Supp 2d 1116 (CD Cal 2002) 1189.

crimes cannot satisfy the threshold criterion for application of the 'act of state' doctrine.[175]

Second, as the key question seems to be whether a court decision might impede US foreign relations policy, the doctrine would not seem to apply in a human rights context if the foreign State's human rights record has already been publicly denounced by the US government.[176]

Third, the doctrine is not likely to apply where the impugned foreign act is that of a former government. For example, the 'act of state' doctrine did not apply in *Bigio v Coca-Cola*,[177] *Wiwa 2002*,[178] or *Bodner v Banque Paribas*,[179] where the acts of the former governments of, respectively, Egypt, Nigeria, and France, were at issue. Indeed, in each case, the impugned acts had been repudiated by the current governments of those countries.

In *Liu v Republic of China*, the Ninth Circuit noted as a relevant consideration whether the impugned acts of the foreign State were somehow performed 'in the public interest'.[180] The *Liu* court noted how such reasoning could apply to expropriations performed for the purpose of justly reallocating resources. Many of the complaints against corporations raised in US courts concern abuses committed by their government partners on joint venture development projects, which are arguably pursued to boost the public interest in economic development. Whilst the latter argument may be true, it cannot be contended that grave abuses, such as tortures and killings, are necessary in the public interest to allow such projects to proceed.[181]

In a number of cases where 'act of state' has arisen, the views of the US State Department have been sought. The purpose of such submissions is to provide evidence of the executive government's own view of whether the litigation at hand would unduly interfere in its conduct of foreign affairs. The Court does not inquire as to whether the view is 'wise or unwise, or whether it is based on misinformation or faulty reasoning'.[182] In a number of these cases, such as *Kadic v Karadzic*, the State Department has not objected to the continuation of the litigation. However, in *Rio Tinto*, the State Department, possibly reflecting a new hostility by the Bush administration to transnational human rights litigation, submitted an opinion that the continuation of the litigation would harm US foreign policy interests in promoting the Bougainville peace process. This opinion was crucial to the court's decision to dismiss the case. The court stated:

---

[175] See also M Bühler, 'The Emperor's New Clothes: Defabricating the Myth of 'Act of State' in Anglo-Canadian Law' in Scott, above n 19, at 343, 364. See below however, on how other allegations in *Rio Tinto* were dismissed for 'act of state' (text below at n 184).
[176] See *Republic of Philippines v Marcos* 862 F 2d 1355 (9th Cir 1988) 1360; *Unocal 2002*, above n 40, at 14233.
[177] 239 F 3d 440 (2d Cir 2000) 451.
[178] No 96 Civ 8386, 2002 US Dist LEXIS 3293 (SDNY Feb 22, 2002) 93–94.
[179] 114 F Supp 2d 117 (EDNY 2000) (official acts of Vichy France rejected by current French government).
[180] 892 F 2d 1419 (9th Cir 1989) 1432. The case did not concern an ATCA claim.
[181] See *Unocal 2002*, above n 40, at 14234–35.
[182] *Sarei v Rio Tinto* 221 F Supp 2d 1116 (CD Cal 2002) 1182.

42 *The Alien Tort Claims Act*

[P]laintiffs have not cited, and the court has not found, a single case in which a court permitted a lawsuit to proceed in the face of an expression of concern such as that communicated by the State Department here. This is probably because to do so would have the potential to embarrass the executive branch in the conduct of its foreign relations, and 'the major underpinning of the act of state doctrine is . . . [to] foreclose' such a possibility.[183]

The Court ultimately dismissed allegations of racial discrimination and breaches of UNCLOS against Rio Tinto due to 'act of state'.[184] *Rio Tinto* seems at odds with *Kadic* dicta from the Second Circuit, where it had been asserted that 'expressions of concern' by the US government 'would not necessarily preclude adjudication'.[185] *Rio Tinto* may also be criticised for its overemphasis on the need to prevent 'embarrassment' for the legislature and executive. Embarrassment per se does not rise to the level of the mischief that the act of state doctrine is designed to prevent, that is undue interference with or substantial impact on foreign policy.

In current litigation in the DC Circuit against Exxon Mobil regarding its alleged actions in Aceh, Indonesia,[186] the State Department has submitted a brief to the Court, advising that continuation of the litigation would be detrimental to US foreign policy interests.[187] The State Department argues that the litigation could destabilise Indonesia's economy by discouraging foreign direct investment, and thus create a more fertile environment for the growth of international terrorism. The State Department added that the litigation would be seen by Indonesia as interference in its internal affairs in a particularly sensitive area, its dealings with the Aceh secessionist movement. The offence caused by the litigation could therefore threaten US diplomatic efforts to secure crucial Indonesian cooperation in the ongoing war against terrorism. The brief also contends that the litigation would jeopardise the efforts of US entities, includ-

---

[183] *Sarei v Rio Tinto* 221 F Supp 2d 1116 (CD Cal 2002) 1192, citing *Alfred Dunhill of London, Inc v Republic of Cuba* 425 US 682 (SCt 1976) 697.

[184] *Rio Tinto* was the first 'true' ATCA case to be dismissed for act of state, as it was the first such case where the claims at hand had been found to concern the law of nations. 'Act of state' was used to dismiss allegations in *Roe v Unocal* 70 F Supp 2d 1073 (CD Cal 1999) and *Nat'l Coalition Gov't of the Union of Myanmar v Unocal, Inc* 176 FRD 329 (CD Cal 1997) of, respectively, forced conscript labour, and expropriation of a national's property. In neither dismissal however were the alleged acts found to be violations of the law of nations, so ATCA would not have been activated anyway.

[185] *Kadic v Karadzic* 70 F 3d 232 (2d Cir 1995) 250. In that case, the government did not oppose adjudication, thus 'reinforc[ing the Court's] view that adjudication may properly proceed'. Powell J of the Supreme Court in *First National City Bank v Banco Nacional de Cuba* 406 US 759 (SCt 1972) 773 stated that he would be 'uncomfortable with a doctrine which would require the judiciary to receive the Executive's permission before invoking its jurisdiction'.

[186] *Doe v Exxon Mobil* Docket No 01–1357 CIV (DDC 2002). See, generally, M Saint-Saens and AJ Bann, 'Using National Security to undermine Corporate Accountability Litigation: The Exxon-Mobil v Doe Controversy', (2003) 11 *University of Miami International and Comparative Law* 39.

[187] Details of the *Exxon Mobil* complaint, and the State department memo of 29 July 2002 can be found at <http://www.labourrights.org/> (30 September 2002). See also M McGrory, 'Powell's Awkward Position' *Washington Post* (Washington, August 29 2002) A31.

ing companies, to improve human rights in Indonesia. The litigation would result in preference being given in contracts and tenders to non-US companies, particularly companies from the People's Republic of China, that 'would be far less concerned about human rights abuses, or about upholding best business practices'. Furthermore, any resultant preference given to US corporate competitors would jeopardise the US foreign interest in US companies increasing their overseas investment opportunities.

The effect of this brief on the *Exxon Mobil* litigation remains to be seen. The *Rio Tinto* precedent indicates that it could derail the plaintiffs' case. On the other hand, the brief may be distinguished from the *Rio Tinto* brief in that the latter identified specific harm that the actual litigation could cause to a particular aspect of US foreign policy, its promotion of peace in Bougainville. The Exxon Mobil brief cites more generalised and speculative concerns, which relate less to the specific litigation and more to *any* human rights litigation concerning the Indonesian government, or indeed against a US company regarding its overseas activities. The only specific consequence that is cited as a likely *direct* result of the *Exxon Mobil* litigation is the extra offence Indonesia could feel over a case concerning events in Aceh. This contention is made even though the US State Department and the Congress have published accusations of grave human rights abuse by Indonesia in Aceh.[188] The concerns regarding the 'war on terrorism' could be expressed in litigation concerning any of the numerous lukewarm US allies in a war that presently has no foreseeable end. The concerns over possible damage to human rights in Indonesia seem at best ironic in the context of litigation against a US corporation allegedly complicit in gross human rights violations, including murder and rape, in Aceh.[189] Finally, the concerns regarding the financial interests of US businesses abroad should be irrelevant. Civil litigation against a US corporation concerning its US activities cannot be dismissed on the basis that the decision might adversely affect the business interests of other US corporations; the transnational element does not justify a different result in transnational cases. Routine deference to such wide-ranging policy preferences would amount to an abdication of judicial power in favor of judicial apologism for the policies of the political arms of the government.[190]

The defendants in *Presbyterian Church v Talisman* also argued that the case, which concerned allegations of gross human rights violations in Sudan, should be dismissed for act of state. The court refused, noting that the alleged acts (genocide, war crimes, torture, and enslavement) were so universally condemned that they could not be properly classified as acts of state. The court in *Talisman* also took a sceptical view of the impact that the litigation would have

---

[188] See Affidavit of Harold Hongju Koh in the matter of *John Doe I v Exxon Mobil Corporation* Docket No 01–1357 CIV (LFO) paras 14–15. Note also that litigation against an Indonesian general regarding his alleged abuses in East Timor is proceeding in the capital in *Doe v Major General Johnny Lumintang* Civ Action No 00-674 (DDC 2001).
[189] See Collingsworth, above n 16, at 190–91, outlining the contentions in the Exxon litigation.
[190] See also Tzeutschler, above n 32, at 369–70.

44 The Alien Tort Claims Act

on US foreign policy. Though the US government was attempting to broker peace in the Sudanese civil war, the court found that no reasons had been submitted as to why the litigation would jeopardise those diplomatic efforts. Further, any ultimate finding of liability against Talisman, which would implicitly involve a factual finding that the Sudanese government had perpetrated atrocities, would not undermine US policy towards Sudan. The US congress had already declared Sudan to be guilty of genocide,[191] while the US executive government had condemned Sudan as a state sponsor of terrorism. Therefore, 'any criticism of Sudan that would arise as a result of the adjudication of [the] case would be a mere drop in the bucket'.[192] The defendant's unsuccessful arguments in *Talisman* concerning the alleged impact the litigation might have on foreign peace initiatives were very similar to those successfully made by the defendants in *Rio Tinto* about the Bougainville Peace Process. A key difference between the two cases is that a US State Department brief, which supported the defendants' arguments, was submitted in *Rio Tinto*, but was not requested by the court in *Talisman*.

Political Question

The courts will refrain from exercising jurisdiction if they resolve that the dispute at issue concerns a non-justiciable political question.[193] The Supreme Court spelt out the relevant considerations for the purposes of a 'political question' analysis in *Baker v Carr*:

> Prominent on the surface of any case held to involve a political question is found a textually demonstrable constitutional commitment of the issue to a coordinate political department; or a lack of judicially discoverable and manageable standards for resolving it; or the impossibility of deciding without an initial policy determination of a kind clearly for nonjudicial discretion; or the impossibility of a court's undertaking independent resolution without expressing lack of the respect due coordinate branches of government; or an unusual need for unquestioning adherence to a political decision already made; or the potentiality of embarrassment from multifarious pronouncements by various departments on one question. . . . Unless one of these formulations is inextricable from the case at bar, there should be no dismissal for non-justiciability on the ground of a political question's presence. The doctrine of which we treat is one of 'political questions,' not one of 'political cases.'[194]

The above criteria are unfortunately quite vague. Professor Brilmayer has aptly summed up the doctrine by noting that it arises when the litigation raises

---

[191] See *Sudan Peace Act* (2002) Pub L No 107–245, 21 October 2002.
[192] *Presbyterian Church of Sudan v Talisman Energy* 244 F Supp 2d 289 (SDNY 2003) 346.
[193] See NS Williams, 'Political Question or Judicial Query: An Examination of the Modern Doctrine and its Inapplicability to Human Rights Mass Tort Litigation' (2001) 28 *Pepperdine Law Review* 849 for a critique of the use of the political question doctrine in human rights litigation in the US.
[194] 369 US 186 (SCt 1962) 217.

matters that are simply 'too political . . . to handle'.[195] The political question doctrine arises when a case will force a court to intrude too much into the political realm cordoned off for the legislature and/or the executive, so the doctrine, like that of 'act of state', is also linked to the notion of the separation of powers. The classic instance of application of the 'political question' doctrine again arises when a case impinges on the area of foreign policy. Though 'political question' and 'act of state' often arise together, they are distinguishable in that the former issue can arise in the absence of the necessity to 'judge' a foreign government's official act.

In *Iwanowa v Ford Motor Co*, a complaint against a US company concerning use of slave and forced labour in Nazi Germany in World War II, the Court dismissed the case, inter alia, on political question grounds because the issue of compensation for grievances arising out of the War had been dealt with by the political branches of government in concluding post-war reparations treaties.[196] Claims against Japanese companies for alleged forced labour in the Far East during World War II were similarly dismissed.[197]

In *Rio Tinto*, the State Department brief was again very influential in the Court's decision to dismiss the case for 'political question':

> Were the court to ignore this statement of position, deny the motion to dismiss, and retain jurisdiction over this action, it would surely 'express . . . lack of respect for the

---

[195] L Brilmayer, 'International Law in American Courts: A Modest Proposal' 100 (1991) *Yale Law Journal* 2277, 2305.

[196] 67 F Supp 2d 424 (DNJ 1999) 483–91. Other grounds for dismissal included statute of limitations grounds, and non-conformity with the post-war treaties. See also *Burger-Fischer v Degussa AG* 65 F Supp 2d 248 (DNJ 1999), and D Vagts and P Murray, 'Litigating the Nazi Labour Claims: The Path not Taken' 43 (2002) *Harvard International Law Journal* 503. The latter article explains at 503 how these labour claims against corporations active under Nazi occupation have now been settled by the 'United States-Germany Agreement Concerning the Foundation "Remembrance, Responsibility and the Future"' (2000) 39 *International Legal Materials* 1298. All pending litigation was subsequently dismissed: *In re Nazi Era Cases against German Defendants* 198 FRD 429 (DNJ 2001). See also Ramasastry, above n 151, at 122–24.

An action against German and Japanese companies for utilising slave labour during World War II in *Deutsch v Turner Corp* 324 F 3d 692 (9th Cir 2003) was dismissed for statute of limitations reasons. A California statute which purported to remove that bar for such victims of the Nazis and their allies was ruled unconstitutional for intruding upon the federal government's exclusive foreign affairs powers. Note that claims against companies based outside Germany were not the subject of the Post-War settlements. Hence, cases such as *Bodner v Banque Paribas* 114 F Supp 2d 117 (EDNY 2000) against a French bank for collusion in the looting of the property of victims of the Nazis were initially allowed to proceed. The *Banque Paribas* litigation has now settled under the 'Washington Agreement', an Agreement between the Government of the United States and the Government of France concerning payment for certain losses suffered during World War II, 18 January 2001, see generally <http://www.wiesenthal.com/swiss/index.cfm> (22 October 2002). See also Vagts & Murray, above n 196, at 508, note 33, on the similar actions by Holocaust victims to recover assets from Swiss Banks which were settled in 1998; see *In re Holocaust Victim Assets Litigation* 105 F Supp 2d 139 (EDNY 2000). See generally, A Ramasastry, 'Secrets and Lies? Swiss Banks and International Human Rights' (1998) 31 *Vanderbilt Journal of Transnational Law* 325.

[197] See *In re World War II Era Japanese Forced Labour Litigation* 114 F Supp 2d 939 (ND Cal 2000); *Japanese Forced Labour Litigation II* 164 F Supp 2d 1160 (ND Cal 2001). See also Ramasastry, above n 151, at 127–29.

coordinate branches of government', and cause 'the potentiality of embarrassment from multifarious pronouncements by various departments on one question'.[198]

Unlike the 'act of state' dismissals in *Rio Tinto*, the 'political question' dismissal related to the entire case, including the allegations of crimes against humanity and war crimes. Thus, the political question doctrine applies to permit dismissal of claims regarding even the most heinous human rights crimes.

As with the act of state doctrine, it is possible that the *Rio Tinto* court placed too much emphasis on the importance of complying with the State Department's contentions so as to avert executive embarrassment, resulting in an overextension of the political question doctrine. Determination of Rio Tinto's liability for human rights abuses in PNG would not have caused 'multifarious pronouncements . . . on *one question*'. The US executive had addressed the issue of PNG's behaviour in Bougainville (and indeed had criticised PNG for human rights abuses committed during the relevant period), but had not dealt with the behaviour and actions of Rio Tinto itself. Furthermore, the litigation was not *about* the 'question' the US executive was addressing, the Bougainville peace process. Rather, it was about whether a corporation had contravened a statute, normally a patently justiciable question.

Again, the *Talisman* court came to a very different conclusion to that in *Rio Tinto*, with regard to the application of the political question doctrine. On the issue of embarrassing the other arms of government, the court stated that this only arose if the 'judicial resolution of a question would contradict prior decisions taken by the political branch in those limited contexts where such contradiction would seriously interfere with important governmental interests'.[199] Again, given the recent condemnation of Sudan by the Congress and the executive, any judicial findings regarding the behaviour of the Sudanese government would not undermine those policy stances.

As in *Rio Tinto* but not *Talisman*, the State Department has submitted a brief supporting the dismissal of the *Exxon Mobil* litigation for reasons of political question. That case will therefore be instructive with regard to the effect of such briefs upon future political question arguments in transnational human rights litigation.

Comity

The doctrine of international comity has been defined as 'the recognition one nation allows within its territory to the legislative, executive or judicial acts of another nation, having due regard both to international duty and convenience'.[200] Comity essentially applies where the exercise of jurisdiction would

---

[198] *Sarei v Rio Tinto* 221 F Supp 2d 1116 (CD Cal 2002).
[199] *Presbyterian Church of Sudan v Talisman Energy* 244 F Supp 2d 289 (SDNY 2003) 348, quoting *Kadic v Karadzic* 70 F 3d 232 (2d Cir 1995) 250.
[200] *Hilton v Guyot* 159 US 113 (SCt 1895) 164.

be unreasonable in light of the connections to and interests of another affected State in the litigation.[201]

Comity arose in *Rio Tinto*, where the court balanced the US policy interests in exercising jurisdiction with the PNG policy interests in the court refraining from such an exercise.[202] Again, the State Department brief was influential in the Court's determination that both the US and PNG policy interests favoured denial of jurisdiction in the US forum. Parts of the case, those relating to racial discrimination and environmental harms contrary to UNCLOS, were therefore dismissed on grounds of comity. However, the Court did not dismiss the allegations of crimes against humanity and war crimes on comity grounds. As such offences are considered particularly odious by the international community, policy considerations favored the maintenance of jurisdiction over those offences.[203]

In *Talisman*, the court rejected a contention that the court should dismiss the case out of respect for Sudan. The case concerned allegations of *Talisman's* involvement in genocidal acts in Sudan. The court found that comity could not justify dismissal of claims of genocide. 'Such acts are fundamentally different than a foreign court's determination in, for example, a bankruptcy matter'.[204] As in *Rio Tinto*, comity was not granted in respect of claims of the most egregious human rights violations.

Talisman also argued that the case should be dismissed for reasons of comity out of 'deference to Sudan's ongoing peace negotiations'.[205] The court rejected this contention, noting that 'any adjudication of private plaintiffs' rights in [the New York] court would certainly have far less impact' on the peace negotiations than the US government's public identification of Sudan as a sponsor of state terrorism, and a perpetrator of genocide. The *Talisman* court was more rigorous than the *Rio Tinto* court in evaluating the likely political consequences of the litigation within the relevant foreign country. Of course, the two cases can again be distinguished on the basis that a State Department brief was submitted in favour of the defendants in *Rio Tinto* but not in *Talisman*.

---

[201] *Restatement (Third) of the Foreign Relations Law of the US* § 403(1) (1987).
[202] *Sarei v Rio Tinto* 221 F Supp 2d 1116 (CD Cal 2002) 1208. This 'balancing' analysis resembles the 'balancing of interests' performed for the purposes of determining whether a stay on the basis of forum non conveniens [FNC] should be granted; see ch 4, pp 92–94, and also *Sequihua v Texaco* 847 F Supp 61 (SD Tex 1994) 63–4, on the close links between comity and FNC analysis. See also *Jota v Texaco Inc* 157 F 3d 153 (2d Cir 1998) 160 and *Torres v Southern Peru Copper* 965 F Supp 899 (SD Tex 1996) 908–9.
[203] *Sarei v Rio Tinto* 221 F Supp 2d 1116 (CD Cal 2002) 1207; the allegations relating to war crimes and crimes against humanity were dismissed on the grounds of political question (see above, text at n 198).
[204] *Presbyterian Church of Sudan v Talisman Energy* 244 F Supp 2d 289 (SDNY 2003) 342.
[205] *Ibid* at 343.

PRIVATE ACTOR ABUSES

Most human rights abuses are only prohibited by customary international law if committed by or in collusion with a governmental public actor. However some human rights violations, such as genocide, certain war crimes, piracy, slavery,[206] forced labour,[207] and aircraft hijacking[208] are prohibited by the law of nations, even in the absence of state action. Furthermore, acts committed *in furtherance* of such 'private actor' abuses are also actionable without state action.[209] On the other hand, US courts have found that rape, summary execution, torture,[210] cruel inhuman and degrading treatment,[211] pollution of international waters contrary to UNCLOS,[212] crimes against humanity,[213] rights to associate and organise,[214] and racial discrimination[215] are presently proscribed by the law of nations only when state action is present (unless committed in furtherance of one of the 'private actor' abuses). The topic of direct human rights duties for private bodies, including corporations, is a dynamic area of international law, and it is likely that the recognised customary duties of corporations and other private entities will increase in the near future.[216] Certainly, the classification of crimes against humanity by a US court as abuses requiring state action appears overly conservative, considering the existence of international criminal tribunals with jurisdiction over individuals who have committed that crime.

In the *Unocal* litigation, all Judges apart from Reinhardt J (who felt that such a determination was unnecessary), confirmed that forced labour was a private actor abuse; state action is not a prerequisite to actionability. The Circuit Court found that Unocal could be held responsible for the forced labour allegedly perpetrated by the Myanmar military if it 'aided and abetted' the relevant actions of the military. The Circuit majority used 'aiding and abetting' principles from the international criminal tribunals at Nuremberg, Tokyo, Yugoslavia, and Rwanda, thus indicating that international law rather than §1983 provides the

---

[206] Hall, above n 121, at 410; *Kadic v Karadzic* 70 F 3d 232 (2d Cir 1995) 241–43.
[207] Eg, *Doe I v Unocal Corp* 963 F Supp 880 (CD Cal 1997) 891–92.
[208] *Burnett v Al Baraka Investment and Development Corporation* 274 F Supp 2d 86 (DDC 2003).
[209] *Unocal* 2002, above n 40, at 14223; *Kadic v Karadzic* 70 F 3d 232 (2d Cir 1995) 243–44; *Presbyterian Church of Sudan v Talisman Energy* 244 F Supp 2d 289 (SDNY 2003) 328.
[210] *Kadic v Karadzic* 70 F 3d 232 (2d Cir 1995) 243.
[211] This is implicit from the finding regarding torture. See also *Abdullahi v Pfizer* No 01 Civ 8118, 2002 US Dist LEXIS 17436 (SDNY 2002) 14–15 (medical experimentation without informed consent requires state action to activate ATCA).
[212] *Sarei v Rio Tinto* 221 F Supp 2d 1116 (CD Cal 2002) 1187.
[213] *Wiwa v Royal Dutch Petroleum Co*, No 96 Civ 8386, 2002 US Dist LEXIS 3293 (SDNY Feb 22, 2002) 39.
[214] *Estate of Rodriguez v Drummond* 256 F Supp 2d 1250 (WD Al 2003) 1264–65.
[215] *Sarei v Rio Tinto* 221 F Supp 2d 1116 (CD Cal 2002) 1153.
[216] ICHRP, above n 150, especially at 73–76.

standard for establishing a private actor's accomplice liability for a 'private actor' abuse.[217]

The Circuit Court adopted the standard for the actus reus of aiding and abetting from the ICTY decision in *Prosecutor v Furundzija* as "knowing 'practical assistance [or] encouragement . . . which has a substantial effect on the perpetration of the crime'".[218] Unocal had possibly 'encouraged' or 'provided practical support' by hiring the military to perform pipeline-related duties, and by showing the Myanmar military where to perform those tasks. Furthermore, the abuses 'most probably would not have occurred in the same way' unless Unocal had so engaged the military, so Unocal's actions had a substantial effect on the commission of the impugned acts.[219] Unocal also had a case to answer regarding the mens rea of aiding and abetting, as evidence had been adduced that Unocal had 'actual or constructive (ie reasonable) knowledge' that its conduct 'would assist or encourage' the Myanmar military 'to subject Plaintiffs to forced labour'.[220] Notably, it was not necessary to prove that Unocal intended for the human rights abuses to occur.[221] The Court made similar findings regarding the allegations of murder and rape, which, in this case, fell within the ambit of 'private actor abuses' as they were allegedly committed in furtherance of forced labour.[222]

The 'aiding and abetting' test used by the Circuit majority for joint liability for private actor abuses in *Unocal 2002* is similar to the tort test used in the same case by Reinhardt J to determine a private actor's joint liability for all abuses committed by a State.[223] Both tests impose broader joint liability than the 'active participation' tests imposed by Lew J in *Unocal 2000*,[224] and increase the risk of ATCA liability for corporations engaged in commercial projects in partnership with notoriously brutal governments, who may foreseeably go overboard in performing partnership tasks.

---

[217] The opposite conclusion appears to have been reached in *Rio Tinto* at note 122 therein, where § 1983 was used to determine Rio Tinto's responsibility (for the purposes of a motion to dismiss) for private actor abuses allegedly committed by the PNG government. This District Court decision predates *Unocal 2002* and was influenced by the jurisprudence in *Unocal 2000*.
[218] IT-95-17/1-T, 10 December 1998 (ICTY), reprinted at (1999) 38 *International Legal Materials* 317, [235].
[219] *Unocal 2002*, above n 40, at 14222.
[220] *Ibid* at 14222.
[221] *Ibid* at 14218.
[222] *Ibid* at 14223.
[223] The Circuit Court noted that the *Furundzija* test as adopted accorded with US tort law, *ibid* at p 14219. Indeed, the majority implicitly supported tort law as an alternative potential basis for Unocal's liability at p 14212, n 20.
[224] Lew J also used international law principles to determine Unocal's liability for the 'private actor abuse' of forced labour. However, he focused only on the Nuremburg precedents rather than more modern case law, and wrongly construed them as requiring Unocal's active 'participation and cooperation in the forced labour practices (*Unocal 2000*, above, n 124, at p 1310).

A SUMMARY OF CORPORATE COMPLICITY UNDER ATCA

The majority of ATCA cases against TNCs have concerned alleged corporate complicity in human rights abuses committed by governments. The law under ATCA regarding corporate complicity is in a state of some uncertainty, given the overemphasis on § 1983 in most ATCA litigation, conclusory reasoning that sheds little light on the issue,[225] the overturning of *Unocal 2000* by a split court in *Unocal 2002* (from which an appeal is now pending), and the possible application of different standards regarding corporate complicity for abuses committed by governments according to the classification of the relevant abuses as 'private actor' abuses or abuses which require state action. A brief summary of the probable position follows, notwithstanding the pending *Unocal* appeal.

A corporation will definitely be held liable as an accomplice if it directly assists a government in perpetrating a relevant human rights violation. This is so even under the narrow judgment of Lew J in *Unocal 2000*. It also appears that corporations may be held liable if they engage in action which foreseeably leads to the perpetration by a government of a relevant human rights abuse. This is most clearly the case with 'private actor' abuses after *Unocal 2002*, though international criminal law and tort principles, as well as more liberal interpretations of § 1983 such as that of Professor Forcese, would lead to a similar result for all breaches of the law of nations. Lew J's requirement that a corporation actively assist in the perpetration of the actual abuse is probably too strict.

Where a TNC benefits from a State's human rights abuses, it is unlikely that that circumstance alone attracts ATCA liability. Mere benefit does not forge a causal link to foreseeable abuse. For example, in *Bigio v Coca-Cola*, the Second Circuit denied that Coca-Cola could be held to have participated in the expropriation of the plaintiffs' property by Egypt simply because it derived an indirect economic benefit from its eventual purchase and lease of the expropriated land.[226] Similarly, in *Ge v Peng*, Adidas could not be held complicit in the manufacture of soccer balls in China by forced prison labour, due to the simple fact that its logo eventually appeared on those balls.[227]

The outer limits of corporate complicity might be tested in litigation that was launched in November 2002 against a number of companies regarding their dealings in and with South Africa during the apartheid years, *Khulumani et al v*

---

[225] See, eg, *Beanal v Freeport-McMoran, Inc* 969 F Supp 362 (ED La 1997) 380; *Abdullahi v Pfizer* No 01 Civ 8118, 2002 US Dist LEXIS 17436 (SDNY September 16, 2002) 16; *Wiwa v Royal Dutch Petroleum Co* No 96 Civ 8386, 2002 US Dist LEXIS 3293 (SDNY Feburary 22, 2002) 40.

[226] 239 F 3d 440 (2d Cir 2000) 449. The Court did not confirm whether expropriation of property with State action could activate ATCA. It probably does not; see above, text at n 68.

[227] 201 F Supp 2d 14 (DDC 2000) 22. In any case, forced prison labour was held not to breach the law of nations.

*Barclays National Bank et al.*²²⁸ The plaintiffs are victims, and victims' survivors, of the apartheid regime, including Khulumani, a South African organisation representing 32,000 members. The defendants are oil companies, banks, arms manufacturers, transportation companies, technology companies, and mining companies.

The claims against the mining companies mirror ATCA claims made in other cases. Mining companies such as Rio Tinto have been accused of directly colluding with the South African government in the violation of the rights of workers, including suppression of the freedom of association of workers, racist practices, 'subhuman' and dangerous working conditions, denial of medical treatment to workers, and the payment of 'meager wages'.²²⁹

The remaining claims are distinguishable from other ATCA claims against businesses due to the indirect nature of the link between the companies and the alleged abuse. Essentially, a number of the defendants are accused of aiding and abetting the South African government in its perpetration of the apartheid system, and associated human rights abuses related to the oppressive nature of that regime, including killings and tortures. Most of the defendants have been accused of supplying money or goods to the South African military and police, with constructive knowledge that the police and military would use those resources in order to maintain the apartheid system. However, the complaints, especially those against the banks and the oil companies, go further in attempting to attribute liability to the defendants vis persons harmed by those defendants' decisions to invest in South Africa per se. Absent such investment, the plaintiffs argue that the apartheid regime would have crumbled earlier, so the defendants' business dealings effectively propped up the regime, permitting the perpetuation of apartheid and its associated inherent abuses.²³⁰

The *Khulumani* complaint manifests a common criticism of TNCs, that is that they help to maintain certain unsavory regimes by virtue of their investment presence in a country. It seems unlikely that such actions attract ATCA liability in the absence of a clear causal connection between the TNC's actions and an identifiable ATCA 'tort'. It seems very likely that the plaintiffs will be able to 'prove' to a requisite legal standard that corporate trade and/or investment per se actually caused, or even had a substantial effect on, the perpetration of foreseeable human rights abuses by a repressive government.²³¹ For example, it

---

²²⁸ Case CV 25952 (EDNY 2002), filed before the District Court for the Eastern District of New York, 11 November 2002 [Khulumani complaint] <http://www.nyed.uscourts.gov/coi/cases_of_interest.html> (15 September 2003). See GC Hufbauer and NK Mitrokostas, *Awakening the Monster: The Alien Tort Statute of 1789* (Washington DC, International Institute of Economics, 2003), describing similar pending cases at pp 72–73.

²²⁹ See Khulumani complaint, *ibid* at paras 603–29. It is uncertain whether all of these alleged human rights breaches violate 'the law of nations'.

²³⁰ See, eg, *ibid* at paras 271, 289, 391, 399, 413, 424.

²³¹ See ICHRP, above n 150, at 132; see also T Collingsworth, 'Separating Fact from Fiction in the Debate over Application of the Alien Tort Claims Act to Violations of Fundamental Human Rights by Corporations' (2003) 37 *University of San Francisco Law Review* 563, 585. In *Burnett v Al*

is difficult to prove on the balance of probabilities a hypothetical contention that a government would necessarily fall if denied access to certain resources. For example, one can only guess at the extent to which organised crime and the black market may step in to fill hypothetical financial voids. The attribution of liability for foreign investments linked directly to the maintenance of the South African army and police may be easier to establish, being a step closer to the perpetration of concrete abuses. Furthermore, it may be easier to prove corporate complicity in human rights abuses by virtue of trade/investment per se for certain types of businesses, such as arms dealers, compared to others.

The *Khulumani* complaint nevertheless represents a worrying development in ATCA litigation, as it may discourage foreign investment in many impoverished States that need such investment, as many such States have governments with unsatisfactory human rights records. It may always be arguable that such investment facilitates the extended tenure of a bad government, and therefore the continuance of that government's human rights violations.[232] TNCs should not be liable for merely investing in 'bad' countries, unless such investment is itself a breach of domestic or international law. In the latter case, relevant investment must be prohibited by customary international law, a treaty, or by a Security Council resolution. In the absence of national or international prohibitions on investment, companies cannot be expected to guess which countries are 'so bad as to warrant complete disengagement'.[233]

In the case of South Africa, the Security Council imposed an arms embargo from 1977 through to 1994,[234] lending credence to the contention that the trade in armaments with South Africa throughout this period was indeed a breach of the law of nations. The UN General Assembly, throughout the entire apartheid era, passed numerous resolutions calling for comprehensive trade sanctions,[235] even condemning transnational corporations for 'political, economic and military collabouration' with the South African government.[236] Though General Assembly resolutions are not per se legally binding, they are nevertheless evidence of customary international law. Indeed, apartheid is recognised in

---

Baraka Investment and Development Corporation 274 F Supp 2d 86 (DDC 2003), a Saudi bank was sued for allegedly providing funds to a terrorist organisation that perpetrated the attacks on New York City on 11 September 2001. Robertson J found that there was 'no support . . . for the proposition that a bank is liable for injuries done with money that passes through its hands in the form of deposits, withdrawals, check clearing services, or any other routine banking service' (at p 109).

[232] See also Anita Ramasastry, 'Banks and Human Rights: Should Swiss Banks be liable for Lending to South Africa's Apartheid Government?' *Findlaw Legal Commentary*, 3 July 2002 <writ.news.findlaw.com/ramasastry/20020703.html> (15 September 2003).

[233] S Joseph, 'Taming the Leviathans: Multinational Enterprises and Human Rights' (1999) 46 *Netherlands International Law Review* 171, 188.

[234] See, eg, UN doc. S/RES/418, 4 November 1977; UN doc. S/RES/473, 13 June 1980; UN doc S/RES/591, 28 November 1986.

[235] See Khulumani complaint, above n 228, at para 224 ff.

[236] See, eg, UN doc A/RES/38/39A, 5 December 1983, UN doc, A/RES/39/15, 23 November 1984, UN doc A/RES/44/27 C & D, 22 November 1989.

customary international law as a crime against humanity.[237] The International Convention on the Suppression and Punishment of the Crime of Apartheid 1973, which now has 101 States parties, defines a number of crimes relating to apartheid, including, in Article III(b), directly abetting, encouraging or cooperating in the commission of the crime of apartheid. Thus, it may be that general trade with the South African apartheid government, and investment in the country during the period of that regime, amounted to breaches of customary international law and thus a contravention of 'the law of nations' attracting ATCA liability. Such international illegality cannot however easily be translated to apply outside the South African context, even with regard to trade with the most oppressive regimes such as the military dictatorship currently in power in Myanmar, or the military junta led by General Pinochet in Chile from 1973 to 1989. Unlike the apartheid regime, those military dictatorships are not *of themselves* a manifestation of an international crime, nor has trade with those regimes ever been comparably condemned in international forums. It therefore may be that the South African litigation has a sui generis character with limited precedent value, given the very specific and unique international condemnation of the relevant regime and its apartheid system.[238]

TNCs should be held liable for aiding and abetting human rights abuse when their actions foreseeably lead to the perpetration of identifiable grave human rights abuses by another. However, courts must retain a sense of proportion in establishing the causal link between a TNC and an abuse perpetrated by a third party. Corporations should not be held liable under ATCA for simply doing business with 'bad' people, including 'bad' governments, except in the rare situations where such engagement is per se a breach of the law of nations.

THE INTERNATIONAL TREATY LIMB OF ATCA

Almost all ATCA cases have focused on the first limb of jurisdiction: torts committed 'in violation of the law of nations'. Very few cases have even raised the second limb: torts committed in violation 'of a treaty of the United States'. This is because courts have generally assumed that the second limb refers exclusively to self-executing treaties. Self-executing treaties become part of US law without the need for statutory incorporation, whereas non self-executing treaties must be statutorily incorporated before they grant private rights of action.[239] Most

---

[237] Apartheid is classified as a crime against humanity under the *Statute of the International Criminal Court*, Article 7(j). See also *Restatement (Third) of the Foreign Relations Law of the United* States, § 702, n 11, stating that 'systemic racial discrimination' is a *jus cogens* violation.

[238] See also A McBeth, 'The role and responsibilities of the finance industry in relation to human rights: a legal analysis' (unpublished paper, copy on file with the author) 16.

[239] See *Sei Fujii v California* 38 Cal 2d 718 (SCt Cal 1952) and also KDA Carpenter, 'The International Covenant on Civil and Political Rights: A Toothless Tiger?' (2000) 26 *North Carolina Journal of International Law and Commercial Regulation* 1, esp at 11–16.

human rights treaties are 'non self–executing', so they do not grant private rights of enforcement.[240] However, the restriction of the treaty limb of ATCA to self-executing treaties renders that limb of ATCA a nullity, as self-executing treaties can be enforced apart from ATCA. The treaties prong serves no purpose unless it applies to non self-executing treaties.[241] Therefore, it seems more logical to interpret the treaties prong so as to refer to any treaty ratified by the US. So far, no US court has adopted such a teleological interpretation of the treaty limb of ATCA. If a court was to take such an approach, actions under an expanded treaties limb would probably only lie with regard to events inside the US, and against the actions of US government agents at home or abroad. The US's ratification of a treaty should not give a green light to US courts to enforce that treaty's norms in an extraterritorial context against an alien or even a private US citizen if the treaty does not otherwise represent customary international law.[242]

In *Ralk v Lincoln County, Ga*,[243] the court found that a person can bring an action under ATCA for violation of the ICCPR.[244] This dicta was based on an earlier decision in *Abebe-Jira v Negewo*.[245] It is not clear from either decision whether this is because the ICCPR itself constitutes a part of 'the law of nations', or because it is 'a treaty of the United States'. In *Estate of Rodriguez v Drummond*,[246] the cases were interpreted as construing the ICCPR as evidence of customary norms, therefore relegating the potential significance in the cases of the treaties limb of ATCA.

CHOICE OF LAW UNDER ATCA

In transnational litigation, the issue of 'choice of law' commonly arises. That is, what law is to be applied to resolve the issues in the case at hand: the law of the forum or the law of the site of the impugned actions? This issue can be crucial in transnational proceedings, for example where one of the potential choices of law is significantly more lenient to the defendant than the other.

[240] Stephens and Ratner, above n 22, at 59.
[241] *Ibid* at 59–60; see also Carpenter, above n 239, at 49, and Paust, above n 16, at 823–24. Indeed, the potentially expansive reach of the treaties prong, when read in accordance with its natural language, was one justification given by Bork J in *Tel-Oren v Libyan Arab Republic* 726 F 2d 774 (DC Cir 1974) 812 for his narrow interpretation of the whole of ATCA (see below, text at n 265).
[242] Carpenter, above n 239, at 38–39 argues that the treaties prong should only be enforceable against US defendants per se. However, I argue that the US's obligations under a human rights treaty are normally limited to controlling government actions at home and abroad, and to controlling private actors *within* jurisdiction. Thus, the behaviour of a US private citizen abroad is rarely the subject matter of a US treaty obligation, and should not generally fall within the treaties prong. See S Joseph, J Schultz and M Castan, *The International Covenant on Civil and Political Rights: Cases, Commentary and Materials* (Oxford, Oxford University Press, 2004), 92. See also ch 1, n 85.
[243] 81 F Supp 2d 1372 (SD Ga 2000).
[244] *Ralk v Lincoln County* 81 F Supp 2d 1372 (SD Ga 2000).
[245] 72 F 3d 844 (11th Cir 1996), affirming *Abebe-Jiri v Negewo* 1993 WL 814304 (ND Ga 1993) 4.
[246] 256 F Supp 2d 1250 (WD Al 2003).

ATCA cases have suggested several alternative approaches to the choice of law question. Some US federal judges have concluded that ATCA prescribes 'international law' as the law governing the substance of the claim, while federal law governs procedural matters.[247] Other judges have opted for federal common law as the appropriate choice of law.[248] Other courts have applied the law of the law of the foreign site of the relevant acts, where that law is compatible with 'international law and provides a remedy compatible with the purposes of the ATCA and pertinent international norms'.[249] The most important thing to note, regarding choice of law under the ATCA, is that courts have not applied foreign laws so as to frustrate the purpose of ATCA, by for example applying a foreign law that grants immunity to the perpetrator of a gross human rights abuse,[250] or that imposes a punishment that plainly fails to reflect the gravity of the offence.[251]

THE FUTURE FOR ATCA

At the time of writing, ATCA was under significant threat from two fronts. First, attempts are being made to 'roll back' the *Filartiga* interpretation of ATCA so as to deprive the statute of any contemporary relevance. Second, significant segments of the business community, which has undoubtedly been spooked by the cases against corporations, have begun to lobby Congress to secure the repeal or amendment of ATCA. These two developments will be discussed in turn.

Rolling back *Filartiga*: Attacks upon the ATCA in Litigation

There is no doubt that the Bush administration has exhibited greater hostility to the litigation generated under ATCA than its predecessors, as indicated by the State Department briefs submitted in *Rio Tinto* and *Exxon Mobil*. The *Exxon Mobil* brief in particular raises issues far beyond the scope of the particular fact situation in the relevant litigation, such as the alleged detrimental effect of such litigation on the prosecution of the war on terror, and the harm caused by such

---

[247] See, eg, *Xuncax v Gramajo* 886 F Supp 162 (D Mass 1995) 182–84; see also Tzeutschler, above n 32, at 403; B Stephens, 'Corporate Liability: Enforcing Human Rights Law through Domestic Litigation' (2001) 24 *Hastings International and Comparative Law Review* 401, 408–9.

[248] See, eg, *Alvarez-Machain v US* 331 F 3d 604 (9th Cir 2003) 635, and Reinhardt J in *Unocal* 2002, above n 40.

[249] *Tachiona et al v Mugabe and ZANU-PF* (2002) 234 F Supp 2d 401, at 418. In some instances, Zimbabwean law was used to determine liability in that case.

[250] *Ibid* at 415; see also *Filartiga v Peña-Irala* 577 F Supp 860 (EDNY 1984) 863 (decision of District Court upon remittance from the Circuit Court).

[251] *Tachiona et al v Mugabe and ZANU-PF* 234 F Supp 2d 401 (SDNY 2002) 414; the issue of choice of law in ATCA cases was comprehensively canvassed by Marrero J in this case at pp 406–20.

56 *The Alien Tort Claims Act*

litigation to the promotion of overseas investment opportunities for US businesses. These general concerns could be repeated in almost any transnational ATCA case against a US corporation. The effect of the *Rio Tinto* brief indicates that State Department intervention could prove decisive in such human rights litigation, to the detriment of plaintiffs. As noted above, the outcome of the current attempt by the *Exxon Mobil* defendants to have the litigation dismissed will be instructive in signaling the normative effects of such briefs upon the viability of such litigation.

The US Department of Justice (DOJ) has submitted a further *amicus* brief in the *Exxon Mobil* litigation,[252] as well as an *amicus* brief in the *Doe v Unocal* appeal before the *en banc* panel of the Ninth Circuit.[253] Both briefs put the argument that the *Filartiga* interpretation of ATCA is wrong, and should therefore be departed from. In analysing this argument, I will focus on the *Unocal* brief.

In the *Unocal* brief, the DOJ argues that ATCA does not provide a cause of action; it merely ensures that federal courts, as opposed to the more parochial State courts at the time of ATCA's enactment in 1789, have jurisdiction over torts in breach of the law of nations. The DOJ conceded that this interpretation deprives ATCA of contemporary relevance, due to the enactment of later statutes granting broader jurisdiction to federal courts.[254] Certainly, the ATCA does not *explicitly* create a private cause of action, so the existence of such has been inferred by courts. Furthermore, there is no legislative history available for ATCA to give indications of the intent of the enacting Congress.[255] Counsel for the *Unocal* plaintiffs responded by noting that such an interpretation would not only render ATCA redundant now, but also redundant at its inception, as no statutes were subsequently passed to explicitly create such causes of action.[256]

In its *Unocal* brief, the DOJ argues that the inference that ATCA creates private causes of action gives municipal teeth to international obligations that the US government has clearly refused to incorporate into domestic law.[257] Upon ratification of all of the human rights treaties to which it is a party, the US government has issued a declaration clarifying that the treaty is not self-executing, and therefore is not part of US domestic law. Its failure to ratify other treaties

---

[252] The brief, submitted in July 2003, is available via <http://www.labourrights.org> (25 September 2003).

[253] The 'Unocal brief', dated 8 May 2003, is available via <http://www.earthrights.org/atca/dojbrief.pdf> (25 September 2003).

[254] In particular, federal courts have jurisdiction over issues 'arising under' the Constitution and federal laws under 28 USC § 1331. 'Federal laws' include customary international law incorporated into US law. See ch 3, pp 77–78.

[255] See DJ Kochan, 'Constitutional Structure as a Limitation on the Scope of the "Law of Nations" in the Alien Tort Claims Act' (1998) 31 *Cornell International Law Journal* 153, 161. See also Bork J in *Tel-Oren v Libyan Arab Republic* 726 F 2d 774 (DC Cir 1984) 812–13.

[256] See generally, Response to the DOJ (Unocal Response), 2 June 2003 <http://www.earthrights.org/atca/dojbrief.pdf> (25 September 2003) 12–13. See also Anne-Marie Burley, 'The Alien Tort Statute and the Judiciary Act of 1789: A Badge of Honor' (1989) 83 *American Journal of International Law* 461.

[257] Unocal Brief, above n 253, at 12–19.

obviously manifests an intent not to be bound by those treaties' norms in either international or domestic law. Therefore, the DOJ contends that the indirect enforcement of such norms through the instrument of the ATCA in US courts undermines the clear intentions of the US government regarding the domestic enforceability of international human rights norms. This argument however exhibits fundamental misunderstandings about the nature of international law and of ATCA decisions.[258] The DOJ arguments indicate that treaties are the only source of the US's international obligations. That is patently untrue, as the US is also bound by customary international law and *jus cogens*. The enforcement of a human rights norm under ATCA arises because a US court has identified that norm as a norm of customary international law or, in some cases, *jus cogens*. The fact of US ratification of a particular treaty is relevant to but is not decisive in the identification process. The fact that the intentions of the executive government regarding the enforceability of certain treaty norms may be thwarted is irrelevant, as the enforcement by courts of customary international law under ATCA has been authorised by the legislature in enacting ATCA.

The DOJ also disputed the extraterritorial application of ATCA, as US statutes are ordinarily presumed not to apply outside US territory, in the absence of explicit words to the contrary.[259] Plaintiffs' counsel responded by referring to the plain language of the statute, which invokes no geographic restriction. Furthermore, ATCA refers to torts, which were and are recognised at common law as being 'transitory', in that tort liability follows tortfeasors across national borders.[260] Therefore, the word 'tort' in ATCA incorporates the characteristics of a tort, including its transitory nature, so ATCA, in the view of the plaintiffs, must apply in an extraterritorial context.[261]

The DOJ also argued that the current interpretation of ATCA allows courts to interfere too much in the arena of foreign relations, which is constitutionally reserved to the political branches of government.[262] In response, plaintiffs' counsel notes that such considerations did not justify an interpretation of ATCA that would wipe out 'an entire class of cases'.[263] Rather, courts could eject cases that seriously interfered with foreign relations on a case-by-case basis by utilising the abstention doctrines of act of state political question, and comity.[264]

---

[258] Unocal Response, above n 256, at 17–24; see also Carpenter, above n 239, at 39–40.
[259] Unocal brief, above n 253, at 27–29.
[260] *McKenna v Fisk* 42 US 241 SCt (1843) 248. See also ch 3, pp 65–66.
[261] Unocal response, above n 256, at 14–15, and 27.
[262] Unocal brief, above n 253, at 20–22. See, for a view that the *Filartiga* interpretation is unconstitutional, Kochan, above n 258, and CA Bradley, 'The Alien Tort Statute and Article III' (2002) 42 *Virginia Journal of International Law* 587. See, for a response to Bradley, arguing in favour of the constitutionality of the *Filartiga* approach, WS Dodge, 'The Constitutionality of the Alien Tort Statute: Some Observations on Text and Context' (2002) 42 *Virginia Journal of International Law* 687. Many of the arguments therein are encompassed in the DOJ's *Unocal* brief, but others are beyond the scope of this book.
[263] Unocal Response, above n 256, at 30.
[264] *Ibid*.

58   The Alien Tort Claims Act

The DOJ arguments essentially support the narrow reading given to ATCA by Bork J in his concurring judgment in a decision in 1984, *Tel-Oren v Libyan Arab Republic*.[265] Bork J had added that the ATCA, if it was indeed interpreted as providing for a cause of action, should only apply to those breaches of the law of nations that were recognised in 1789: violation of safe conducts, infringement of the rights of ambassadors, and piracy.[266] The framers of ATCA certainly would not have contemplated the vast expansion of the law of nations that has arisen since 1789, particularly in the area of human rights law. However, the US judiciary has generally refrained from interpreting statutes using the strict originalist doctrines famously advocated by Robert Bork.[267] Furthermore, the expansive language used in the ATCA cannot be ignored, especially when compared with narrower contemporaneous legal provisions, such as s. 13 of the First Judiciary Act,[268] which explicitly conferred jurisdiction upon the Supreme Court to hear suits brought by ambassadors. As noted by counsel for the *Unocal* plaintiffs, the early Congress 'knew full well how to craft' narrower provisions.[269]

Since *Filartiga*, the Second Circuit and Ninth Circuit in numerous cases, as well as the Eleventh Circuit in *Abebe-Jira v Negewo*[270] and the Fifth Circuit in *Beanal v Freeport-McMoran*,[271] have accepted that ATCA is constitutional, that it creates causes of action, that the law of nations is interpreted in accordance with its contemporary meaning, and that it applies to extraterritorial acts. Acceptance of the DOJ arguments in *Unocal* will require the Ninth Circuit to depart from that virtually constant line of authority. The only Circuit to address ATCA that has been unclear in its interpretation is the DC Circuit, where Bork J in *Tel-Oren*,[272] and Randolph J more recently in *Al Odah v United States*,[273] have advocated narrow interpretations of ATCA in line with the DOJ's current arguments. No DC Circuit majority has approved of either the narrow or the broad view of ATCA.[274]

---

[265]   726 F 2d 774 (DC Cirt 1984).
[266]   *Ibid* at 813.
[267]   See generally, RH Bork, *The Tempting of America: The Political Seduction of the Law* (New York, The Free Press, 1990) chs 7–8.
[268]   1 Stat 73, 76–77 (1789).
[269]   Unocal response, above n 256, 26.
[270]   72 F 3d 844, 847 (11th Cir 1996).
[271]   197 F 3d 161 (5th Cir 1999). Though the Fifth Circuit dismissed the ATCA claim in that case, it did not suggest that it departed from the case law of the other Circuits.
[272]   Though all three judges in *Tel-Oren v Libyan Arab Republic* 726 F 2d 774 (DC Cir 1984) dismissed the plaintiff's case (an ATCA case against alleged terrorists), they all did so for different reasons and fundamentally disagreed with each other. Its holding has not 'had a strong precedential value', due to the lack of agreement amongst the court's members; see Zia-Zarifi, above n 23, at 103.
[273]   321 F 3d 1134 (DC Cir 2003) 1146–49. The case concerned an allegation, inter alia, that the detention of terrorist suspects in Guantanamo Bay without judicial process breached ATCA. The majority of the Court dismissed the plaintiffs' case on other grounds.
[274]   Robb J in *Tel-Oren v Libyan Arab Republic* 726 F 2d 774 (DC Cir 1984) argued in note 5 at 826 therein that *Filartiga* 'is at odds with the reality of the international structure'. However, Robb J's reasoning was based on the idea that almost all ATCA cases would, in his opinion, breach the political question doctrine. Therefore, Robb J's reasoning was quite different to that of Bork J, so

The Future for ATCA 59

The DOJ brief mirrors a brief submitted by the Reagan government in *Trajano v Marcos*.[275] However, it contradicts briefs submitted by the DOJ in *Filartiga*[276] and *Kadic v Karadzic* under the respective administrations of Jimmy Carter and Bill Clinton, when the DOJ argued for an expansive interpretation of ATCA. The attitude of successive US administrations to the ATCA has changed according to the party in power, reflecting the likely political motivation behind DOJ briefs in general.[277] Given the rejection of the DOJ arguments in *Trajano*, it seems likely that they would be similarly rejected in *Unocal*, where the Ninth Circuit could be expected to uphold its own previous support for the broad interpretation of ATCA.

However, the *Unocal* appeal is now on hold, pending a similar challenge to ACTA in the US Supreme Court. The Supreme Court has never pronounced its view on the interpretation or constitutionality of ATCA. Since *Filartiga*, the Supreme Court has consistently declined to hear appeals in ATCA cases, thus allowing over twenty years of ATCA jurisprudence to develop without its guidance.[278] However, on 1 December 2003, the US Supreme Court granted certiorari in two related cases, *US v Alvarez-Machain* and *Sosa v Alvarez-Machain*.[279] The cases are linked, and concern the abduction from Mexico to the US of one Dr Alvarez-Machain [Alvarez] by Mexican nationals (including one Jose Francisco Sosa) at the direction of the US Drug Enforcement Agency [DEA] in 1990. Alvarez was prosecuted in the US for the murder of a DEA agent in Mexico in 1985, and acquitted. Alvarez then brought suit against the DEA and the Mexican kidnappers under, inter alia, the ATCA. On 3 June 2003, the Ninth Circuit *en banc* decided that ATCA claims properly lay against both the US (which was substituted for the DEA agents) and the Mexican nationals (including Sosa) regarding Alvarez's arbitrary detention in Mexico prior to his transportation across the border.[280] Sosa and the US successfully sought an order for certiorari from the US Supreme Court. Two grounds of appeal are that the ATCA is unconstitutional, or that it is merely jurisdictional. It is possible that

---

the two do not combine to create a Circuit majority (cf Randolph J in *Al-Odah v US* 321 F 3d 1134 (DC Cir 2003) 1146). The DC Circuit in *Sanchez-Espinoza v Reagan* 770 F 2d 202 (DC Cir 1985), concerning allegations about US actions in Nicaragua under the Reagan administration, did not have to decide on the scope of ATCA as they dismissed the allegations for sovereign immunity.

It may be noted that the DC District Court has upheld the expansive interpretation of ATCA in *Doe v Islamic Salvation Front* 993 F Supp 3 (DDC 1998) 8 and *Burnett v Al Baraka Investment and Development Corporation* 274 F Supp 2d 86 (DDC 2003).

[275] This litigation culminated in the decision in 978 F 2d 493 (9th Cir 1992).

[276] The *Filartiga* brief is reproduced at (1980) 19 *International Legal Materials* 585.

[277] See *Trajano v Marcos* 978 F 2d 493 (9th Cir 1992) 500. See also E Schrage, 'Judging Corporate Accountability in the Global Economy' (2003) 42 *Columbia Journal of Transnational Law* 153, 161.

[278] The Supreme Court considered an ATCA claim in *Argentine Republic v Amerada Hess Shipping Corp* 488 US 428 (SCt 1989), where it held that the *Foreign Sovereign Immunities Act* acts as a bar on ATCA claims.

[279] *US v Alvarez-Machain* 2003 US LEXIS 8573 (SCt 2003) and *Sosa v Alvarez-Machain* 2003 US LEXIS 8572 (SCt 2003).

[280] Once in the US, Alvarez's detention was lawful under US law, and thus was not arbitrary according to the Ninth Circuit. See *Alvarez Machain v US* 331 F 3d 604 (9th Cir 2003) 90–93.

the Supreme Court, if indeed it should uphold the appeal, will decide the *Alvarez-Machain* case on a narrower ground of appeal.[281] It is futile to predict the outcome of the Supreme Court case. An update regarding this case will be available on the publisher's website soon after the decision is handed down: www.hartpub.co.uk/updates.html.

Potential Legislative Amendments

The business world is clearly concerned by the ongoing human rights litigation, and a number of business groups are preparing to make a concerted effort to lobby Congress to repeal or amend the ATCA[282] if the *Alvarez* case should fail to effectively 'repeal' the statute. In particular, 'USA-Engage', a group formed under the auspices of the National Foreign Trade Council, a group of US companies which generally advocates for the removal of barriers to global trade, has taken the lead in attacking ATCA.[283] A peruse of the USA-Engage website at www.usaengage.org reveals a wealth of material that criticises ATCA litigation, particularly its extension since *Unocal* to encompass corporate defendants.[284] Arguments regarding the desirability of ATCA litigation against corporations, and indeed all forms of transnational human rights litigation against corporations are discussed in Chapter 8, and therefore will not be addressed here.

Large and influential sections of corporate America are clearly preparing for a lobbying assault on the ATCA. They are likely to receive support from the Bush administration, which may help to sway the Republican majority (as at January 2004) in both houses of Congress. On the other hand, forces are gathering to 'save' the ATCA, including high profile NGOs such as the Lawyers' Committee for Human Rights and Earthrights. Furthermore, legislators may baulk at tampering with the law, and risk being portrayed as supporters of gross human rights abuses, especially in an election year. It is futile at this stage to attempt to predict the legislative fate of the ATCA.

---

[281] For example, the US Supreme Court could decide that Alvarez's detention in Mexico, which lasted less than 24 hours, does not constitute a breach of the law of nations. Alternatively, the Court could decide that the abduction in Mexico of Alvarez was authorised under US law (Alvarez had been indicted under US law). See also Hufbauer and Mitrokostas, above n 228, at 50.

[282] See T Blass, 'Alien Tort Claims Act and Multinational Corporations' (2003) 57 (2) *International Bar News* 9; see also Collingsworth, above n 231, esp at 564–66.

[283] The NFTC, USA-Engage, and other business groups submitted an *amicus* brief in the Unocal litigation, which raised similar arguments to those of the DOJ in the Unocal Brief. The 'NFTC' brief, lodged 29 April 2003, is available via <http://nftc.org/default/usa%20engage/4-29-03%20Brief.pdf> (25 September 2003). A similar brief was filed on 6 October 2003 in the *Alvarez-Machain* litigation, available via <http://www.uschamber.com/nclc/caselist/issues/reform.htm> (17 December 2003).

[284] See <http://www.usaengage.org/legislative/2003/alientort/index.html> (25 September 2003).

Consequences of Defusing the ATCA

At the time of writing, the future of the ATCA is unclear. ATCA could be 'defused' by a judicial reinterpretation, judicial pronouncement of its unconstitutionality, or by legislative amendment. Whilst the defusing of ATCA would remove an important and perhaps the most effective tool in the armory of human rights litigation, it would not spell the end of such litigation. For example, TVPA would likely assume greater prominence, and is discussed directly below. As is discussed in Chapters 3 and 5, further alternative causes of action, which would probably multiply in ATCA's absence, are available in the US to persons seeking redress from corporations regarding alleged human rights abuses committed overseas. In particular, 28 USC § 1331 may represent a complete replacement for ATCA. The ATCA revival in *Filartiga* let the 'human rights litigation' genie out of the bottle, but its removal will not put her back in.[285]

THE TORTURE VICTIM PROTECTION ACT

TVPA entrenches the *Filartiga* cause of action, by explicitly legislating for a civil cause of action for acts of torture and extra-judicial killings, when committed by individuals 'under actual or apparent authority, or color of law, of any foreign nation' against aliens or US citizens. TVPA thus covers only a sub-set of the causes of action apparently available under ATCA. It does extend ATCA jurisdiction in one respect, as the latter statute is explicitly limited to alien plaintiffs.

There is some doubt over whether TVPA binds corporations. In *Beanal v Freeport-McMoran Inc*,[286] the court found that private corporations could not be so liable. On appeal, the Circuit Court in *Beanal v Freeport-McMoran* explicitly did not decide whether causes of action lay against corporations under TVPA.[287] More recently in *Sinaltrainal v Coca Cola*[288] and *Estate of Rodriguez v Drummond*,[289] the respective courts refused to dismiss TVPA actions against corporations. Both courts noted that the term 'individual', which was used to describe persons liable under TVPA, was consistently interpreted in US law as encompassing an artificial person, including a corporation. The balance of extant case law indicates therefore that corporations are vulnerable to TVPA suits.

TVPA of course covers only a portion of the human rights abuses currently actionable under ATCA. Furthermore, no actions would be available for

---

[285] See also LCHR Brief, above n 76, at 18; see also Schrage, above n 277, at 156 and 162–63.
[286] 969 F Supp 362 (ED La 1997) 382–83.
[287] 197 F 3d 161 (CA5, La, 1999), 169.
[288] 256 F Supp 2d 1345 (SD Fla 2003) 1359.
[289] 256 F Supp 2d 1250 (WD Al 2003) 1266–67.

'private' acts of torture or extra-judicial killing, as TVPA explicitly includes a state action requirement. It could be anticipated that, in the absence of ATCA, the outer limits of the meaning of 'torture' under TVPA would be rigorously explored by counsel.[290] In any case, TVPA could provide a substitute cause of action for a significant number of the pending ATCA claims against TNCs, including claims of torture and/or extra-judicial killing against Shell in Nigeria, Chevron in Nigeria, Unocal in Myanmar, Exxon-Mobil in Indonesia, and Talisman in the Sudan. TVPA claims would have similarly been available in some of the cases that have been dismissed, such as the claim against Rio Tinto for its actions in Papua New Guinea.

Two further points of difference exist between TVPA and ATCA. First, TVPA contains an explicit statute of limitations clause. Second, TVPA explicitly requires plaintiff to 'exhaust adequate and available remedies in the place in which the conduct giving rise to the claim occurred' prior to bringing a TVPA claim in a US court.[291] These two requirements are discussed directly below.

An action cannot be maintained under TVPA unless it is commenced within ten years of the cause of action arising. Many of the pending actions against TNCs under ATCA include claims relating to alleged acts committed within the past ten years so it would be possible to file new claims under TVPA. To the extent that current ATCA cases are apparently excluded from TVPA actionability due to lack of timeliness, plaintiffs may be able to benefit from equitable tolling if the relevant ATCA actions were commenced within ten years of the occurrence of the relevant acts. However, certain pending claims under ATCA, such as a new claim filed in January 2004 against Mercedes-Benz for complicity in torture by the Argentine government in the 1970s,[292] would not be permitted under TVPA.

The requirement to exhaust domestic remedies was discussed in *Estate of Rodriguez v Drummond*, where the plaintiffs failed to pursue any remedies in Colombia for the alleged wrongful death of trade unionists in that country prior to filing the TVPA claim in Alabama. The Court found that the burden of proof was upon defendants to establish that the plaintiffs had failed to exhaust relevant remedies.[293] Furthermore, the Court found that the plaintiffs, at least for the purposes of preliminary rulings, had adequately pleaded that pursuance of remedies in Colombia would be futile, and would even place them at risk of persecution and retaliation.[294] A similar decision was reached in *Sinaltrainal v Coca Cola*.[295] It appears therefore that US courts will follow the approach taken

---

[290] TVPA essentially incorporates the meaning of 'torture' as defined in article 1 of the Convention against Torture and other Cruel, Inhuman or Degrading Treatment or Punishment (1984) [CAT]. See, for a discussion of the meaning of 'torture' under CAT, Joseph, Schultz, and Castan, above, note 242, pp 195–213.
[291] In *Sarei v Rio Tinto* 221 F Supp 2d 1116 (CD Cal, 2002), at 1132–39, the Court discussed the 'exhaustion' requirement of TVPA and found that it did not implicitly apply to ATCA claims.
[292] See D Kravets, 'Argentine War Victims sue Mercedes-Benz', 15 January 2004, *Associate Press*.
[293] 256 F Supp 2d 1250 (WD Al 2003), 1267
[294] *Ibid*, 1267–68.
[295] 256 F Supp 2d 1345 (SD Fla, 2003), 1357–58.

in international law to the issue of exhaustion of domestic remedies, where it has been readily accepted that in certain circumstances, especially when people are seeking redress for gross violations of human rights, it is simply futile and even dangerous to exhaust local remedies, if they indeed exist at all.[296] In most cases, it will be difficult for defendants to shift their burden of proof regarding exhaustion of remedies when faced, as they must be under TVPA, with allegations of such egregious acts as torture and extra-judicial killing.[297]

Many of the same concepts that are relevant under ATCA law, such as the tests for determining 'state action' and for establishing corporate complicity in the acts of governments,[298] as well as the application of 'principles of abstention' such as the doctrines of act of state or political question, are similarly relevant in the context of TVPA.

CONCLUSION

ATCA imposes civil liability on TNCs for breaches of customary international law. TNCs can be held directly liable for the small but possibly growing number of private actor abuses, as well as acts committed in furtherance of such abuses. Other ATCA claims are only actionable if accompanied by State action. With respect to the latter claims, most courts have used § 1983 tests to determine whether collusion between an TNC and a government has been adequately pleaded so as to ground a claim against that TNC, though alternative tests derived from international law and tort law have also been used. Finally, as ATCA claims against TNCs will often concern the actions of foreign governments, a number of principles of abstention may be relevant, namely the doctrines of act of state, political question, and comity.

Apart from the substantive issues discussed above, a number of procedural issues routinely arise in ATCA cases, and are discussed below in Chapter 4.

Post-Script: The US Supreme Court handed down its decision in *Sosa v Alvarez-Machain* on 29 June 2004. The majority confirmed that ATCA provides a basis for civil suits by victims of violations of 'the law of nations', wherever they occur. An update regarding this case will be available via <http://www.hart pub.co.uk>.

---

[296] Persons are commonly required to exhaust available national remedies before making a complaint under an international law mechanism against a State, under a procedure such as that available under the Optional Protocol to the ICCPR. See, on exhaustion of domestic remedies in international law, Joseph, Schultz, and Castan, above note 242, ch 6.

[297] See *Sinaltrainal v Coca Cola* 256 F Supp 2d 1345 (SD Fla, 2003) at 1357, quoting the Senate Committee Report on TVPA: '[A]s an initial matter, the committee recognises that in most instances the initiation of litigation under this legislation will be virtually prima facie evidence that the claimant has exhausted his or her remedies in the jurisdiction in which the torture occurred.'

[298] For example, in *ibid*, the Court noted at 1357 that '[t]he color of law element of a TVPA claim is identical to that under the ATCA'.

3
Other Jurisdictional Bases in the US

THE ALIEN TORT Claims Act (ATCA) is the most well-known jurisdictional basis for transnational human rights claims against TNCs in US courts. However, other jurisdictional bases are important as they provide subject matter jurisdiction for the numerous human rights claims which fall outside ATCA.

TORT JURISDICTION

Human rights abuses can be classified as ordinary torts. For example, loss of life can give rise to wrongful death suits; torture or cruel and inhuman treatment give rise to assault and battery claims.[1] The tort of negligence may also be relevant, for example where a TNC fails to take due care to ensure adequate safety standards in its factories, resulting in loss of life or damage to health, or when a TNC engages military personnel to defend its installations when it should be aware that such an engagement is likely to result in human rights abuses and injuries to others.[2]

US State courts have subject matter jurisdiction over 'transitory torts', torts committed in other countries which are unlawful under the law of that foreign country, and where that country's law is consistent with the policies of the US forum.[3] US federal courts also have 'diversity jurisdiction' to consider civil law complaints arising between aliens and US citizens if the claim is over $75,000 USD, and thus have subject matter jurisdiction to hear complaints by aliens

---

[1] See B Stephens and M Ratner, *International Human Rights Litigation in US Courts* (New York, Transnational Publishers Inc, 1996) 88; see also C Scott, 'Translating Torture into Transnational Tort: Conceptual Divides in the Debate on Corporate Accountability for Human Rights Norms' C Scott (ed) *Torture as Tort* (Oxford, Hart Publishing, 2001) 62.
[2] See C Forcese, 'Deterring 'Militarized Commerce': The Prospect of Liability for 'Privatized' Human Rights Abuses' (2000) 31 *Ottawa Law Review* 171, 208–10.
[3] See JM Blum and RG Steinhardt, 'Federal Jurisdiction over International Human Rights Claims: The Alien Tort Claims Act after Filartiga v Peña-Irala' (1981) 22 *Harvard International Law Journal* 53, 63, and *Filartiga v Peña-Irala* 630 F 2d 876 (2d Cir 1980) 885. See generally, on transnational tort liability, M Anderson, 'Transnational Corporations and Environmental Damage: Is Tort Law the Answer?' (2002) 41 *Washburn Law Journal* 399; A Rosencranz and R Campbell, 'Foreign Environmental and Human Rights Suits Against US Corporations in US Courts' (1999) 18 *Stanford Environmental Law Journal* 145, 171–79.

against US citizens, including corporations, and by US citizens against foreign corporations.[4]

ATCA has a number of advantages for human rights litigants over ordinary transnational tort litigation. First, the 'tort' in an ATCA claim is classified as a breach of 'the law of nations' rather than a 'garden variety' tort,[5] escalating the opprobrium associated with a finding of liability. Second, ATCA applies regardless of whether the conduct is unlawful in the State where the tort arose, as ATCA implicitly resolves difficult 'choice of law' issues in favor of US federal common law and/or international law.[6] When a court exercises ordinary transnational tort jurisdiction, it often decides such cases according to the law of the site of the tort, which may be more lenient to the tortfeasor than US law.[7] Finally, it appears that transitory tort claims are more vulnerable to dismissal on the ground of *forum non conveniens*, a doctrine which permits the dismissal of a case on the grounds that it should be litigated in another forum, than ATCA claims.[8]

Ordinary transnational tort jurisdiction nonetheless acts as an important supplement to ATCA jurisdiction. Ordinary transnational tort jurisdiction often lies in cases where the alleged human rights abuse fails to rank as a breach of the law of nations. For example, litigation concerning intrastate environmental harm, an action that has been found not to activate ATCA may probably proceed as a transitory tort claim.[9] Transnational tort jurisdiction may also lie in regard to human rights abuses committed by corporations in the numerous circumstances where customary law fails to recognise liability absent State action.

---

[4] 28 USC § 1332 (1988). There must be complete diversity in the case. For example, a diversity action against a US corporation could not involve even one US plaintiff; see Stephens and Ratner, above n 1, at 36; PI Blumberg, 'Asserting Human Rights Against Multinational Corporations under United States Law: Conceptual and Procedural Problems' (2002) 50 *American Journal of Comparative Law* 493, 527. In *Abu-Zeineh v Federal Laboratories Inc* 975 F Supp 774 (WD Pa 1994), a claim by Palestinians regarding the deaths of family members from CS gas sold to Israel by the defendants was dismissed, as the plaintiffs were stateless, and therefore did not have foreign citizenship for the purposes of diversity jurisdiction: J Green and P Hoffman, 'US Litigation Update' in M Kamminga and S Zia-Zarifi (eds) *Liability of Multinational Corporations under International Law* (The Hague, Kluwer Law International, 2000) 237–38.

[5] *Xuncax v Gramajo* 886 F Supp 162 (D Mass 1995) 183; see also B Stephens, 'Translating Filartiga: A Comparative and International Law Analysis of Domestic Remedies for International Human Rights Violations' (2002) 27 *Yale Journal of International Law* 1, 31–32.

[6] See ch 2, p 55.

[7] See below, on choice of law, text at nn 62–73.

[8] See ch 4, text at pp 92–94.

[9] The Circuit Court referred transitory tort claims in *Bano v Union Carbide Corp* 273 F 3d 120 (2d Cir 2001), concerning groundwater pollution caused by the abandoned Union Carbide plant in India, back to the District Court. That case was subsequently dismissed in *Bano v Union Carbide* 2003 WL 1344884 (SDNY 2003) on 18 March 2003, on statute of limitations grounds. However, the claims relating to the property damage, as opposed to personal injury, were reinstated and remanded to the lower court in *Bano v Union Carbide* 2004 WL 516238 (CA2, NY 2004).

A Brief Overview of Relevant Tort Principles

A TNC may be liable in tort for its overseas human rights practices in a number of ways. A TNC may *intentionally* cause tortious harm to others.[10] However, it will normally be difficult to prove that a TNC has intended to violate a plaintiff's human rights. It will be easier to establish that a TNC has been *reckless*, in that it has acted in wanton or willful disregard for the likely consequences of its actions for others.[11] Finally, a TNC may be *negligent* about the effects of its actions upon another, in that it may cause reasonably foreseeable harm to another by failing to exercise reasonable care.[12] Negligent conduct is not as morally culpable as intentional or reckless conduct. Courts have acknowledged this increased moral culpability by being more prepared to find that a defendant's intentional or reckless conduct has caused the alleged harm to a plaintiff, than to find causation entailed in a defendant's negligent conduct.[13] For example, a TNC that intentionally causes harm is liable even for harm that is unlikely to occur.[14] In contrast, negligent conduct only attracts liability for harms that are reasonably foreseeable.

In many cases where a TNC has been accused of breaching human rights, the allegation essentially relates to the TNC's liability for the acts of a third party. For example, as discussed in Chapter 2, TNCs have been accused in numerous ATCA cases of culpably acting in concert with governments in perpetrating gross human rights abuses. As discussed in Chapter 7, plaintiffs are commonly attempting to attribute liability to parent companies for the acts of their subsidiary companies in the developing world.

Therefore, it is important to discern when an actor, including a TNC, is responsible in tort for the acts of another. An actor will be *vicariously* liable for the acts of its agents under the theory of *respondeat superior*.[15] Thus, an employer is normally liable for the tortious acts of an employee acting within the apparent scope of his/her authority; a principal is responsible for the acts of an agent in the same circumstances. Alternatively, an actor may *act in concert* with another party, in which case both parties will be liable for the tortious acts of each other that are perpetrated in furtherance of their joint enterprise.[16]

Generally, a person has no duty to *control* the acts of a third party so as to prevent the perpetration of a tort by that person, unless the former person has a special relationship with the tortfeasor, or with the person who is likely to be

---

[10] *Restatement (Third) of Torts: Liability for Physical Harm (Basic Principles) (Tentative Draft)* § 1 (2001).
[11] *Ibid* at § 2.
[12] *Ibid* at § 3.
[13] *Restatement (Second) of Torts* § 501; § 33(b) (1965).
[14] *Ibid* at § 33(a).
[15] *Restatement (Third) of Torts: Apportionment of Liability* § 13 (2000).
[16] *Restatement (Second) of Torts* § 876 (1965). See also discussion of *Bowoto v Chevron Texaco Corp* No C 99–2506 SI, 2004 US Dist LEXIS 4603 (ND, Cal 2004), in ch 7, at pp 132–33.

harmed by the third party tortfeasor.[17] For example, a special relationship exists between a person and a third party tortfeasor when the two are in master/servant relationship,[18] or a parent/minor child relationship.[19] These are merely examples of 'special relationships': the category of such relationships is not closed, and will depend on the facts of each case.

Doe v Unocal

Some of the above tort principles may be illustrated by a discussion of the litigation in *Doe v Unocal*. Unocal has been sued in the Central District Court of California and the Superior Court of California under a variety of causes of action. Both the federal and State cases concern Unocal's alleged legal responsibility for gross human rights abuses, including killings, tortures, forced labour, destruction of property and forced removals of entire villages, perpetrated by the Myanmar military whilst it provided security for the Yadana pipeline project, of which Unocal was a participant.

The federal litigation has largely revolved around Unocal's liability under the ATCA.[20] It is worth setting out the chronology of the federal litigation. The case was dismissed by Lew J in 2000 [*Unocal 2000*],[21] but reinstated by the Ninth Circuit in 2002 [*Unocal 2002*].[22] That decision was vacated on 14 February 2003, and Lew J's decision reinstated, pending an appeal to an eleven judge *en banc* panel within the Ninth Circuit.[23]

In the State court, the plaintiffs have argued that Unocal is liable for the torts of wrongful death, battery, false imprisonment, intentional infliction of emotional distress, negligent infliction of emotional distress, negligence per se, and conversion.[24] A motion to dismiss the tort claims by the defendants was rejected by Chaney J in June 2002. Chaney J's interim decision is instructive in examining the potential liability of TNCs under ordinary tort law. Some of the decisions in the federal *Unocal* litigation are also relevant to this question. In particular, Reinhardt J used ordinary tort principles in *Unocal 2002* to establish whether Unocal could be held liable under the ATCA for the actions of the Myanmar military.[25]

---

[17] *Ibid* at § 315.
[18] *Ibid* at § 317; this relationship is of course reflected in the principle of vicarious liability.
[19] *Ibid* at § 316
[20] See ch 2, p 22, pp 35–38, and 48–50.
[21] *Doe I v Unocal Corp* 110 F Supp 2d 1294 (CD Cal 2000) (*Unocal 2000*).
[22] *John Doe I v Unocal Corp* 2002 US App LEXIS 19263 (9th Cir 2002) (*Unocal 2002*).
[23] *Doe v Unocal Corp* 2003 WL 359787 (9th Cir Feb 14, 2003).
[24] The plaintiffs' complaint is available via <http://www.earthrights.org/unocal/index.shtml> (4 September 2003). In addition, the plaintiffs made claims under a Californian business law statute, and an equitable claim of unjust enrichment.
[25] The other judges did not decide the case on the basis of tort law. Rather, they resorted to international law (see ch 2, pp 48–50). However, they conceded that Unocal's liability might also be established under tort principles, but declined to definitively answer this question (see *ibid* at 14212, n 20).

In order to examine the decisions of Chaney J and Reinhardt J, it is necessary to briefly outline certain aspects of the corporate arrangements governing the Yadana pipeline project. The project involved offshore exploration and development, and onshore projects within Myanmar. The litigation concerned activities perpetrated by the Myanmar military, which had been hired to provide security for the onshore construction and operation of an oil pipeline. The participants in the joint venture are the Myanmar government-owned oil company, the Myanmar Oil and Gas Enterprise (MOGE), the French corporate group Total, a Thai Petroleum company known as PTTEP, and Unocal. Responsibility for the onshore part of the project, the construction and operation of the pipeline, was vested in the Myanmar Gas Transportation Company (MGTC), which was owned by the joint venturers. Unocal set up a wholly owned subsidiary, Unocal International Pipeline Corporation (UIPC), to own its 28 per cent interest in MGTC.[26]

One of Unocal's contentions before the California court was that it was not involved in the construction of the pipeline, which was the responsibility of MGTC.[27] Chaney J held that Unocal, as one of the joint venturers, could potentially be held liable for the tortious actions of its subsidiary, MGTC, as the court found that there was sufficient evidence to indicate that the latter was the alter ego of each of the joint venturers. In law, the acts of a company's alter ego are treated as the acts of the company itself.[28] Chaney J went on to find that there was sufficient evidence, for the purposes of an application for summary dismissal, to establish that the Myanmar military had been hired by the joint venturers or their alter ego MGTC to provide security for the pipeline, and therefore that Unocal, as one of the joint venturers, could be vicariously liable as a principal for the acts of its agent, the Myanmar military.

In *Unocal 2002*, Reinhardt J also found that the Myanmar military could feasibly be classified as an agent of Unocal, giving rise to vicarious liability on the part of Unocal. Unlike Chaney J, Reinhardt J was also prepared on the facts to find that the Myanmar military was potentially part of the joint venture itself, rather than only an agent.[29] Under that analysis, Unocal could also be held liable as a person 'acting in concert' with the Myanmar military.

[26] This recitation of the facts is taken from *Unocal 2002*, above n 22, at 14193–95.

[27] See 'Ruling on Unocal Defendants' Motion for Summary Judgment based on (1) Absence of Vicarious Liability and (2) Failure to Join Indispensable Parties' [Vicarious Liability Ruling], Decision of the Superior Court of California, County of Los Angeles, 10 June 2003, available via <http://www.earthrights.org/unocal/index.shtml> (11 September 2003).

[28] If an entity is found to be the alter ego of another entity, the actions of the former entity are treated as those of the latter. The 'alter ego' principle is particularly relevant in corporate law, for example in piercing the veil so as to expose shareholders, including parent companies, to the liabilities of companies in which they hold shares. The Vicarious Liability Ruling indicates that there was sufficient evidence available to hold Unocal liable for the actions of UIPC, as only the latter subsidiary company was directly connected to MGTC. In January 2004, Chaney J ruled that UIPC was not Unocal's alter ego. However, she 'left the door open for plaintiffs to continue the trial under other theories of liability', such as agency. See, on this latest decision in the State litigation, http://www.earthrights.org/news/unocalupdate.shtml (14 April 2004). See also, ch 7, p 130.

[29] See ch 2, text at n 141.

Chaney J only allowed the plaintiffs to proceed on the basis of Unocal's alleged vicarious liability. For example, Chaney J summarily dismissed the tort actions against Unocal regarding *its own* actions, such as allegedly aiding and abetting the Myanmar military in its impugned actions.[30] To a large extent, these dismissals were based on the doctrine of collateral estoppel, which 'bars a party from relitigating an issue that a court has already adjudicated'.[31] The relevant prior adjudication, at the time of Chaney J's decision, was Lew J's decision in the federal court in *Unocal 2000* to dismiss the ATCA claims because he could not find a sufficient link between Unocal and the actions of the Myanmar military.[32] Of course, Lew J's decision may be reversed by the en banc panel of the Ninth Circuit, which could lead to a re-arguing of some parts of the State case. Chaney J however refused to revisit this decision upon application of the plaintiffs after the decision, now vacated, in the federal case of *Unocal 2002*. She evidently took a narrower view on the facts of Unocal's potential liability under tort principles than did the judges in *Unocal 2002*.

Chaney J dismissed the allegation of Unocal's direct liability for the alleged intentional torts (ie battery, assault, false imprisonment, intentional infliction of emotional distress, conversion) on the basis that Unocal was not the actual alleged perpetrator of the acts, and therefore was not the alleged tortfeasor. Interestingly, the claim was not dismissed on the basis of a lack of intent. Though there was no suggestion that Unocal intended or desired the perpetration of the intentional torts, the evidence was nevertheless sufficient 'to create a triable issue of fact' as to whether Unocal was substantially certain that the impugned acts would occur.[33]

Chaney J also dismissed the negligence claims against Unocal, as she could not uncover a relevant duty of care owed by Unocal to the plaintiffs. The negligence claims related to Unocal's failure to control the Myanmar military. As noted above, a person owes no duty to prevent a third party from harming another, unless a special relationship exists between the defendant and the third party.[34] A special relationship exists where the defendant is able to control the third party.[35]

---

[30] 'Ruling on Defendants' Motion for Summary Judgment, or in the Alternative, Summary Adjudication on each of the Plaintiffs' Tort Claims' [Tort Ruling], Decision of the Superior Court of California, County of Los Angeles, 7 June 2003, available via <http://www.earthrights.org/unocal/index.shtml> (11 September 2003).

[31] Tort Ruling, *ibid* at 4.

[32] *Unocal 2000*, above n 21.

[33] See also *Gomez v Aquistaspace* 50 Cal App 4th 740 (1996) 743, on how the existence of substantial certainty regarding an outcome, as opposed to 'mere' recklessness, denotes sufficient 'intent' for the purpose of establishing the perpetration of intentional torts.

[34] In this respect, Chaney J cited *Wise v Superior Court* 222 Cal App 3d 1009 (1990) 1013.

[35] In this respect, Chaney J cited at p 13 *Lopez v McDonald's Corp* 193 Cal App 3d 495 (1987) 515. The principle from *Lopez* does not, with respect, appear to be so wide as expressed by Chaney J. The case concerned the potential liability of McDonald's Corporation for the actions of a person who perpetrated a massacre in one of its restaurants. On the facts, McDonald's was not held liable for the gunman's actions. The discussion of the potential liability of McDonald's for a third party's actions focused on the liability of a business proprietor for the reasonably foreseeable acts of a third party which harm the proprietor's customers. Thus, the discussion did not relate to the *general* duty of a person to control a third party.

Chaney J followed the federal decision in *Unocal 2000* to establish that Unocal did not control the Myanmar military.[36] Unocal did owe the plaintiffs a duty 'not to place [them] in a situation in which [they are] exposed to an unreasonable risk of harm through the reasonably foreseeable conduct . . . of a third person'.[37] Alternatively, Unocal had a duty not to create a foreseeable risk of harm to the plaintiffs from the Myanmar military, or exacerbate the risk of harm posed by the Myanmar military.[38] Chaney J could not find, in the circumstances, that Unocal owed a relevant duty to the plaintiffs. The evidence could only establish that Unocal knew of the risk posed by the Myanmar military to the plaintiffs, and that it knowingly benefited from the harm caused, and even, perhaps, that its 'investment perpetuated the risk'.[39] With respect to Chaney J, it seems arguable that the perpetuation of a risk, that is the extension of the period of time during which a risk is present, essentially amounts to the increase or exacerbation of a risk.[40]

Chaney J also denied that Unocal had been negligent in investing in the project, and hiring the Myanmar military to provide security for the project. The plaintiffs' contention was that these actions exposed the plaintiffs to a foreseeable risk of damage. Chaney J found, on the evidence, that the project and the employment of the Myanmar military would have happened at the behest of the other joint venturers, such as Total, regardless of Unocal's involvement in the project. Thus, Unocal's impugned decisions did not *cause* the harm to the plaintiffs; that harm would have arisen anyway.[41]

In contrast, Reinhardt J found that Unocal could be held liable for recklessly disregarding the likely risk of harm posed by the Myanmar military to the plaintiffs.[42] As noted above, a judge is more likely to find that reckless behaviour has caused harm than negligent behaviour. Chaney J did not explicitly address claims regarding recklessness.

Chaney J also dismissed the contentions that Unocal had aided and abetted the Myanmar military by providing substantial assistance or encouragement in the commission of the torts.[43] In contrast, the majority in *Unocal 2002* found that, on the facts presented, Unocal could potentially be held to have aided and abetted the Myanmar military under principles drawn from international criminal law. The test for aiding and abetting in international criminal law is similar, if not more strict, than that in US tort law.[44] Therefore, Chaney J has again taken a narrower view of the facts than the Circuit Court judges in *Unocal 2002*.

---

[36] See Lew J's decision in *Unocal 2000*, above n 21, at 1306–7.
[37] *Lugtu v California Highway Patrol* 26 Cal 4th 703 (SCt Cal 2001) 716.
[38] *Pamela L v Farmer* 112 Cal App 3d 206 (1980) 209, 211–12.
[39] Tort Ruling, above n 30, at 14.
[40] See further, ch 7, pp 137–38.
[41] Tort Ruling, above n 30, at 8–11.
[42] See ch 2, text at n 144.
[43] Tort Ruling, above n 30, at 6–8.
[44] Compare the test from *Prosecutor v Furundzija* Case no IT–95–17/1–T, Judgment, 10 December 1998 (ICTY) of 'knowing 'practical assistance [or] encouragement . . . which has a substantial effect on the perpetration of the crime' (which was used by the majority in *Unocal 2002*; see ch 2, text at n 218), with *Restatement (Second) of Torts* § 876(b) (1965), which states that a person

Other Examples of Transitory Tort Cases

There are a number of other examples of salient transitory tort claims in the US. The most famous perhaps is the litigation concerning the Union Carbide gas plant disaster in Bhopal, India.[45] On 2 December 1984, a lethal gas methyl isocyanate leaked from Union Carbide's Bhopal subsidiary and killed thousands of people in Bhopal, and maimed or disabled hundreds of thousands more. A personal injuries action was brought by the Indian government and a number of private plaintiffs against the parent corporation in New York.[46] The plaintiff claimed that the parent company was liable under the tort of negligence. The plaintiff also argued, in the alternative, that Union Carbide had a strict duty to ensure that its hazardous plant did not cause harm in its activities.[47] The substantive tort claims were never tested in New York, as the case was dismissed for *forum non conveniens* (FNC) on the ground that it should more appropriately be heard in India.[48]

A series of transnational tort claims have been brought by Ecuadorian plaintiffs against Texaco regarding its alleged responsibility for contamination of the environment in the Amazon region, which has caused associated health problems.[49] The first claim, *Sequihua v Texaco*, filed in Texas, was dismissed for FNC.[50] A subsequent claim, *Aguinda v Texaco*, was similarly dismissed in New York.[51] Similar claims against Southern Peru Copper with regard to alleged environmental damage in Peru have also been dismissed for FNC.[52]

In contrast to the litigants against Union Carbide and Texaco, plaintiffs in another series of transitory tort claims concerning Shell Oil, Dow Chemicals, Standard Fruit, and Dole have had some comparative success, at least in overcoming FNC. The litigation concerned the use of the pesticide dibro-

---

is liable for the tortious conduct of another 'where the former person gives substantial assistance or encouragement to the other'.

[45] See generally, P Muchlinski, 'The Bhopal Case: Controlling Ultrahazardous Industrial Activity undertaken by Foreign Investors' (1987) 50 *Modern Law Review* 545.

[46] *In re Union Carbide Corp Gas Plant Disaster at Bhopal* 634 F Supp 842 (SDNY 1986) and *In re Union Carbide Corp Gas Plant Disaster at Bhopal* 809 F 2d 195 (2d Cir 1987). All claims in the US arising out of that disaster were finally dismissed in *Bano v Union Carbide* 273 F 3d 120 (2d Cir 2001).

[47] See MJ Rogge, 'Towards Transnational Corporate Liability in the Global Economy: Challenging the Doctrine of Forum non Conveniens in Re: Union Carbide, Alfaro, Sequihua, and Aguinda' (2001) 26 *Texas International Law Journal* 299, 302, 323.

[48] See ch 4 on FNC. See ch 7, n 76, on the outcome of the proceedings in India.

[49] See Rogge, above n 47, at 306–12.

[50] *Sequihua v Texaco, Inc* 847 F Supp 61 (SD Texas 1994).

[51] *Aguinda v Texaco* 945 F Supp 625 (SDNY 1996). This initial dismissal was reversed and remitted in *Jota v Texaco* 157 F 3d 153 (2d Cir 1998), but a new decision to dismiss for FNC was issued in *Aguinda v Texado* 142 F Supp 2d 534 (2001) (affirmed in 303 F 3d 470 (2002)).

[52] *Torres v Southern Peru Copper* 965 F Supp 899 (SD Tex 1996). Upon refiling in New York, the case was again dismissed for FNC in *Flores v Southern Peru Copper* 253 F Supp 2d 510 (EDNY 2002) The Circuit Court did not review the FNC decision in *Flores v Southern Peru Copper* 343 F 3d 140 (2d Cir 2003).

mochloropropane [DBCP] on banana plantations in Central America, Africa and South East Asia; exposure to DBCP allegedly caused injuries, especially sterilisation, to the plaintiffs.[53] Shell Oil and Dow Chemicals were sued as manufacturers of DBCP, while Standard Fruit and Dole were sued as users of the product. DBCP was banned in the US in 1977 after instances of sterilisation arose in California, yet the chemical was exported and used in other countries after that date. An action for wrongful death and personal injury was brought in 1990 under Texas State jurisdiction in *Dow Chemicals v Castro Alfaro*.[54] The inevitable FNC argument by the defendants was dismissed by Supreme Court of Texas on the basis that Texas had statutorily removed FNC in transnational personal injury cases. The legal significance of Castro Alfaro's victory was however short-lived. The defendants promptly settled the case with three plaintiffs, while the Texas legislature repealed the relevant statute, thus reintroducing FNC for future litigation in Texas.[55] A subsequent tort claim in *Delgado v Shell Oil*[56] was dismissed for FNC by a Texas District Court in 1995.

The persistent plaintiffs filed again in Louisiana in *Martinez v Dow Chemicals*.[57] In 2002, Barbier J dismissed the defendants' FNC arguments in *Martinez*,[58] so the status quo is that the case will proceed to be heard on the merits, pending an appeal or perhaps a settlement. Barbier J's decision to keep the litigation within jurisdiction is reflective of a recent trend in FNC jurisprudence in transnational human rights litigation, as is discussed in Chapter 4.

Thus far, most litigation in transitory human rights tort claims in the US has focused on the procedural issue of FNC. Substantive issues such as the existence, nature and scope of the duty of care owed by a TNC to transnational human rights victims have not yet been extensively addressed in the US. To what extent does a parent company owe a duty of care to its subsidiary's employees, or to persons in the vicinity of a factory owned by a subsidiary, or persons harmed directly or indirectly by the subsidiary's work practices?[59] Does that duty vary if the operations of the subsidiary are extraordinarily hazardous, as in the *Union Carbide* case? The substantive potential of tort law to provide remedies for transnational human rights victims of TNCs has not been clarified by courts.[60]

Transnational tort cases have also arisen in the US with regard to alleged tortious actions in other *developed* countries, particularly products liability cases

---

[53] See Rogge, above n 47, at 303–6.
[54] 786 786 S W 2d 674 (SCt Tex 1990).
[55] See Rogge, above n 47, at 306.
[56] 890 F Supp 1324 (SD Tex 1995).
[57] 219 F Supp 2d 719 (ED La 2002).
[58] See ch 4, text at n 97.
[59] See ch 7.
[60] For example, despite the scale of the Bhopal catastrophe, it is uncertain whether Union Carbide could have been proven negligent under US or Indian law; see Rogge, above n 47, at 321: 'No one knew precisely how the Bhopal disaster occurred. . . . Duty, fault, and causation would be extraordinarily difficult to prove.' See also Anderson, above n 3, at 416.

against US pharmaceutical companies.[61] These cases do not however raise human rights issues to the same extent as the transnational cases discussed herein, as developed countries are more likely to have adequate legislative standards (eg health and safety, environmental standards) and/or common law standards (eg well-developed tort law) for preventing corporate human rights abuse, even if litigation in such States is not as favorable to the plaintiff as litigation in the US. Therefore, such cases are distinguishable from the cases discussed herein, and are beyond the scope of this book. It may be noted that most of these product liability cases have been dismissed for FNC.

Choice of Law

The issue of 'choice of law', the law to be applied in a case, is likely to prove much more complex and problematic in such cases, compared to ATCA cases.[62] Contemporary rules applied throughout the US regarding choice of law in transnational tort cases are 'diverse' and inconsistent.[63] A variety of approaches are taken across the various US jurisdictions. The most common approach is for a court to apply the test outlined in §145 of the *Restatement (Second) of Conflict of Laws*. That test dictates that the law to be applied is that of the jurisdiction with 'the most significant relationship to the occurrence [ie. the act or acts at issue] and the parties'. The identity of this forum is worked out by referring to factors enumerated in §6: the needs of the international legal system; the relevant policies of the forum; the relevant policies of other interested States; justified expectations; certainty, predictability, and uniformity; ease in determining the applicable law. A significant number of US States however tend to favour the law of the site of the alleged wrong. Yet another group of US States adopts the so-called 'interest' approach, whereby the court will apply the law of the forum, if it has 'an interest' in the outcome.[64] The law of another

---

[61] For example, a number of product liability cases have been instigated against US for injuries caused in the UK; see *Watson v Merrell-Dow Pharmaceuticals Inc* 769 F 2d 354 (6th Cir 1985); *Dowling v Richardson-Merrell* 727 F 2d 608 (6th Cir 1984); *Harrison v Wyeth Laboratories* 510 F Supp 1 (ED Pa 1980) (aff'd 676 F 2d 685 (3rd Cir 1982)); *Chambers v Merrell Dow Pharmaceuticals* 519 NE 2d 370 (SCt Ohio 1988). See also *In re Silicon Gel Breast Implant Litigation* 887 F Supp 1469 (ND Ala 1995) (products liability litigation by injured parties from the UK, Australia, New Zealand, and Canada); *Ison v E I DuPont de Nemours* 729 A 2d 832 (SCt Del 1999), (fungicide exposure in UK and New Zealand); *Carlenstolpe v Merck* 819 F 2d 33 (2d Cir 1987) (pharmaceutical products case brought by a Swedish consumer); *Picketts v International Playtex* 576 A 2d 518 (SCt Conn 1990). See also Blumberg, above n 4, at 502, n 35 and 511–13.

[62] See ch 2, pp 54–55.

[63] See GB Born, *International Civil Litigation in United States Courts* (3rd edn, The Hague, Kluwer Law International, 1996) 635–36. See also Anderson, above n 3, at 415–18.

[64] See M Whincop and M Keyes, *Policy and Pragmatism in the Conflict of Laws* (Aldershot, Ashgate, 2001) 17–18; see also Born, *ibid* at 632–33 and 635. The 'interest' approach was initially put forward by Brainerd Currie in his *Selected Essays in Choice of Law* (1963) (cited in Born at p 632, n 145). See also extracts of B Currie, 'Notes on Methods and Objectives in the Conflict of Laws', [1959] *Duke Law Journal* 171, extracted in Born, *ibid*, at pp 636–39. Currie's approach has been described as 'unabashedly parochial' and 'little more than a complicated pretext for applying the *lex*

jurisdiction will only apply if that other State has a genuine interest in the case, while the forum's interest is negligible. Furthermore, a number of US States do not adopt a consistent approach, with, for example, the choice of law rules in New York having been described as utterly confused, and 'incoherent'.[65] US choice of law rules are further complicated by the fact that a foreign law will not be applied if it is deemed to contravene 'public policy' within the forum.[66] Given all of the above, it is trite to say that choice of law in the US essentially involves analysis on a case-by-case basis. Even the apparent certainty of the rule that forum law governs procedural issues in a case[67] is undermined by the fact that the dividing line between procedural and substantive issues is not clear-cut.[68]

In *Doe v Unocal*, the California Superior Court has rejected the defendants' argument that Myanmar law should govern the case.[69] Chaney J appeared to use a combination of the interest test and the *Restatement's* 'most significant relationship test' as the appropriate choice of law principles for the State of California. Chaney J found that, on the basis of the evidence before her, Myanmar law was 'radically indeterminate' on the relevant issues in the case.[70] In that case, the court assumed that the foreign law was 'not out of harmony with [Californian law]',[71] so Californian law was applied to resolve the issues. Importantly, Chaney J also found that public policy considerations barred the application of Myanmar law to the extent that it might have precluded the plaintiffs' tort claims concerning forced labour. This ruling signals that a US court will not enforce a foreign law that shields companies from egregious human rights allegations, such as those made in *Unocal*. Public policy may not however eject foreign laws that are lenient regarding 'lesser' human rights abuses.

The site of the tort will always be a relevant, if not decisive, consideration in determining the appropriate law to be applied in a transnational human rights case. However, the 'site' of the wrong in transnational human rights tort cases against corporations may not be clear. An alleged wrong may be caused by many acts, which occur across jurisdictions. The cases may commonly involve a decision being made in one jurisdiction, but being implemented with allegedly foreseeable disastrous outcomes in another. For example, an alleged contributory cause of the Bhopal accident was the decision, apparently made in Connecticut but implemented in Bhopal, to cut costs at the Bhopal plant by shutting off the refrigeration unit on the 'ill-fated tank' of deadly gas, 'thus

fori', in Juenger, 'General Course of Private International Law' (1983) 193 *Recueil des Cours* 119, 218, cited in Born at p 633, n 154.

[65] Juenger, *ibid* at 223, cited in Born, *ibid* at p 636, n 176.
[66] See Born, *ibid* at 629 and 651–52.
[67] *Restatement (Second) Conflict of Laws* § 122 (1971).
[68] Born, above n 63, at 652.
[69] Transcript available via <http://www.ccr-ny.org/> (4 September 2003).
[70] For example, defendants had argued that Myanmar law was different to Californian law on the issue of whether Unocal's Myanmar subsidiary was its alter ego.
[71] See also *Gagnon Co Inc v Nevada Desert Inn Inc* 45 Cal 2d 448 (SCt Cal 1955) 454.

allowing the gas to warm from [zero degrees] Celsius to the more volatile ambient temperature'.[72] Plaintiff lawyers are now commonly targeting the decisions made at a TNC's headquarters, as well as the implementation of those decisions in host countries. This tactic has consequences for choice of law analyses, and of course for the attribution of substantive liability within corporate groups.[73]

Do Tort cases against Private Sector Parties Raise Human Rights Issues?

Unlike ATCA claims, ordinary transnational tort claims will not normally be drafted in human rights language. Rather, reference will be made to ordinary tort principles. Nevertheless, these cases raise important human rights issues. For example, the cases concerning Union Carbide and the fertilizer DBCP, noted above, concern rights to life and health.

Of course, that argument taken to its logical extent could label every personal injuries case a 'human rights' case, which might devalue the currency of human rights language. However, the transnational tort cases against companies cited above are clearly distinguishable from ordinary tort claims. Each of the corporate defendants in the 'transnational human rights' cases has been accused of causing severe, even catastrophic, damage to local populations in the course of taking advantage of lax regulatory regimes in developing countries. Such circumstances clearly have a qualitatively different human rights dimension to ordinary personal injury cases, which normally lack the element of the failure in State protection.

It is now well recognised that international human rights treaties (and maybe customary international law) require States to regulate private parties so as to prevent human rights abuses by those parties.[74] For example, a State should enact and enforce appropriate laws to prevent companies within jurisdiction from exposing their workers to unreasonable dangers which harm those workers' rights to life or freedom from inhuman treatment. Unfortunately, States may be unwilling or unable to control powerful elements in their domestic private sector, as is often the case with developing nations and TNCs. TNCs have been tempted to take advantage of this lack of domestic regulatory control to the detriment of the enjoyment of certain rights by individuals within those States, as alleged for example in the DBCP cases. Therefore, the enforcement of human rights norms (in the guise of transnational tort law) against a defendant corporation represents an implementation of the plaintiff victim's right to be protected from those abuses, albeit by a party (the US) other than the party that

---

[72] Anderson, above n 3, at 416.
[73] See generally, ch 7.
[74] See above, ch 1, p 9, and ch 2, p 39. See also Scott, above n 1, at 47–49. This duty is sometimes known as the doctrine of horizontality, or the horizontal application of human rights. Cf *Restatement (Third) of the Foreign Relations Law of the US* § 207 (1987), which indicates that States are not liable in international law for the actions of private individuals.

has the international obligation to protect the plaintiff (the host State). A more radical extension of the latter argument is that States have duties to control the extraterritorial actions of their private citizens, including corporations. In that case, enforcement of transnational tort law against a US corporation for abusing human rights abroad represents an implementation of the US's own human rights obligations.[75]

JURISDICTION UNDER § 1331

Transnational human rights cases may also arise in federal courts as claims for violations of international law, including international human rights law,[76] because federal courts have jurisdiction over matters arising under the Constitution and federal laws under 28 USC § 1331. 'Federal laws' include self-executing treaties ratified by the US.[77] The relevance of federal 'treaty' jurisdiction in human rights matters has been curtailed by the US executive practice of issuing a declaration upon ratification that human rights treaties are not self-executing.[78]

The orthodox view in US law is that customary international law constitutes enforceable federal common law, so long as there is no relevant statutory law in the area.[79] Federal statutes prevail over inconsistent custom.[80] As federal law

---

[75] This author has previously doubted that such a position exists generally under existing international treaties, let alone customary law; see S Joseph, 'Taming the Leviathans: Multinational Enterprises and Human Rights' (1999) 46 *Netherlands International Law Review* 171, 177–78. See also ch 1, text at n 85. However, see M Sornarajah, 'Linking State Responsibility for Certain Harms caused by Corporate Nationals Abroad to Civil Recourse in the Legal Systems of Home States' in Scott, above n 1.

[76] See generally Armin Rosencranz & Richard Campbell, 'Foreign Environmental and Human Rights Suits Against US Corporations in US Courts' (1999) 18 *Stanford Environmental Law Journal* 145, 171–75.

[77] A self-executing treaty is treated as if it is a federal statute, so later statutes will override them to the extent of any inconsistency. See ch 2, pp 53–54.

[78] KDA Carpenter, 'The International Covenant on Civil and Political Rights: A Toothless Tiger?' (2000) 26 *North Carolina Journal of International Law and Commercial Regulation* 1, 5–7.

[79] *The Paquete Habana* 175 US 677 (SCt 1900) 700; *Ex Parte Quirin* 317 US 1 (SC 1942); see also *Filartiga v Peña-Irala* 630 F 2d 876 (2d Cir 1980) 885–87. This orthodox position has been strongly challenged in CA Bradley and JL Goldsmith, 'Customary International Law as Federal Common Law: A Critique of the Modern Position' (1997) 110 *Harvard Law Review* 815 (denying that customary international law is part of federal law), and CA Bradley and JL Goldsmith, 'The Current Illegitimacy of International Human Rights Litigation' (1997) 66 *Fordham Law Review* 319 (consequently challenging the *Filartiga* interpretation of ATCA). See also The 'Unocal brief', dated 8 May 2003, <http://www.earthrights.org/atca/dojbrief.pdf> (25 September 2003) 22–25. See, in response to Bradley and Goldsmith, GL Neuman, 'Sense and Nonsense about Customary International Law: A Response to Professors Bradley and Goldsmith' (1997) 66 *Fordham Law Review* 371, and B Stephens, 'The Law of Our Land: Customary International Law after Erie' (1997) 66 *Fordham Law Review* 393. This debate is beyond the scope of this book.

[80] See Born, above n 63, at 21. The judiciary endeavors to interpret US statutes so as to conform with custom, unless such a construction is impossible (Born, *ibid*, at p 22). Custom should prevail over all State laws due to its status as federal law. However, '[p]arties have rarely argued that [custom] preempts state law, so there is little judicial precedent on the issue' (Born, *ibid*, at p 21).

is quite comprehensive, there is little scope for the application of customary international law. Nevertheless, custom provided a basis for federal jurisdiction in *Bodner v Banque Paribas*, where the complaints of the US plaintiffs against a French Bank for looting of their possessions during World War II (a war crime) were accepted under § 1331.[81] However, the opposite conclusion has been reached in other human rights cases, such as *Xuncax v Gramajo*, where Woodlock J denied that customary international law could provide an autonomous right to sue in a federal court.[82] The *Bodner* view probably accords more with Supreme Court authority that custom is part of federal common law, as federal common law incorporates a right to sue for vindication of the rights therein.[83]

Claims under § 1331 largely overlap with ATCA claims. Currently, its main importance lies in providing a cause of action to human rights victims who are US nationals, who lack standing under ATCA. Of course, § 1331 would assume greater importance if the ATCA should be repealed or amended, or emasculated by the pending Supreme Court decision in *Sosa v Alverez Machain*. Indeed, it might provide a ready-made replacement for ATCA causes of action if it is settled that it provides a cause of action as well as federal jurisdiction for violations of customary international law.[84] In that case, the ATCA jurisprudence on the meaning of the term 'law of nations' within that statute, which has generally been interpreted to mean 'customary international law',[85] would be very relevant for future actions based solely on § 1331.

LIABILITY UNDER RICO

In a number of transnational human rights cases, plaintiffs have claimed relief under the *Racketeer Influenced and Corrupt Organizations* [RICO] statute.[86] Paragraph (c) thereof states:

> It shall be unlawful for any person employed by or associated with any enterprise engaged in, or the activities of which affect, interstate or foreign commerce, to conduct or participate, directly or indirectly, in the conduct of such enterprise's affairs through a pattern of racketeering activity or collection of unlawful debt.

Paragraph (d) prohibits conspiracy to commit offences under, inter alia, paragraph (c).

---

[81] *Bodner v Banque Paribas* 114 F Supp 2d 117 (EDNY 2000) 127. The substantially identical claims of foreign plaintiffs in the case gave rise to ATCA jurisdiction.
[82] 886 F Supp 162 (D Mass 1995) 193–94.
[83] Stephens and Ratner, above n 1, at 35. See also JJ Paust, 'Human Rights Responsibilities of Private Corporations' (2002) 35 *Vanderbilt Journal of Transnational Law* 801, 821.
[84] See also *Kadic v Karadzic* 70 F 3d 232 (CA 2, NY, 1995), at 246 on the uncertainty surrounding this issue.
[85] See generally, ch 2 at pp 25–33.
[86] 18 USC § 1962 (2002).

An enterprise must consist of a 'group of persons associated together for a common purpose of engaging in a course of conduct'.[87] Breyer J in the Supreme Court held in *Cedric Kushner Promotions Ltd v King* that a corporation and its agent employee (also its president and its sole shareholder) could constitute an enterprise for the purposes of RICO.[88] Corporate acts are therefore always committed by 'enterprises' as a corporation cannot act without the assistance of a human being. Thus, the doctrine of separate legal personality for corporations, normally a boon in avoiding liability,[89] could have a double-edged effect as it increases a corporation's chances of falling foul of RICO.

Racketeering activity is defined as any act or threat involving a long list of crimes, including murder, arson, extortion, bribery, peonage, involuntary servitude, and slavery. Two or more instances of 'racketeering' constitute a 'pattern' of racketeering activity.[90] In order to recover damages, a plaintiff must suffer loss to property or business.[91] A defendant found liable under RICO is susceptible to triple damages, as well as a plaintiff's legal costs.[92]

RICO was originally enacted to deal with organised crime. Certainly, it was enacted to deal with crimes that are somehow related to commercial aims. The perpetration of personal injuries per se is not sufficient to trigger a RICO claim.[93] However, RICO's potential scope is very broad, considering the scope of the definition of 'racketeering'. It has now been invoked as an alternative cause of action in a number of ATCA cases against corporations. Importantly, for the purposes of transnational human rights litigation, the courts have confirmed that RICO does not require that the racketeering activities be committed inside the US.[94] A Court can exercise RICO jurisdiction over extraterritorial acts so long as extraterritorial damage was caused by intra-territorial conduct (the conduct test), or such acts have substantial effects inside the US (the effects test).[95]

In *Wiwa v Royal Dutch Petroleum Co (Wiwa 2002)*, the plaintiffs claimed that the defendants violated RICO in that they engaged in an enterprise in the Ogoni oilfields with the Nigerian military and an unaffiliated company, Willbros West Africa,[96] to perform acts such as murder (eg of environmental

---

[87] *Procter & Gamble Co v Big Apple Industrial Bldgs* 879 F 2d 10 (2d Cir 1989) 15.
[88] 533 US 158 (SCt 2001); see discussion in *Wiwa v Royal Dutch Petroleum Co* No 96 Civ 8386, 2002 US Dist LEXIS 3293 (SDNY Feb 22, 2002) 74–78.
[89] See generally below, ch 7.
[90] 18 USC § 1961(5).
[91] 18 USC § 1964(c).
[92] 18 USC § 1964(c).
[93] See *Burnett v Al Baraka Investment and Development Corporation* 274 F Supp 2d 86 (DDC 2003) 100–2, where the injuries and deaths caused by the terrorist attacks of 11 September 2001 were found not to give rise to a RICO claim.
[94] *Wiwa v Royal Dutch Petroleum Co* No 96 Civ 8386, 2002 US Dist LEXIS 3293 (SDNY Feb 22, 2002) 81–83.
[95] *Unocal 2002*, above n 22, at 14241.
[96] No 96 Civ 8386, 2002 US Dist LEXIS 3293 (SDNY Feb 22, 2002); the Court thus did not need to define the enterprise as consisting only of persons within the Shell group.

80 *Other Jurisdictional Bases in the US*

protesters), arson, extortion, and bribery. As the defendants' racketeering activities allegedly forced the plaintiffs to flee and therefore abandon their property and businesses, the plaintiffs had suffered relevant damage for the purposes of RICO. The relevant effects inside the US were that (i) 40 per cent of the oil extracted from the relevant operations was exported to the US, and (ii) the defendants hoped to gain a significant competitive advantage from the lower production costs entailed in their 'unlawful exploitation of the Ogoni oil fields'.[97] The Court accepted that these economic effects inside the US could give rise to RICO jurisdiction. Furthermore, these allegations clearly satisfied the 'commercial nexus' requirement of RICO, paragraph (c), as well as a prima face claim of conspiracy under paragraph (d).[98] Barring appeals or settlement, the RICO claims against the *Wiwa* defendants will be assessed on the merits by the District Court of Southern New York.

A similar RICO claim in relation to forced labour, characterised as 'extorted' labor, was rejected in *Unocal 2002*. While the Court accepted that forced labour could be classified as racketeering activity, and that loss of '[t]he right to make personal and business decisions about one's own labor' constituted damage to a property right,[99] it found that the allegations did not satisfy the 'conduct' or the 'effects' test for the extraterritorial application of RICO. Regarding the conduct test, Unocal's transferal of moneys to parties in Myanmar to finance the Yadana pipeline project did not 'directly cause' injuries in Myanmar.[100] The allegation that Unocal's impugned activities in Myanmar would give it an unfair advantage in US oil markets was not accepted as satisfaction of the effects test, as the plaintiffs had failed to outline specific facts to support their 'conclusory allegations'.[101]

The unsuccessful *Unocal 2002* effects claim mirrored the successful claim (for the purposes of staving off summary dismissal) in *Wiwa 2002*. Future cases will help clarify the law regarding the application of RICO to extraterritorial acts.[102] At the least, the two cases confirm that RICO claims may lie against corporate defendants when they, or their commercial partners, engage in certain human rights abuses to further the aims of a commercial project, so long as the test for extraterritorial application of RICO can be satisfied.[103]

---

[97] *Ibid* at 70–71.
[98] *Ibid* at 85–86.
[99] *Unocal 2002*, above n 22, at 14240.
[100] *Unocal 2002*, above n 22, at 14242.
[101] *Unocal 2002*, above n 22, at 14242.
[102] In *Sinaltrainal v Coca-Cola Co* 256 F Supp 2d 1345 (SD Fla 2003), the RICO claim was dismissed as the plaintiffs failed 'to allege any conduct satisfying either [the conduct or the effects] test' (at 1359). In *Bowoto v Chevron Texaco Corp* No C 99-2506 SI, 2004 US Dist LEXIS 4603 (ND, Cal 2004), the court has allowed RICO claims to proceed against the company, though the reasoning in that regard has not been publicly released.
[103] See also *Doe v The Gap* No CV–01–0031, 2001 WL 1842389 (DN Mar I Nov 6, CD Cal 2001) where the plaintiffs were permitted to pursue RICO claims for 'peonage' against garment manufacturers and retailers, in that plaintiff workers were allegedly forced to work in appalling conditions to pay off exorbitant recruitment fees paid to their employers. The alleged property damage was lost

CONCLUSION

There are a number of significant alternative bases for suing corporations for their overseas breaches of human rights. These alternative bases will become more important and prominent if ATCA should be repealed, or significantly reinterpreted. 28 USC § 1331 could provide a wholesale replacement for ATCA, though its meaning has not yet been clarified within US law. The outer limits of RICO in transnational human rights litigation will undoubtedly be explored, though it appears likely that it will only be actionable in rare cases. Finally, ordinary US tort law provides an avenue for challenging human rights abusive behaviour by TNCs that extend beyond the extraordinary circumstances envisaged by ATCA, TVPA, § 1331, and RICO.

moneys in the form of lost wages, excessive payments for employer-provided food, and payment of recruitment fees. The site of the alleged racketeering was the US commonwealth territory of Saipan in the Marianas Islands, so the plaintiffs did not have to satisfy the test for extraterritorial application of RICO. The *Gap* case settled in late 2002 against all defendants except Levis (see International Restructuring Education Network Europe (IRENE), *Lawsuits against Multinational Corporations for Labor Rights Violations* (Amsterdam, copy on file with the author, September 2002) 56–58).

4
Procedural Obstacles in the US

THE TWO PREVIOUS chapters concern the bases of subject matter jurisdiction for US courts over transnational human rights violations by corporations. Plaintiffs must also overcome formidable procedural obstacles. First, US courts cannot exercise jurisdiction over defendants unless they can establish 'personal jurisdiction' over them. Second, a US court may refuse to exercise jurisdiction on the discretionary ground of *forum non conveniens*. These two procedural issues are discussed in turn.

PERSONAL JURISDICTION

A US Court can generally exercise personal jurisdiction over a defendant to the extent permitted by the due process clauses of the US Constitution.[1] A defendant must have 'certain minimum contacts with [a forum] 'such that the maintenance of the suit does not offend "traditional notions of fair play and substantial justice"'.[2]

General jurisdiction 'permits a court to adjudicate any claim against a defendant'.[3] US courts may exercise general jurisdiction over US nationals, including companies incorporated in the US, even for their extraterritorial activities.[4] Foreign corporations are subject to general jurisdiction in US courts if they 'do business' in the forum, that is they have substantial, ongoing business relations in the forum.[5] Given its significance, it is unfortunate that the standard of 'substantial business dealings' is quite vague, and its satisfaction can only be determined on a case-by-case basis.[6] Examples of the application of the test in

---

[1] In some States, the jurisdictional reach of courts is further restricted by statutory laws. See GB Born, *International Civil Litigation in United States Courts* 3rd edn, (The Hague, Kluwer Law International, 1996) 69–70.

[2] *International Shoe Co v State of Washington* 326 US 310 (SCt 1945) 316, quoting *Milliken v Meyer* 311 US 457 (SCt 1940) 463. See also *World-Wide Volkswagen Corp v Woodsen* 444 US 286 (SCt 1980) 295.

[3] Born, above n 1, at 77.

[4] Ibid at 100; *Blackmer v US* 284 US 421 (SCt 1932).

[5] Born, *ibid*; *Wiwa v Royal Dutch Petroleum* 226 F 3d 88 (2d Cir 2000) 95; and *Doe I v Unocal Corp* 27 F Supp 2d 1174 (CD Cal 1998) 1184 (*Unocal 1998*).

[6] Born, *ibid* at 104; SM Hall, 'Multinational Corporations' Post-Unocal Liabilities for Violations of International Law' (2002) *George Washington International Law Review* 401, 406.

ATCA cases are given below. The issue has not yet arisen in the other salient transnational human rights cases.

General jurisdiction may be distinguished from specific jurisdiction; the latter only permits 'the adjudication of claims that are related to or arise out of a defendant's contacts with the forum'.[7] A lesser level of forum contact is required for specific jurisdiction than for general jurisdiction, as the relevant contact is established by the impugned act itself.[8] 'Specific jurisdiction' is unlikely to be relevant in transnational human rights complaints against non-US corporations, as such complaints rarely relate to actions inside the US.[9]

An important factor in considering personal jurisdiction over TNCs is the extent to which US courts will ground personal jurisdiction over foreign parent companies upon the existence within jurisdiction of subsidiaries or agents. This issue has been important in three ATCA cases, *Doe v Unocal (Unocal 1998)*,[10] *Wiwa v Royal Dutch Petroleum (Wiwa 2000)*,[11] and *Presbyterian Church of Sudan v Talisman Energy*.[12]

Personal jurisdiction will be established where the parent is held to be the 'alter ego' of its local subsidiary, a test which is interchangeable with that of 'piercing the corporate veil' so as to expose a parent 'behind' its subsidiary.[13] 'Alter ego' is established when a parent and its subsidiary fail to comply with the formal requirements of corporate separateness, or when a parent exercises an extreme level of control over its subsidiary, such that they are 'not really separate entities'.[14] For example, a parent's exercise of 'day-to-day' control over a subsidiary's operations usually suffices to establish alter ego.[15] The 'alter ego' test is difficult to satisfy, as indicated in the *Unocal* litigation.

---

[7] Born, *ibid* at 78.
[8] *Ibid* at 78.
[9] See S Zia-Zarifi, 'Suing Multinational Corporations in the US for Violating International Law' (1999) 4 *University of California at Los Angeles Journal International Law and Foreign Affairs* 81, 126. The plaintiffs in *Unocal 1998*, above n 5, at 1188, failed to establish that the California court had specific jurisdiction over Unocal's French partner Total by virtue of the latter's contractual relationship with Unocal, a Californian company.
[10] 27 F Supp 2d 1174 (CD Cal 1998).
[11] *Wiwa v Royal Dutch Petroleum* 226 F 3d 88 (2d Cir 2000).
[12] *Presbyterian Church of Sudan v Talisman Energy* 244 F Supp 2d 289 (SDNY 2003). The Bolivian corporate defendant in *Eastman Kodak Co v Kavlin* 978 F Supp 1078 (SD Fla 1997) was dismissed for lack of personal jurisdiction in an evidentiary hearing; the transcript of reasoning is not available. On *Eastman Kodak*, see J Green and P Hoffman, 'US Litigation Update' in M Kamminga and S Zia-Zarifi (eds) *Liability of Multinational Corporations under International Law* (The Hague, Kluwer Law International, 2000) 234–35. Personal jurisdiction has not been explicitly addressed in court decisions in other cases against foreign corporations, such as *Sarei v Rio Tinto* 221 F Supp 2d 1116 (CD Cal 2002) or *Bodner v Banque Paribas* 114 F Supp 2d 117 (EDNY 2000).
[13] PI Blumberg, 'Asserting Human Rights Against Multinational Corporations under United States Law: Conceptual and Procedural Problems' (2002) 50 *American Journal of Comparative Law* 493, 497, n 12.
[14] *Unocal 1998*, above n 5, at 1187; PI Blumberg, 'Accountability of Multinational Corporations: The Barriers Presented by Concepts of the Corporate Juridical Entity' (2001) 24 *Hastings International and Comparative Law Review* 297, 305.
[15] Blumberg, above n 13, at 498.

In *Unocal 1998*, the District Court had to decide if it had jurisdiction over Unocal's corporate partner in the Yadana project, the French energy company Total SA [Total]. The plaintiffs attempted to establish that the court had general jurisdiction over Total by virtue of the presence of a number of Total subsidiaries in California. Ultimately, the plaintiffs 'establishe[d] only that Total is an active parent corporation involved directly in decision-making about its subsidiaries' holdings'.[16] The level of control was not however so extreme as to establish 'alter ego' status.

An alternative basis for jurisdiction is to establish that a subsidiary is a parent's agent under the common law.[17] Under this test, the agent must act for the benefit of the parent with the parent's knowledge and consent. Furthermore, the parent must have a high degree of control over the agent's actions. Finally, the agent must act within its authority. Common law agency has not arisen as a basis for jurisdiction over parent corporations in respect of the actions of their subsidiaries in transnational human rights litigation.[18]

An alternative jurisdictional test of agency, a *sui generis* doctrine found in the Second and Ninth Circuits,[19] arose in both *Unocal 1998* and *Wiwa 2000*. Under this doctrine, an entity is a corporation's agent if it performs services that are 'sufficiently important to the [parent] that if it did not have a representative to perform them, the [parent's] own officials would undertake to perform substantially similar services'.[20]

In *Unocal 1998*, Paez J found that Total's subsidiaries were not Total's agents under this test, due to insufficient evidence of the importance of the subsidiaries' activities to Total.[21] Therefore, the plaintiffs failed to establish that the California court had jurisdiction over Total. Zia-Zarifi has described this decision as a 'triumph of corporate formality over reality'.[22] Certainly, it seems unlikely that Total would forego operations in the lucrative Californian market in the absence of its subsidiaries. The strictness of the Ninth Circuit's *Unocal 1998* decision regarding sui generis agency can be contrasted with the Second Circuit's decision in *Wiwa 2000*.

The plaintiffs in *Wiwa 2000* argued that the District Court of New York had general jurisdiction over the defendants Royal Dutch Petroleum Company and Shell Transport and Trading Company, two companies incorporated, respectively, in the Netherlands and the UK. They submitted that two bodies located

---

[16] *Unocal 1998*, above n 5, 1188.
[17] Born, above n 1, at 164; Blumberg, above n 14, at 307–8.
[18] Blumberg, *ibid*, notes at 307 that 'few parent/subsidiary relationships satisfy the common law requirements for an "agency" relationship'.
[19] Blumberg, above n 13, at 499.
[20] *Chan v Society Expeditions, Inc* 39 F 3d 1398 (9th Cir 1994) 1405, as quoted by Paez J in *Unocal 1998*, above n 5, at 1188. See also *Wiwa v Royal Dutch Petroleum* 226 F 3d 88 (2d Cir 2000) 95, citing *Frummer v Hilton Hotels International Inc* 19 NY 2d 533 (NY App 1967) 537.
[21] *Unocal 1998*, above n 5, at 1189. Paez J's decision was affirmed in *Doe I v Unocal Corp* 248 F 3d 915 (9th Cir 2001).
[22] Zia-Zarifi, above n 9, at 128.

in New York were the defendants' agents: an Investor Relations Office (IRO) and its manager, James Grapsi. While Grapsi and the IRO were 'nominally' part of Shell Oil, a Delaware-based subsidiary of the defendants, the Court determined that they 'devoted one hundred percent of their time to the defendants' business'.[23] The Second Circuit went on to find that the work of Grapsi and the IRO was of sufficient importance to establish agency, even though they were not involved in the defendants' core business of operating in the oil trade.

> The defendants are huge publicly-traded companies with a need for access to capital markets. The importance of their need to maintain good relationships with existing investors and potential investors is illustrated by the fact that they pay over half a million dollars per year to maintain the Investor Relations Office. In our view, the amount invested by the defendants in the US investor relations activity substantially establishes the importance of that activity to the defendants.[24]

The Court concluded that the exercise of personal jurisdiction over the defendants was fair and reasonable, and therefore conformed with constitutional due process requirements:

> The defendants control a vast, wealthy, and far-flung business empire which operates in most parts of the globe. They have a physical presence in the forum state, have access to enormous resources, face little or no language barrier, have litigated in this country on previous occasions, have a four-decade long relationship with one of the nation's leading law firms, and are the parent companies of one of America's largest corporations [Shell Oil], which has a very significant presence in New York. New York City, furthermore, where the trial would be held, is a major world capital which offers central location, easy access, and extensive facilities of all kinds. We conclude that the inconvenience to the defendants involved in litigating in New York City would not be great and that nothing in the Due Process Clause precludes New York from exercising jurisdiction over the defendants.[25]

Wiwa 2000 was followed in this respect by *Presbyterian Church of Sudan v Talisman Energy*.[26] The defendant Talisman is a Canadian company traded on the New York Stock Exchange. That fact alone was insufficient to establish the Southern New York District Court's jurisdiction over Talisman, but was 'a factor militating in favour of conferring jurisdiction'.[27] Further links, the combined effect of which was to establish sufficient links between Talisman and the State of New York so as to ground jurisdiction, were manifested by Talisman's total control over a New York based subsidiary, Fortuna.[28]

---

[23] *Wiwa v Royal Dutch Petroleum* 226 F 3d 88 (2d Cir 2000) 95–96.
[24] *Ibid* at 96. The mere fact of stock exchange listing is however not enough to establish a presence in New York: *ibid* at 97.
[25] *Ibid* at 99.
[26] 244 F Supp 2d 289 (SDNY 2003) 330–31.
[27] *Ibid* at 330.
[28] 'Talisman's officers and directors dominate the Fortuna board, . . . Fortuna has no separate financial standing, . . . Fortuna and Talisman share the same address, and . . . Talisman posts corporate bonds for Fortuna': *ibid*.

Most major TNCs desire to have some presence inside the US, so many corporations are potentially vulnerable to the jurisdiction of US courts. The jurisdictional inquiry will amount to an analysis of the significance of business conducted in the forum by the corporation itself, or the extent of control exercised by a company over its subsidiaries or agents within jurisdiction or, regarding agency within the Second and Ninth Circuits, the importance of the agent's activities to the parent. Under the latter principle, many foreign corporations listed on the New York Stock Exchange will be subject to New York jurisdiction by virtue of their investor relations offices in that forum. *Wiwa 2000* also indicates that the richest corporations are more likely than other corporations to fall within the personal jurisdiction of US courts, as the exercise of such jurisdiction is less likely to be deemed unfair and thus unconstitutional.

It is important to distinguish the tests for *jurisdiction* over a corporation based on alter ego/agency from the tests for *liability* over a corporation based on alter ego/agency. The former establishes a connection between the corporation and the forum such that a case against the corporation can proceed within the forum. There is no need to establish that the alter ego or agent is in any way related to the issues in the relevant litigation.[29] The latter relates to whether the corporation can actually be held liable for the actions of its alter egos/agents. While it may be clear that a Court has personal jurisdiction over a corporate parent, problems may arise in establishing the parent's responsibility for the alleged wrongs of its subsidiary. For example, in *Alomang v Freeport-McMoran*,[30] the Louisiana Court of Appeal dismissed a claim under State tort law because the plaintiffs failed to establish that the defendant's Indonesian subsidiary, which had allegedly engaged in human rights abuses, was the alter ego of the New Orleans-based defendant. The test for alter ego/agency jurisdiction is easier than the test for alter ego/agency liability.[31] The issue of establishing parent corporation liability for the consequences of actions taken by their subsidiaries is discussed below in Chapter 7.

FORUM NON CONVENIENS

Forum non conveniens (FNC) is a common law doctrine which permits US courts to dismiss cases on the basis that the balance of relevant interests weighs in favour of trial in a foreign forum.[32] FNC only arises on the defendant's application; judges do not consider the doctrine upon their own motion. As the doctrine is essentially applied at the discretion of the trial judge, with little scope

---

[29] See *Presbyterian Church of Sudan v Talisman Energy* 244 F Supp 2d 289 (SDNY 2003) 331.
[30] *Alomang v Freeport-McMoran* 811 So 2d 98 (La App 2002).
[31] Born, above n 1, at 153.
[32] See *Gulf Oil v Gilbert* 330 US 501 (SCt 1947); *Piper Aircraft v Reyno* 454 US 235 (SCt 1981). US States typically adopt the federal FNC test from *Gulf Oil*. However, see Blumberg, above n 13, at 524–25, on the few State variations to the FNC test.

for review of that decision,[33] only trends rather than strict rules can be uncovered governing application of the FNC doctrine.[34] A baseline proposition is that deference is to be given to the plaintiff's choice of forum. A two-step test is then applied. The first step is to establish that there exists an adequate available alternative forum. The second step is to weigh up the respective public and private interests at issue to decide which forum is the most convenient for the litigation. The FNC doctrine is obviously a relevant consideration in transnational human rights cases where most if not all of the salient events occur outside US territory. Dismissal for FNC usually has a devastating effect on a plaintiff's case; cases are rarely re-litigated in the putative available foreign forum after FNC dismissal by a US court.[35]

The earliest transnational human rights cases, a series of ordinary tort claims in the US against Union Carbide, Texaco, and Dow Chemicals (and its corporate predecessors in the DBCP litigation), were almost all dismissed for FNC.[36] However, as will be discussed below, it appears that FNC motions are easier for plaintiffs to overcome in ATCA and certainly TVPA cases. Furthermore, the latest case in the DBCP saga, *Martinez v Dow Chemicals*, has recently survived an FNC challenge, and signals several developments that may keep more transitory tort claims inside the US.

I now turn to examine the various considerations taken into account by judges when faced with a motion to dismiss for FNC, and how these considerations have impacted on transnational human rights litigation against corporations.

Deference to Plaintiff's Choice

The court confers a measure of deference on the plaintiff's choice of forum, which increases according to the strength of the connection between the plaintiff and the forum. For example, greater deference is given to the forum choice of a resident plaintiff rather than a non-resident plaintiff, as it is generally more inconvenient for a resident to pursue litigation in an overseas forum. This greater deference applies to all residents of the US, whether or not they are US citizens, and regardless of whether they reside in the district in which they seek to bring a case. For example, substantial deference was given to the plaintiffs'

---

[33] See *Piper Aircraft v Reyno* 454 US 235 (SCt 1981) 251.
[34] A Rosencranz and R Campbell, 'Foreign Environmental and Human Rights Suits Against US Corporations in US Courts' (1999) 18 *Stanford Environmental Law Journal* 145, 180.
[35] See generally, J Duval-Major, 'One Way Ticket Home: The Federal Doctrine of Forum non Conveniens and the International Plaintiff' (1992) 77 *Cornell Law Review* 650, 671–72. See also DW Robertson, 'Forum Non Conveniens in America and England: "A Rather Fantastic Fiction"' 103 (1987) *Law Quarterly Review* 398. See however, text at nn 102–3 below.
[36] See ch 3, pp 72–73; see also C Scott, 'Multinational Enterprises and Emergent Jurisprudence on Violations of Economic Social and Cultural Rights' in A Eide, C Krause and A Rosas (eds) *Economic Social and Cultural Rights* 2nd edn, (The Hague, Kluwer Law International, 2001) 587–90.

claims in *Wiwa 2000* as some of those alien plaintiffs were US residents, even though they were not residents of New York, the US state in which they had brought the case.[37] Therefore, a US resident's transnational case is more likely to survive an FNC motion.

Adequate Alternative Forum

FNC is not available unless an adequate alternative forum exists. The defendant must be susceptible to the jurisdiction of the relevant forum, and the forum must permit litigation on the subject matter of the dispute.[38] In transnational human rights litigation, the most obvious alternative forum is the State where the alleged abuses took place. An alternative forum may also lie in the State of the defendant's domicile when the defendant is an alien.

The 'subject matter of the lawsuit must be cognisable in the alternative forum',[39] so the case must be arguable and a remedy available if the case should succeed. However, US courts do not necessarily give much weight to the comparative possibility of *success* for the plaintiff in deciding if an alternative forum is adequate. For example, both the District and Circuit Courts in the *Wiwa* litigation found that England, the home State of one of the defendants, was an adequate alternative forum, even though substantial evidence was introduced to indicate that the chances of success for the plaintiffs were very low.[40]

On the other hand, the Court in *Sarei v Rio Tinto* applied quite a strict test of 'adequacy' in determining that Australia, the home State of one of the defendant companies, was not an adequate forum for the litigation. The Court noted that the exact ATCA claims were not cognisable in Australia. This is not surprising as ATCA is a unique US statute. The fact that the claims might be actionable under Australian tort law was insufficient to support a finding that Australia was an adequate forum.[41] The *Rio Tinto* decision, unusually, verges close to a decision that ATCA-like claims must be available to justify dismissal of an ATCA case for FNC. If so, the *Rio Tinto* standard of 'adequacy' is too high; it should not be necessary for the *same* avenue of legal redress to be available so long as a satisfactory alternative avenue exists.

---

[37] *Wiwa v Royal Dutch Petroleum* 226 F 3d 88 (2d Cir 2000) 101; the Circuit Court found that the lower Court had not sufficiently deferred to the forum choice of the two US resident plaintiffs in this case. See also *Presbyterian Church of Sudan v Talisman Energy* 244 F Supp 2d 289 (SDNY 2003) 338–39.

[38] *Flores v Southern Peru Copper Corp* 253 F Supp 2d 510 (SDNY 2002) 526.

[39] *Sarei v Rio Tinto* 221 F Supp 2d 1116 (CD Cal 2002) 1165; see also *Bodner v Banque Paribas* 114 F Supp 2d 117 (EDNY 2000) 132.

[40] *Wiwa v Royal Dutch Petroleum Co* No 96 Civ 8386, 1998 US Dist LEXIS 23064 (SDNY Sept 25, 1998) 15–16; the Circuit Court also found England to be 'adequate' without addressing the success issue: 226 F 3d 88 (2d Cir 2000). See also Zia-Zarifi, above n 9, at 141.

[41] *Sarei v Rio Tinto* 221 F Supp 2d 1116 (CD Cal 2002) 1178.

In *Presbyterian Church of Sudan v Talisman Energy*, the Court assumed that Canada, the defendant Talisman's home country, was an adequate alternative forum because Canada's adequacy was not challenged by the plaintiffs. However, the court strongly hinted that, had Canada's adequacy been contested, it might have decided otherwise. The court noted that Canada commonly applied the law of the situs state in transnational litigation, and was therefore likely to apply Sudanese law, which conferred inferior rights on non-Muslims such as the plaintiffs.[42] Furthermore, Canada did not permit ATCA-type claims,[43] and 'did not have a well-developed class action procedure'.[44] The court strongly hinted that it was tempted to declare Canada an inadequate forum for similar reasons to those given in *Rio Tinto* regarding Australia.

As noted in Chapter 1, the US is an especially 'plaintiff friendly' forum for civil litigants. This consideration is not enough to result in the designation of an alternative forum as inadequate.[45] For example, Keenan J found that the non-availability of contingency fees and juries in India did not establish India as an inadequate forum for the mass tort litigation arising out of the 1984 Bhopal industrial disaster in *In re Union Carbide Corp Gas Plant Disaster at Bhopal (Union Carbide Bhopal)*.[46]

ATCA jurisdiction will usually only lie, and TVPA jurisdiction will only lie, when the human rights abuse at issue has been committed by or in collusion with a government. Where foreign government collusion is alleged in TNC human rights abuse, this must give rise to a danger of corruption in the adjudication of claims arising from that abuse in that foreign forum, and/or victimisation of the plaintiff in that State. 'Most countries with poor human rights records are highly unlikely to provide a fair forum, if one at all, for the adjudication of human rights claims'.[47] Arguments based on the alleged corruption of alternative forums nevertheless have an unsuccessful history in FNC cases in the US.[48]

However, that trend may have been reversed in recent years. In *Presbyterian Church of Sudan v Talisman Energy*, the plaintiffs alleged that Talisman was

---

[42] *Presbyterian Church of Sudan v Talisman Energy* 244 F Supp 2d 289 (SDNY 2003) 337. See, on choice of law in Canada, ch 6, p 127.

[43] *Presbyterian Church of Sudan v Talisman Energy* 244 F Supp 2d 289 (SDNY 2003) 337.

[44] Ibid at 337, n 39, quoting *Derensis v Coopers & Lybrand Chartered Accountants* 930 F Supp 1003 (DNJ 1996) 1007.

[45] *Blanco v Banco Industrial de Venezuela, SA* 997 F 2d 974 (2d Cir 1993) 982, quoting *Shields v Mi Ryung Constr Co* 508 F Supp 891 (SDNY 1981) 895: 'The unavailability of beneficial litigation procedures similar to those available in the federal district courts does not render an alternative forum inadequate' (see also *Magnin v Teledyne Continental Motors* 91 F 3d 1424 (11th Cir 1996) 1430. See Blumberg, above n 13, at 508.

[46] 634 F Supp 842 (SDNY 1986) 850–51; aff'd 809 F 2d 195 (2d Cir 1987). See also *Sarei v Rio Tinto* 221 F Supp 2d 1116 (CD Cal 2002) 1170; and *Aguinda v Texaco, Inc* 142 F Supp 2d 534 (SDNY 2001) 540–41.

[47] MR Skolnik, 'Comment: The Forum non Conveniens Doctrine in Alien Tort Claims Act Cases: A Shell of its Former Self after Wiwa' (2002) 16 *Emory International Law Review* 187, 207.

[48] See list of cases at *Eastman Kodak Co v Kavlin* 978 F Supp 1078 (SD Fla 1997) 1084; *Flores v Southern Peru Copper Corp* 253 F Supp 2d 510 (SDNY 2002) 538–40.

liable for genocide, war crimes, and torture perpetrated by the Sudanese government. The court refused to accept the defendant's contention that Sudan was an adequate alternative forum, and took the following common sense approach to the question:

> [I]t would be perverse to say the least, to require plaintiffs to bring this suit in the courts of the very nation that has allegedly been conducting genocidal activities to try to eliminate them. . . . One of the difficulties that confront victims of torture under colour of a nation's law is the enormous difficulty of bringing suits to vindicate such abuses. Most likely, the victims cannot sue in the place where the torture occurred. Indeed, in many instances, the victim would be endangered merely by returning to that place. . . . In light of the almost self-evident fact that, if plaintiffs' allegations are true, plaintiffs would be unable to obtain justice in Sudan and might well expose themselves to great danger in trying to do so, the Court finds that Sudan is not an appropriate forum under forum non conveniens analysis.[49]

In *Bridgeway Corp v Citibank*,[50] the Second Circuit confirmed that courts may use US State Department human rights reports to determine whether an alternative forum is too corrupt to be adequate.[51] Such reports were highly influential in *Eastman Kodak Co v Kavlin*,[52] *Wiwa v Royal Dutch Petroleum (Wiwa 2002)*,[53] and the non-ATCA case of *Martinez v Dow Chemicals*[54] in the courts' respective findings that certain putative alternative forums were not adequate.[55] These decisions may be contrasted with that of Rakoff J in *Aguinda v Texaco*, who dismissed adverse State Department reports regarding Ecuador as 'broad, conclusory assertions as to the relative corruptibility or incorruptibility of the Ecuadorian courts, with scant reference to specifics, evidence, or application to the instant cases'.[56] Rakoff J's skeptical characterisation of State Department reports was replicated by Pauley J in *Abdullahi v Pfizer*.[57] This

---

[49] *Presbyterian Church of Sudan v Talisman Energy* 244 F Supp 2d 289 (SDNY 2003) 336.
[50] 201 F 3d 134 (2d Cir 2000), approving a District Court judge's extensive use of State Department reports regarding the state of the Liberian judiciary. The case concerned an action to enforce a judgment rendered by the Supreme Court of Liberia.
[51] See also *Guidi v Intercontinental Hotels Corp* 203 F 3d 180 (2d Cir 2000), and LW Newman, 'Passing Judgment on other Countries' Courts' (May 30, 2000) 223 *New York Law Journal* 3.
[52] 978 F Supp 1078 (SD Fla 1997) 1085–6.
[53] *Wiwa v Royal Dutch Petroleum Co* No 96 Civ 8386, 2002 US Dist LEXIS 3293 (SDNY Feb 22, 2002) 56–57.
[54] 219 F Supp 2d 719 (ED La 2002).
[55] The relevant forums were Bolivia (*Eastman Kodak*), Nigeria (*Wiwa*), the Philippines and Honduras (*Martinez*). In *Martinez*, State Department reports helped to establish that Costa Rica was an adequate alternative forum. Costa Rica however was not an available forum, see below, text at n 97.
[56] 142 F Supp 2d 534 (SDNY 2001) 544.
[57] *Abdullahi v Pfizer* No 01 Civ 8118, 2002 US Dist LEXIS 17436 (SDNY Sept 16, 2002) 26. Pauley J decided to dismiss the case for forum non conveniens. However, Pauley J's decision was vacated by the Second Circuit on 9 October 2003 in *Abdullahi v Pfizer* Nos 02-9223(L), 02-9303 (XAP) (2d Cir 2003). In the period of time between Pauley J's decision and that of the Circuit Court, parallel proceedings in Nigeria had been dismissed. The case was remitted to the District Court for it to consider the circumstances of that dismissal, to discern whether that dismissal was evidence that Nigeria was in fact a corrupt jurisdiction (as contended by the plaintiffs), or whether it had simply been dismissed for acceptable reasons (as contended by Pfizer).

schism between courts is unfortunately characteristic of the inconsistency generated across the spectrum of exercises of discretion in FNC cases across the US circuits.

Public Interests Considerations

Relevant public interests can include US policy interests in favour of or against the hearing of the case in the US, administrative burdens such as court congestion in either the US or in the foreign forum,[58] and a desire to prevent the flooding of US courts by foreign litigation.[59] Until recently, it appeared as though public interest factors in transnational human rights cases were weighed against the plaintiff, as there was felt to be little local interest in deciding the dispute.[60] For example, in *Union Carbide Bhopal*, which concerned litigation arising out of a catastrophic industrial accident in Bhopal India, Keenan J noted that the US public interest favored dismissal as the litigation, which he characterised as having only a 'tenuous connection' with New York, would impose a considerable burden on the court system and would 'tax the time and resources of citizens directly' as jurors.[61] In contrast, India had a 'very strong interest in the aftermath of the accident which affected its citizens on its own soil'.[62] Additionally, the litigation 'offer[ed] a developing nation the opportunity to vindicate the suffering of its own people within the framework of a legitimate legal system'.[63] This anti-plaintiff trend epitomised by *Union Carbide Bhopal* may have changed with the recent cases of *Bowoto v Chevron* and *Wiwa 2000*.

In *Bowoto v Chevron*, Chevron failed in its bid to have an ATCA claim against it for alleged human rights abuses in Nigeria dismissed for FNC. In his reasoning, Legge J noted the interest that California has in 'regulating the conduct of corporations that are headquartered [t]here, even if the conduct of the corporation . . . is overseas'.[64] Legge J's decision has obvious implications for all extraterritorial human rights actions against US corporations. However, this decision is unreported and is therefore of minimal precedent value. It has not been cited in any reported case.

In the *Wiwa* litigation, which again concerned ATCA claims, the Southern District Court of New York dismissed the case due to FNC, finding that

---

[58] While US court congestion was cited as a policy interest in favour of dismissal for FNC in *Sarei v Rio Tinto* 221 F Supp 2d 1116 (CD Cal 2002) 1175, it was balanced by the lack of evidence of less congestion in the alternative forum of PNG.

[59] See *Piper Aircraft v Reyno* 454 US 235 (SCt 1981) 250.

[60] KL Boyd, 'The Inconvenience of Victims: Abolishing Forum non Conveniens in US Human Rights Litigation' (1998) 39 *Virginia Journal of International Law* 41, 46.

[61] 634 F Supp 842 (SDNY 1986) 862.

[62] *Ibid* at 867.

[63] *Ibid* at 865–66.

[64] Case no C 99-2506, unreported (ND Cal April 7, 2000): transcript available at <http://www.earthrights.org/chevron/0407transcript.rtf> (8 January 2004).

England, the home of one of the defendants, would be a more appropriate forum for the litigation.[65] In reversing the ruling on appeal, the Second Circuit in *Wiwa 2000* decided that the District Court had failed to properly take account of two factors favouring retention of jurisdiction. First, the District Court had not sufficiently deferred to the resident plaintiffs' choice of forum.[66] Second, the Second Circuit found that insufficient weight had been given to the US 'policy interest in providing a forum for the adjudication of international human rights abuses'.[67] The Court found that the enactment in 1991 of the *Torture Victims Protection Act* (TVPA)[68] expressed 'a policy favoring receptivity by [US] courts to such suits'. Before *Wiwa 2000*, 'no court had unequivocally pronounced a US interest in the worldwide enforcement of international human rights norms'.[69] While preserving the relevance of FNC in ATCA cases, it has 'rais[ed] the bar for granting such motions for dismissal in future ATCA [and TVPA] cases'.[70]

The Second Circuit was clearly influenced in its findings regarding US policy interests by the existence of the TVPA which provides an extra legislative basis of jurisdiction for acts of torture and extra-judicial killing. A crucial question therefore arises as to whether the *Wiwa 2000* reasoning applies only to ATCA cases involving the two TVPA causes of action.[71] *Wiwa 2000* is ambiguous on this issue. At times the Circuit Court appeared to confine its reasoning to torture,[72] whereas a number of other passages potentially extend the reasoning to all 'human rights abuses' and 'gross violations'.[73]

Subsequent decisions by District Courts within the Second Circuit initially adopted a narrow reading of the *Wiwa 2000* precedent on US public policy and FNC. In *Aguinda v Texaco*[74] and *Flores v Southern Peru Copper*,[75] the respective district judges clearly limit the *Wiwa 2000* reasoning to fact situations which raise torture and extra-judicial killing.[76] More significantly, in *Abdullahi v Pfizer*, where the facts actually activated ATCA,[77] Pauley J in the Southern District of New York did not even refer to the *Wiwa 2000* realignment of

---

[65] See *Wiwa v Royal Dutch Petroleum Co* No 96 Civ 8386, 1998 US Dist LEXIS 23064 (SDNY Sept 25, 1998).
[66] See above, n 37.
[67] *Wiwa v Royal Dutch Petroleum* 226 F 3d 88 (2d Cir 2000) 103.
[68] See ch 2, p 161.
[69] AX Fellmeth, 'Wiwa v Royal Dutch Petroleum Co: A New Standard for the Enforcement of International Law in US Courts?' (2002) 5 *Yale Human Rights and Development Law Journal* 241, 249; see also Skolnik, above n 47, at 208.
[70] Skolnik, *ibid* at 219.
[71] Blumberg, above n 13, at 521.
[72] *Wiwa v Royal Dutch Petroleum* 226 F 3d 88 (2d Cir 2000) 106.
[73] *Ibid* at 91, 103, 105, 106.
[74] 142 F Supp 2d 534 (SDNY 2001) 554.
[75] 253 F Supp 2d 510 (SDNY 2002) 529. The Circuit Court did not review the FNC decision in *Flores v Southern Peru Copper* 343 F 3d 140 (2d Cir 2003).
[76] The Second Circuit has affirmed the *Aguinda* decision, but the Court did not confirm or deny the limited interpretation of *Wiwa 2000*; see *Aguinda v Texaco* 303 F 3d 470 (2d 2002).
[77] Subject matter jurisdiction did not lie under ATCA in either *Flores* or, at least implicitly, *Aguinda*. See ch 2, p 29.

public interest factors in an FNC determination before dismissing the case for FNC.[78]

However, *Wiwa 2000* was recently followed and endorsed enthusiastically in *Presbyterian Church v Talisman Energy*. The *Wiwa 2000* reasoning was extended so as to apply to any *jus cogens* violation, including the alleged violations in *Talisman*, namely genocide, war crimes, torture and enslavement. '[T]hese acts are universally abhorrent . . . Because of the nature of the alleged acts, the United States has a substantial interest in affording alleged victims of atrocities a method to vindicate their rights'.[79] Thus, the *Talisman* court was able to distinguish *Aguinda* and *Flores*, non-ATCA cases concerning environmental damage (which 'generally does not violate the law of nations') and *Abdullahi*, an ATCA case concerning improper medical experimentation, which does not amount to a *jus cogens* violation.[80]

There is of course no guarantee that courts within the other Circuits will follow the *Wiwa 2000* lead.[81] However, *Wiwa* was cited with approval in *Rio Tinto* in California. In that case, after deciding to dismiss the FNC motion, Morrow J noted that the result was appropriate given that she was dealing with an ATCA case concerning 'violations of international law'.[82] Therefore, Morrow J appeared to extend *Wiwa* beyond torture and extra-judicial killings, and perhaps beyond the *Talisman* definition to all ATCA claims, even those that do not constitute breaches of *jus cogens* norms.

Weighing Respective Private Interests

The factors taken into account in weighing up relevant private interests include the convenience of the plaintiffs and defendants, and the ease of availability of witnesses and evidence. In the similar cases of *Flores* and *Aguinda*, which both concerned alleged gross environmental abuses in foreign States by an American TNC, both courts found that the private interests overwhelmingly favoured the site of the environmental abuses as the most convenient forum (Peru and

---

[78] Note however that the Court in *Abdullahi v Pfizer* No 01 Civ 8118, 2002 US Dist LEXIS 17436 (SDNY Sept 16, 2002) 34 found that the US did have a public interest in litigation involving the safety of a drug developed within jurisdiction, as well as allegations of possible contravention of FDA guidelines. Similar proceedings had already been launched by other plaintiffs in Nigeria, which may have influenced the Court's FNC decision (see also in this respect, *United Bank for Africa v Coker* 2003 WL 22741575 (SDNY 2003), where an FNC dismissal was explicitly influenced by the existence of concurrent proceedings in the alternative forum). Pauley J's decision in *Abdullahi* was vacated by the Second Circuit on 9 October 2003 in *Abdullahi v Pfizer* Nos 02–9223(L), 02–9303 (XAP) (2d Cir 2003). See above, n 57, for the reasoning in the appeal. In the period of time between Pauley J's decision and that of the Circuit Court, the relevant proceedings in Nigeria had been dismissed.
[79] *Presbyterian Church of Sudan v Talisman Energy* 244 F Supp 2d 289 (SDNY 2003) 340.
[80] *Ibid*; see also *Abdullahi v Pfizer* No 01 Civ 8118, 2002 US Dist LEXIS 17436 (SDNY Sept 16, 2002) 5.
[81] Blumberg, above n 13, at 522.
[82] *Sarei v Rio Tinto* 221 F Supp 2d 1116 (CD Cal 2002) 1175.

Ecuador respectively). In both cases, most of the evidence and witnesses, including the plaintiffs, were located in the alternative forum, where an inspection of the allegedly despoiled sites could be more easily arranged. These cases indicate that FNC is a hurdle that transnational environmental litigants will find particularly difficult to overcome.[83]

In *Sarei v Rio Tinto*, the potential hostility of the government of Papua New Guinea (PNG) towards the plaintiffs, who were engaged with other Bougainvilleans against PNG in a civil war, led the Court to conclude that the balancing of 'private interests' favoured retention in the forum.[84] The possible persecution of the plaintiffs in a foreign forum would also tend to cast doubt on the adequacy of the forum. This part of the *Rio Tinto* decision demonstrates how Courts can merge the various elements of the FNC test.

As noted above, the non-availability of US-style procedures does not mean that an alternative forum is inadequate. However, weight will be given to the inconvenience caused to a plaintiff by the non-availability of such procedural advantages.[85] 'The . . . court must be alert to the practicalities of the plaintiff's position, financial or otherwise, and his or her ability as a practical matter to bring suit in the alternative forum'.[86]

The *Wiwa* litigation concerns alleged human rights abuses committed by the defendants in collusion with the Nigerian government. Nigeria was not however the preferable forum cited by the District Court in dismissing the case for FNC; that forum was the UK, the home of one of the defendants.[87] On appeal in *Wiwa 2000*, the Second Circuit weighed up the relative public interests (noted above) as well as the plaintiff's interests in proceeding within New York, against the defendants' interests in having the litigation proceed in the UK due to greater ease of access to documents. The Circuit Court found that 'the defendants [had] not demonstrated that these costs [were] excessively burdensome, especially in view of the defendants' vast resources'.[88] Furthermore, these extra costs were offset by the additional costs for the plaintiffs in reinstituting the litigation in England, 'especially given the plaintiffs' minimal resources in comparison with the vast resources of the defendants'.[89]

---

[83] See also *Torres v Southern Peru Copper* 965 F Supp 899 (SD Tex 1996).
[84] 221 F Supp 2d 1116 (CD Cal 2002) 1174.
[85] See, eg, *Flores v Southern Peru Copper Corp* 253 F Supp 2d 510 (SDNY 2002) 542–43; see also *Fiorenza v United States Steel Int'l* 311 F Supp 117 (SDNY 1969) 120.
[86] *Sarei v Rio Tinto* 221 F Supp 2d 1116 (CD Cal 2002) 1171, citing *Reid-Walen v Hansen* 933 F 2d 1390 (8th Cir 1991) 1398; see also *Wiwa v Royal Dutch Petroleum* 226 F 3d 88 (2d Cir 2000) 108, n 13: 'plaintiffs have already obtained excellent pro bono counsel . . .; there is no guarantee that they will be able to obtain equivalent representation [in another forum]' and *Presbyterian Church of Sudan v Talisman Energy* 244 F Supp 2d 289 (SDNY 2003) 341.
[87] Identical arguments also applied to the Netherlands, the home of the other defendant. In subsequent proceedings upon remittal of the case in *Wiwa v Royal Dutch Petroleum Co* No 96 Civ 8386, 2002 US Dist LEXIS 3293 (SDNY Feb 22, 2002) 56–57, the District court found that Nigeria was an inadequate forum, relying on State Department reports on its justice system.
[88] *Wiwa v Royal Dutch Petroleum* 226 F 3d 88 (2d Cir 2000) 107.
[89] Ibid.

The court in *Talisman* again followed *Wiwa 2000* in determining that the balance of private interests favoured retention of the litigation in New York. The Canadian defendant company Talisman 'routinely litigate[d] cases outside [its] home jurisdiction'.[90] Again, the 'vast resources' of the defendants were compared with the menial resources of the plaintiffs, leading the court to conclude that the defendants had failed to show 'that pertinent factors "tilt strongly" in favour of trial in the foreign forum'.[91]

The analysis in *Wiwa 2000* and *Talisman* indicates that the relative inconveniences of plaintiff and defendant were not accorded equal weight, as the richer (defendant) parties could 'better afford the inconvenience' than the poorer (plaintiff) parties.[92] *Wiwa 2000* and *Talisman* therefore indicate that plaintiffs will start from an advantageous position in any human rights litigation against TNCs regarding the balance of private interests for FNC purposes, as their inconvenience will normally be more personally consequential than that of the TNC.[93] Furthermore, the instant access to information made possible by modern technological advances, which facilitates access to offshore evidence, may also help tip the balance of private interests away from an FNC dismissal.[94]

Retaliatory Legislation: Trumping *Forum non Conveniens*?

A new factor in FNC motions in the US is the recent spate of 'retaliatory legislation', generally enacted in the late 1990s by civil law countries, particularly in Latin America. This legislation typically precludes the exercise of jurisdiction within the legislating State in cases where the litigation has already commenced in another State with jurisdiction. The legislation thus bars the availability of the legislating State for FNC purposes. Such legislation is designed to thwart the dumping of cases on those jurisdictions via FNC, a doctrine which is rejected in civil law countries.[95] Furthermore, such legislation was passed *in response* to the routine dismissal for FNC of mass tort cases against US multinationals

---

[90] *Presbyterian Church of Sudan v Talisman Energy* 244 F Supp 2d 289 (SDNY 2003) 340.

[91] *Ibid* at 341. Talisman's arguments were also undermined by its contention that Sudan, as well as Canada, constituted a more appropriate forum than New York. It was obviously more convenient for Talisman to litigate the case in New York than in Sudan. Furthermore, New York was a convenient forum for Sudanese government officials, who may have been called as witnesses, given the presence in New York of the Sudanese Permanent Mission to the United Nations (see *ibid* p 341).

[92] Fellmeth, above n 69, at 254.

[93] This advantage tops up the head start afforded by the doctrine of deference; see text, above, at n 37.

[94] Skolnik, above n 47, at 204; Blumberg, above n 13, at 525; see also *Bodner v Banque Paribas* 114 F Supp 2d 117 (EDNY 2000) 133: 'The costs to the [French bank] defendants in defending this action in New York are significantly mitigated by the time and money saving tools including e-mail, fax, scanners, digital photography, and global access to the internet'.

[95] See LW Newman, 'Latin America and *Forum non Conveniens* Dismissals' (Feb 4, 1999) 221 *New York Law Journal* 3. The purpose of the laws is reflected in the name commonly given to these laws: 'Ley de Defensa de los Derechos Procesales de Nacionales y Residentes' (Law in Defence of the Procedural Rights of Nationals and Residents).

regarding alleged actions in Latin America. For example, numerous nations were unhappy at the dismissal of the DBCP case against Dow Chemicals and Shell for FNC by a Texas District Judge in one of the early stages of that litigation.[96]

In the latest stage of the DBCP litigation, *Martinez v Dow Chemicals*, Barbier J found that Costa Rica, Honduras, and the Philippines were unavailable forums as they had all enacted legislation which precluded the commencement of litigation that had been previously commenced in another jurisdiction.[97] Thus, it appears that retaliatory legislation has succeeded in its aim of keeping the DBCP litigation within the US. Furthermore, the logical conclusion from Barbier J's decision is that Costa Rica, Honduras and the Philippines are no longer available forums for the purposes of an FNC motion in any case.

Ecuador passed a similar law in its Law 55 of 1998. In *Aguinda*, Rakoff J doubted the constitutionality of the law in Ecuador, and whether the law would retrospectively apply to the litigation at hand. However, he conceded that the District Court could reconsider the FNC issue if Law 55 in fact precludes availability of the Ecuadorian forum.[98] It may therefore also be that Ecuador is no longer an available alternative forum, and the Texaco litigation will return to the forum of New York. The commencement of a trial against Texaco in Ecuador in October 2003[99] may indicate that Rakoff J was correct, and the litigation is not precluded by Law 55.[100]

Conditional FNC Dismissals

It is common practice in transnational human rights cases for courts to attach conditions to FNC dismissals. For example, in *Union Carbide Corp Bhopal*, the court dismissed the case on the condition that Union Carbide submit to the jurisdiction of the Indian courts, and waive any statute of limitations defences it may have had in India.[101] The 'submission' requirement in particular has

---

[96] W Anderson, '*Forum non Conveniens* Checkmated? The Emergence of Retaliatory Legislation' (2001) 10 *Journal of Transnational Law and Policy* 183, 186; see *Delgado v Shell Oil* 890 F Supp 1324 (SD Tex 1995).

[97] 219 F Supp 2d 719 (ED La 2002) 728, 735, 741. Note that Honduras and the Philippines were determined to be inadequate forums as well; see above, text in n 55.

[98] *Aguinda v Texaco, Inc* 142 F Supp 2d 534 (SDNY 2001) 547.

[99] S McNulty, 'Oil Major Forced to Answer Amazon Charge of Damaging the Environment' *Financial Times* (London, United Kingdom, 29 October 2003) 2, reports that proceedings have now opened against Texaco in Ecuador.

[100] However, this author is uncertain as to whether the relevance of Law 55 in the case has yet been considered by the Ecuadorian court.

[101] 634 F Supp 842 (SDNY 1986) 867. On appeal *In re Union Carbide Corp Gas Plant Disaster at Bhopal* 809 F 2d 195 (2d Cir 1987), the Circuit Court removed a condition that Union Carbide comply with any consequent Indian judgment so long as it satisfied 'minimal standards of due process', and a condition that US federal rules of discovery be utilised to uncover evidence in the Indian proceedings.

become commonplace in FNC dismissals.[102] Such conditions are designed to ensure that the litigation can carry on in the designated convenient forum.

Despite these conditions, *Union Carbide Bhopal* remains one of the few instances where litigation of the relevant case recommenced in a foreign forum after an FNC dismissal.[103] However, in October 2003, a class action commenced against Texaco in Ecuador, following Rakoff J's dismissal of their case in New York in *Aguinda*.[104]

Conclusion on FNC in the US

FNC has been pleaded by defendant corporations in virtually all US transnational human rights cases which have not been dismissed for other reasons.[105] In a recent article, Professor Blumberg stated that 'FNC has prove[n] to be an insuperable obstacle to American trial in virtually every [transnational human rights] case'.[106] Recent developments may signal a change to this assessment, especially in ATCA and TVPA cases, though the decision in *Martinez v Dow Chemicals* indicates that there are also increased opportunities for non-ATCA plaintiffs to defeat the motion. First, US courts are showing a greater propensity to accept arguments that alternative forums are inadequate. In particular, many courts have accepted State Department Reports as evidence that an alternative forum is too corrupt to provide justice in a case. Furthermore, *Rio Tinto* may signal a stricter approach to the evaluation of a forum's adequacy, as Australia was found to be an inadequate forum for lack of ATCA-type jurisdiction. Second, the *Wiwa 2000* decision decreases the chance of an FNC dismissal in torture cases, and might even be used to deflect FNC arguments in all ATCA cases. Third, the advent of retaliatory legislation in Latin America may preclude dismissal for FNC in a significant number of cases. Though the outlook for plaintiffs is not as bleak as forecast by Blumberg, FNC nevertheless continues to pose a daunting impediment to transnational human rights litigation in the US, as evinced by the recent decisions in *Flores v Southern Peru Copper*, *Aguinda v Texaco*, and *Abdullahi v Pfizer*.[107]

---

[102] For example, Rakoff J's original FNC dismissal in the *Aguinda* litigation (*Aguinda v Texaco, Inc* 945 F Supp 625 (SDNY 1996)) was overturned by the Circuit Court in *Jota v Texaco* 157 F 3d 153 (2d Cir 1998) on the basis (at p 159), inter alia, that the District Court had not obtained 'a commitment from [the defendant] Texaco to submit to the jurisdiction of the Ecuadorian courts for purposes of this action'. Rakoff issued a new FNC dismissal in 2001 after obtaining a relevant submission from Texaco.

[103] See ch 7, text in n 76, on the extraordinary outcome of the litigation in India.

[104] See McNulty, above n 99.

[105] The *Doe v Unocal* litigation is an exception; the defendants have not seriously contended that Myanmar would provide an adequate alternative forum.

[106] Blumberg, above n 13, at 505.

[107] Note, however, that *Abdullahi* has been remitted back to the District Court due to new developments in that litigation; see above, n 57.

A thorough evaluation of the merits of FNC in the context of transnational human rights litigation necessarily involves an evaluation of the phenomenon of transnational human rights litigation itself, which is contained below in Chapter 8. Only one issue will therefore be addressed here. Court congestion is a reason often given in the US as a reason for granting FNC. In response, one may note that transnational human rights cases represent a miniscule percentage of the caseload of US courts. Indeed, complex FNC arguments may have led to an *increased* workload in courts in the US, as their existence preoccupies courts with preliminary matters.[108] For example, years have been taken up resolving FNC issues in *Wiwa* instead of allowing the claims to proceed to merits or settlement.

---

[108] P Prince, 'Bhopal, Bougainville and Ok Tedi: Why Australia's Forum non Conveniens Approach is Better' (1998) 47 *International and Comparative Law Quarterly* 573, 585.

5
A New Front: The Nike Case

THE CASE OF KASKY V NIKE

KASKY V NIKE[1] CONCERNED an action against sporting goods giant Nike under Californian laws prohibiting unfair competition and false advertising[2] for allegedly making false and misleading statements about its labour practices. The action was brought by a private citizen, who did not claim to have been personally damaged by the statements. The Californian law is perhaps unique in the US in permitting the enforcement of its obligations by 'private attorneys general'.[3] Furthermore, the relevant laws impose strict liability for false statements, without the need to establish negligence or fault.[4]

The impugned statements were made in response to well-publicised allegations of exploitative working conditions in the factories of Nike's suppliers in South East Asia.

> Specifically, Nike and the individual defendants said that workers who make Nike products are protected from physical and sexual abuse, that they are paid in accordance with applicable local laws and regulations governing wages and hours, that they are paid on average double the applicable local minimum wage, that they receive a 'living wage,' that they receive free meals and health care, and that their working conditions are in compliance with applicable local laws and regulations governing occupational health and safety.[5]

These statements were made in 'press releases, in letters to newspapers, in a letter to university presidents and athletic directors, and in other documents distributed for public relations purposes'.[6] Nike also took out full-page advertisements to publicise a report which found no evidence of illegal or unsafe working conditions in Nike's South East Asian factories. The plaintiff alleged that these statements were false and misleading in contravention of Californian law.

---

[1] 27 Cal 4th 939 (SCt Cal 2002).
[2] *Business and Professions Code* § 17204 and § 17535, respectively.
[3] This was noted by Breyer J in his dissenting opinion in the US Supreme Court (with which O'Connor J joined) at *Nike v Kasky* 123 SCt 2554 (SCt US 2003) 2566.
[4] Ibid at 2567.
[5] *Nike v Kasky* 27 Cal 4th 939 (SCt Cal 2002) 947.
[6] Ibid at 947.

Nike demurred to the plaintiff's claim, arguing that application of the Californian law to the statements at issue would breach the constitutional free speech guarantee in the First Amendment of the US Constitution.[7] Nike's arguments in this regard were upheld in the California Court of Appeals. However, that ruling was reversed by a 4:3 majority of the Supreme Court of California in May 2002. On 26 June 2003, the US Supreme Court dismissed an appeal from the Californian Supreme Court decision, ruling by majority that it lacked jurisdiction to hear an application for certiorari at such a preliminary stage of the case.[8] The case settled in September 2003.

No court decisions addressed the question of whether Nike actually contravened Californian law. The crux of the decisions in the Californian courts concerned whether Nike's speech could be classified as commercial or non-commercial. Commercial speech in the US is entitled to considerably less constitutional protection than non-commercial speech.[9] The US Supreme Court has confirmed on a number of occasions that States are entitled to regulate false and misleading statements made in a commercial context.[10] The reasons for the commercial/non-commercial distinction are threefold. First, the truth or falsity of commercial speech is felt to be more easily verifiable by its disseminator, compared to, for example, political speech.[11] Second, commercial speech is more resilient, or 'hardier', than non-commercial speech, because it is necessary to boost profits, and the proper (non-misleading) exercise thereof is less likely to be chilled by regulation.[12] Finally, the regulation of commercial speech is designed to preserve the integrity of commercial transactions,[13] so ultimately its regulation benefits affected speakers in the commercial sector.

There is no precise test for identifying commercial speech; 'ambiguities . . . exist at the margins of the category of commercial speech'.[14] Three factors were considered influential by the California Supreme Court in characterising Nike's impugned statements as commercial speech.[15] First, the speaker was a commercial entity. Second, the target audience of the statements was, largely, potential consumers of Nike products. Third, the statements consisted of 'representations of fact of a commercial nature' about working conditions and labour practices, 'matters within its own knowledge'.[16] The purpose of the statements was probably to maintain or increase sales, profits, and share prices, by convincing

---

[7] Virtually identical arguments were made regarding the free speech guarantee in the Californian Constitution; see *ibid* at 960.
[8] *Nike v Kasky* 123 SCt 2554 (SCt US 2003).
[9] See, eg, *Central Hudson Gas & Electricity v Public Service Commission* 447 US 557 (SCt 1980).
[10] See eg, *In re RMJ* 455 US 191 (SCt 1982) 203.
[11] *Virginia Pharmacy Board v Virginia Consumer Council* 425 US 748 (SCt 1976) 772, n 24.
[12] *Nike v Kasky* 27 Cal 4th 939 (SCt Cal 2002) 970; see also *Ibid*.
[13] See, eg, *Cincinnati v Discovery Network* 507 US 410 (SCt 1993) 426, confirming that the commercial speech doctrine is designed to prevent 'commercial harms'.
[14] *Edenfield v Fane* 507 US 761 (SCt 1993) 765.
[15] *Nike v Kasky* 27 Cal 4th 939 (SCt Cal 2002) 960–65.
[16] *Ibid* at 963.

consumers and investors that Nike's products were, contrary to certain reports, manufactured in an ethical manner.

The majority denied the contention that Nike's statements were 'non-commercial' as they addressed a matter of 'intense public interest'. First, the majority noted that commercial speech can relate to controversial matters.[17] Second, Nike's commercial speech was not 'inextricably entwined' with the non-commercial aspects of its statements, as Nike was not forced to add commercial elements to its speech by legal or practical compulsion.[18] For example, Nike could (and did) respond to its accusers by engaging in a debate over the degree to which it should be liable for the working conditions in factories run by overseas sub-contractors. It was not necessary, in the opinion of the majority, for Nike to add a purported factual description of the actual conditions in those factories.

Chin J, with whom Baxter J concurred, and Brown J dissented. Chin J argued that the First Amendment guarantees that 'both sides in a public debate may compete vigorously—and equally—in the marketplace of ideas'.[19] Chin J was therefore concerned about the asymmetric result of the majority's decision; Nike's detractors benefited from full First Amendment protection whereas Nike did not. 'According to the majority, if Nike utters a factual misstatement, unlike its critics, it may be sued for restitution, civil penalties, and injunctive relief under these sweeping statutes'.[20]

Chin J added that any commercial aspects of Nike's statements were inextricably intertwined with non-commercial aspects, because Nike could hardly respond to its critics without referring to its own practices. Nike's statements were 'prompted and necessitated by public criticism', as its labor practices '*were* the public issue'.[21] Thus, Nike's statements fell outside the definition of commercial speech in the opinion of Chin J.

Brown J essentially agreed with Chin J. She added an explicit call for the US Supreme Court to re-examine the commercial/non-commercial distinction and adopt a more nuanced approach[22] to replace the current rigid dichotomous approach.[23] Brown J felt that such a reevaluation was necessary as 'the gap between commercial and noncommercial speech is rapidly shrinking'.[24]

Brown J makes an important point. As TNCs such as Nike have become more ubiquitous and powerful, their actions have attracted more attention and more criticism, not only at the grassroots level but also at governmental and intergovernmental levels.[25] Hence, commercial issues have become more political, so

---

[17] Ibid at 964.
[18] See also *Board of Trustees, State University of NY v Fox* 492 US 469 (SCt 1989) 474.
[19] *Nike v Kasky* 27 Cal 4th 939 (SCt Cal 2002) 977.
[20] Ibid at 971.
[21] Ibid at 975, emphasis not added.
[22] Ibid at 995.
[23] Ibid at 980.
[24] Ibid at 979.
[25] See generally, D Kinley, 'Human Rights as Legally Binding or Merely Relevant' in S Bottomley and D Kinley (eds), *Commercial Law and Human Rights* (Aldershot, Ashgate, 2002) 25.

Brown J's aforementioned 'gap' is indeed shrinking. A consequent result may be that the First Amendment rights of powerful commercial speakers like TNCs have increased due to the greater political attention garnered by their commercial activities. Ironically, it may be that the greater power of TNCs necessitates an increase under US law of their constitutional rights. From a policy point of view, one might question whether an entity's constitutional rights should increase as an indirect result of its increase in power.

In the US Supreme Court, only the minority (Breyer and O'Connor JJ) expressed any view on the issue of whether the California law might breach Nike's First Amendment rights. The minority stated that outright reversal of the California Supreme Court's decision, in the sense that all of Nike's impugned words would be classified as deserving full First Amendment protection, was a 'highly realistic possibility'.[26] In their view, Nike's words were 'a mixture of commercial and non-commercial' comments. The comments appeared outside 'a traditional advertising format',[27] they 'did not propose the presentation or sale of a product or any other commercial transaction',[28] and they 'concerned a matter ... of significant public interest and active controversy'.[29] Thus, the form and content of the words distinguished them from pure commercial speech. In classifying Nike's speech as non-commercial, the minority did not need to, and indeed did not, take up Brown J's request to overhaul the commercial speech doctrine. The minority also agreed with the California Supreme Court minority's concerns that 'the commercial speaker engaging in public debate suffers a handicap that noncommercial opponents do not'.[30] The Supreme Court minority was particularly perturbed by 'the regulatory context', as the speech regulation permitted enforcement by private persons who had suffered no damage.[31] While conceding that such private causes of action could help 'to maintain an honest commercial marketplace',[32] the 'delegation of state authority [ie to private attorneys general] authorises a purely ideological plaintiff' to wage a political battle in a courtroom, 'unencumbered by the legal and practical checks that tend to keep the public enforcement agencies focused upon more purely economic harm'.[33] This factor, combined with the strict liability imposed by the laws, seemed particularly likely, in the view of the Supreme Court minority, to render the Californian law a disproportionate burden upon speech, consequently prohibited by the First Amendment.[34]

The parties in the *Nike* case settled the case in September 2003, with Nike agreeing to pay US$1.5 million to the Fair Labor Association (FLA), without

---

[26] *Nike v Kasky* 123 SCt 2554 (SCt US 2003) 2565.
[27] Ibid.
[28] Ibid.
[29] Ibid at 2566.
[30] Ibid at 2567.
[31] Ibid at 2566.
[32] Ibid at 2567.
[33] Ibid.
[34] Ibid at 2568.

admitting liability. The FLA intends to use the money to monitor the overseas work practices of US companies, and to promote compliance with international labour standards.[35]

The *Nike* litigation indicates that consumer protection (or 'trade practices') law could represent an important new bow in the armory of human rights litigation against TNCs. Its precedent is being utilized in other human rights cases. For example, the plaintiffs in *Bowoto v Chevron* filed a complaint of misleading and deceptive conduct against Chevron, regarding denials of allegations of gross human rights abuses in Nigeria, in a State court in February 2003.[36] Furthermore, some of the non-binding codes of conduct adopted by TNCs, which have proliferated since the 1990s, could perhaps be challenged as misleading representations of actual adherence to those codes, depending on the text and context of their publication.[37]

The *Nike* litigation is a very important international precedent. For example, section 52 of the *Trade Practices Act* 1974 (Cth) imposes strict liability for misleading and deceptive conduct in trade or commerce in Australia.[38] It is quite possible that misleading or false statements about a corporation's ethical practices, if designed to enhance the attractiveness of one's products to consumers, contravene s 52. Section 53 imposes strict liability for false representations about certain aspects of goods and services. Under s 75AZC, a breach of s 53 can also give rise to criminal penalties.[39] These sections could come into play, for example, if a company made a false statement about the process by which a commodity was manufactured (eg whether or not a product was manufactured by child labourers). As in California, ss 52 and 53 are actionable by any person, regardless of whether he/she has suffered damage from the misrepresentation.[40] Australia has no comparable constitutional guarantee of free speech, so the

---

[35] See B Egelko, 'Nike settles suit for $1.5 million: Shoe giant accused of lying about workers' treatment', *San Francisco Chronicle* (San Fancisco, United States, 13 September 2003) B1.

[36] See *Bowoto et al v Chevron* Case no CGC-03-417580 (Cal 2003), 'Complaint for Injunctive and Declaratory Relief, Restitution and Disgorgement of Profits', February 2003, available via <http://www.earthrights.org/chevron/index.shtml> (12 September 2003). This State complaint parallels a federal case against Chevron under the Alien Tort Claims Act. Note also that a claim regarding misleading and deceptive conduct has been filed by the People for the Ethical Treatment of Animals (PETA), against KFC and its parent company Yum Brands, regarding alleged misstatements about its record regarding animal welfare (details available via <http://www.kfccruelty.com/victory1.html> (19 September 2003)).

[37] See generally, Su-Ping Lu, 'Corporate Codes of Conduct and the FTC: Advancing Human Rights through Deceptive Advertising Law' (2000) 38 *Columbia Journal of Transnational Law* 603.

[38] An honest innocent statement can give rise to s 52 liability: see eg *Thai Silk Co Ltd v Aser Nominees Pty Ltd* (1991) ATPR 41–146 (FCA) 53,089. However, some courts have indicated that a breach of s 52 is more likely to arise where a clear intention to mislead or deceive is evident: see *Nylex Corp Ltd v Sabco Ltd* (1987) ATPR 40–752 (FCA) 48,179 per Woodward J. The federal provision has been replicated at the State level.

[39] See generally, T Spencer, 'Talking about Social Responsibility: Liability for Misleading and Deceptive Statements in Corporate Codes of Conduct' (2004) 30 *Monash University Law Review* (forthcoming).

[40] *Phelps v Western Mining Corp* (1978) 20 ALR 183 (FCA) 187; *Truth about Motorways Pty Ltd v Macquarie Infrastructure Management Ltd* (2000) 200 CLR 591 (FCA) 601–2.

preliminary issues which have preoccupied US judges in the *Nike* litigation would not be likely to arise if a company was sued under the *Trade Practices Act* for making misleading or false representations about its human rights practices.[41]

Within the European Union, States parties were required, by 1 January 2002, to implement The Sale of Consumer Goods Directive of 1999.[42] This Directive provides for various consumer rights against the seller of goods, and includes a requirement that goods conform to 'any public statements on the specific characteristics of the goods made about them by the seller, the producer or his representative, particularly in advertising and labelling'.[43] It is unclear how this provision might apply, if at all, in the context of a misleading statement about a corporation's ethical practices in producing a commodity.[44]

ASSESSMENT OF THE *NIKE* CASE

The *Nike* case is distinguishable from the truly transnational litigation, so its desirability will be assessed now in an interim conclusion, rather than in the general conclusion in Chapter 8. The 'consumer rights tactic' for imposing corporate human rights accountability has considerable potential advantages for plaintiffs over the other litigation strategies. The putative victims are consumers in developed countries, rather than residents in the developing world. The manifest intraterritorial links that will often exist in these cases will diminish the procedural barriers for plaintiffs. For example, forum non conveniens will often be irrelevant in such cases. Furthermore, it may be possible in such cases to target foreign corporations as an exercise of specific jurisdiction, as the impugned behavior, the dissemination of misleading statements, will often occur within territorial jurisdiction. Of course, jurisdictional issues may still arise where the statement is made in one country but published in another. For example, different rules exist between jurisdictions as to the true 'site' of a statement on the internet.[45] Nevertheless, unlike the other types of litigation discussed in this

[41] There is an implied freedom of political expression in the Commonwealth Constitution; see, eg, *Lange v Australian Broadcasting Corporation* (1997) 189 CLR 520 (HCA). However, it is unlikely that false commercial speech, even that motivated by wide-spread criticism, is protected by that constitutional guarantee. In *Tobacco Institute of Australia Ltd v Australian Federation of Consumer Organisations Inc (No 2)* (1993) 41 FCR 89 (FCA), the Full Federal Court refused leave to argue that s 52 was unconstitutional, as the implied right does not support the right to make misleading or deceptive statements, even over a political subject matter.

[42] EU doc. 1999/44/EC.

[43] *Ibid*, art 2(2)(d).

[44] See H Ward, 'Legal Issues in Corporate Citizenship', Swedish Partnership for Global Responsibility, February 2003 <http://www.iied.org/docs/cred/legalissues_corporate.pdf> (29 December 2003) 21.

[45] See *Dow Jones & Company Inc v Gutnick* (2002) 210 CLR 575 (HCA), decision of the High Court of Australia, on the differences between US and Australian law regarding the 'site' of a tort of defamation, in the context of a statement placed on the internet in New Jersey and downloaded in the Australian state of Victoria.

book, consumer rights litigation based on false statements regarding overseas corporate practices can arise in a wholly intra-territorial setting.

Corporate Rights of Freedom of Expression

This section is concerned with the desirability of laws, designed to punish or at least expose corporate human rights 'spin', per se. One relevant issue, from a human rights point of view, must be whether such laws breach the rights to freedom of expression of commercial speakers. Arguments have been raised that the Supreme Court of California misapplied the 'commercial speech' test in the US, such that application of the Californian law would have breached Nike's First Amendment rights under the US Constitution.[46] Such arguments about the technicalities of a unique US legal doctrine are beyond the scope of this book. The US guarantee of freedom of expression is uniquely broad, even perhaps too broad,[47] so such standards are not the most appropriate criteria for deciding whether a measure is desirable.[48] More universal and objective criteria for establishing whether Nike's free speech rights have been breached are found in international human rights law standards, rather than US constitutional standards. International guarantees of freedom of expression, such as Article 19 of the International Covenant on Civil and Political Rights (ICCPR), are considerably narrower than the First Amendment rights in the US constitution.[49]

In the *Nike* case, the counterbalance to Nike's free speech rights could be the rights of consumers and investors to truthful information. Though Nike's comments were not traditional advertisements, they were nevertheless aimed at influencing consumer choice in an age where a growing number of such choices are influenced by consumer perceptions of a corporation's human rights record. Consumer aspirations are thwarted if consumers are bamboozled by corporate falsehoods. Similarly, investors are also becoming more interested in 'socially responsible' investment, and therefore desire truthful information about a company's ethical record.[50] Such consumer/investor interests may be classified as 'the rights of others' or even 'public order' or 'public morals', ends which are routinely cited in international human rights guarantees as legitimate reasons for restricting certain rights, including freedom of expression.[51] For example, in

---

[46] See M Dobrusin, 'Crass Commercialism: Is it Public Debate or Sheer Profit? The Controversy of Kasky v Nike' (2003) 24 *Whittier Law Review* 1139.

[47] For example, it is arguable that the protection offered to hate speech under the First Amendment (see, eg, *RAV v City of St Paul* 505 US 377 (SCt 1992) is undesirable, and certainly contrary to universal standards regarding the regulation of hate speech.

[48] Of course, the parameters of the US 'commercial speech' doctrine are relevant to the question of whether any finding of liability against Nike would have survived a constitutional challenge on appeal to the US Supreme Court.

[49] See S Joseph, 'A Rights Analysis of the Covenant on Civil and Political Rights' (1999) 5 *Journal of International Legal Studies* 57, 79.

[50] See also ch 1, p 7.

[51] Eg, article 19(3) of the International Covenant on Civil and Political Rights (ICCPR).

Casado Coca v Spain, the European Court of Human Rights stated that advertising 'may sometimes be restricted, especially to prevent unfair competition and untruthful or misleading advertising'.[52]

A further issue to consider is whether such restrictions are proportionate. The *strict* liability imposed by the California statutes in this regard may be considered unnecessarily prejudicial to Nike's rights. Perhaps strict liability should be replaced by liability based on a failure to demonstrate that due diligence was exercised in checking the factual basis of a relevant statement. Such a basis of liability could represent a fair balance between a commercial speaker's right to freedom of expression, and a concerned consumer's rights to reliable information regarding a corporation's ethical practices. However, it is worth noting that all of the laws cited above from California, Australia and the European Union, impose strict liability for certain misleading statements, implying an international consensus of opinion that consumer rights should not be qualified by any leeway for commercial speakers to 'get it wrong' when it comes to describing the characteristics of their own commodities or services.

The lopsided consequence of the Californian law, under which criticisms of Nike's human rights record were fully protected by the First Amendment, whereas Nike's responses were not, is a relevant factor in evaluating the proportionality of the restrictions on Nike's speech. Nike is under a duty to carefully research its human rights record to ensure that its responses are not misleading, whereas its critics can take a more cavalier attitude to the veracity of their statements. This one-sidedness may deprive the Californian measure of the proportionality needed to conform to the requirements of international human rights law. In contrast, under international human rights law, the rights of commercial speakers under international human rights law are *equal* to those of others, such as Nike's critics.[53] Both sets of rights may be restricted by proportionate measures designed to achieve a competing legitimate interest.[54] For example, the free speech rights of Nike's critics could be legitimately curtailed if those criticisms are defamatory.[55] The disparity between the free speech rights of Nike and its critics in the *Nike* case is however a peculiarity of US constitutional law, as interpreted by the California Supreme Court. Such imbalance is not a necessary consequence in other countries, if they should adopt or enforce existing laws against corporations for making misleading and deceptive statements about their human rights records.

[52] Series A no 285 (1994) 18 EHHR 1 (ECHR) para 51.

[53] See, eg, *Ballantyne, Davidson and McIntyre v Canada* UN doc CCPR/C/47/D/359/1989 and 385/1989/Rev 1 (HRC 1993), par 11.3, where the Human Rights Committee, the monitoring body under the ICCPR, stated that differing types of expression were not 'subjected to varying degrees of limitation, with the result that some forms of expression may suffer broader restrictions than others'.

[54] Of course, it may be that commercial speech is effectively afforded less protection, as there will be more circumstances in which limitations thereto will be deemed proportionate and therefore legitimate compared to, for example, limitations on political speech.

[55] For example, freedom of speech can be legitimately curtailed in international human rights law to protect 'the rights and reputations of others'; see, eg, article 19(3)(a), ICCPR.

In any case, international human rights law is in fact ambiguous as to whether artificial persons such as Nike have *human* rights. Under the European Convention on Human Rights, artificial persons have standing to enforce their 'human' rights before the European Court of Human Rights, such as their rights to freedom of expression under article 10.[56] In contrast, corporations do not have standing to make complaints about breaches of ICCPR rights under the First Optional Protocol to the ICCPR.[57] However, it is unclear whether corporations are denied substantive rights under the ICCPR, or whether they are simply denied procedural rights to complain about breaches of their substantive rights under the First Optional Protocol. A comprehensive discussion of the pros and cons of granting human rights to corporations is beyond the scope of this book.[58] For now, it will suffice to note that the prohibition of misleading and deceptive conduct in a commercial context per se, especially if balanced by proportionate restrictions on the speech rights of corporate critics, does not breach a corporation's rights, given the above arguments.

Corporate Silence: An Undesirable Consequence of the *Nike* Case?

It is arguable that the *Nike* litigation and its progeny will result in less openness from companies regarding their human rights practices. For example, Nike cancelled the publication of its corporate responsibility report in response to the ruling by the Supreme Court of California.[59] However, given the volume of the current debate about corporations and human rights, it is questionable whether sustained silence is a viable option for Nike or any other commercial actor when consumers and other corporate stakeholders are increasingly demanding information in this regard.[60] Indeed, one may note that Nike has relaunched its corporate responsibility website, complete with new periodic electronic newsletters, since the *Nike* settlement, in spite of the possibility of new litigation by another plaintiff.

Furthermore, silence is not an option if the publication of certain information is compelled by law. For example, France passed legislation in 2001 which requires all French corporations to report on their social and environmental

---

[56] See, eg, *market intern Verlag GmbH and Klaus Beermann v Germany* Series A no 165 (1989) 12 EHRR 161 (ECHR).
[57] See S Joseph, J Schultz and M Castan, *The International Covenant on Civil and Political Rights: Cases, Materials and Commentary* 2nd edn (Oxford, Oxford University Press, 2004) 68–70.
[58] See for such a discussion, eg, M Addo, 'The Corporation as a Victim of Human Rights Violations' in M Addo (ed), *Human Rights Standards and the Responsibility of Transnational Corporations* (The Hague, Kluwer Law International, 1999) 187–96; S Bottomley, 'Corporations and Human Rights', in S Bottomley and D Kinley, above n 25, 61–65.
[59] See <http://www.nike.com/nikebiz> (28 October 2002).
[60] See Ward, above n 44, at 20–21.

performance.[61] Since 1 September 2003, the Johannesburg Securities Exchange in South Africa has required publicly listed companies to report on their social and environmental standards with reference to the Global Reporting Initiative.[62] Indeed, arguments have been raised that information regarding a corporation's social and environmental practices are 'material' disclosures of concern to investors that must therefore be included in a company's annual report.[63] Generally, companies are required to disclose information that 'the reasonable investor might consider important'.[64] The modern-day investor is quite likely to be influenced by a company's social and environmental performance in making decisions about that company. Indeed, such is acknowledged in a current review of company law in the UK.[65] At the time of writing, it is probable that the UK will introduce mandatory social and environmental reporting requirements for companies.[66] Pressure for similar reform of corporate reporting duties is also mounting in other jurisdictions.[67]

Rather than leading to increased corporate silence or evasiveness on human rights issues, the *Nike* litigation may instead simply ensure that TNCs are more careful about disseminating information regarding their human rights practices. Indeed, given the likely growth of legal regimes that mandate social and environmental reporting, the exercise of such care will become increasingly necessary

[61] The New Economics Regulation (Nouvelles Regulations Economiques) (Law No 2001–420) was adopted by the French Parliament in 2001 and came into force in January 2002. Article 116 thereof mandates the disclosure of social and environmental issues in annual company reports. See <http://www.orse.org/gb/home/report_regulation.html> (13 January 2004).

[62] This initiative was introduced pursuant to the King Report on Corporate Governance for South Africa; see *King Committee on Corporate Governance*, March 2002, available via <http://www.iodsa.co.za> (13 January 2004). An alternative to mandatory reporting could be freedom of information for individuals viz corporations: South Africa recognises such a right for citizens when the information relates to the protection of constitutionally recognised rights (see Ward, above n 44, at 35).

[63] See J Nolan, 'Research Summary Report: prepared as part of the Monash Global Initiative's project on Corporate Social Responsibility' (copy on file with the author, December 2003) 15–17.

[64] See *TSC Industries v Northway Inc* 426 US 438 (SCt 1976) 449. See also Nolan, *ibid*, at 15, citing *Coleman v Myers* [1977] 2 NZLR 225 (SCt Auckland).

[65] See Operating and Financial Review (OFR) Working Group on Materiality: A Consultation Document' <www.dti.gov.uk/cld/ofrwgcon.pdf> (13 January 2004) esp para 20. A final report of this Working Group was expected in December 2003, though the Group announced in November that it would be delayed. No report was available as at January 2004. See also UK government White Paper, 'Modernising Company Law', Schedule 2 http://www.dti.gov.uk/companiesbill/whitepaper.htm> (13 January 2004), which also indicates that social and environmental issues are 'material factors' that should be recorded in a company's annual report.

[66] An expanded concept of materiality that includes environmental and social issues could impact on the breadth of a company director's fiduciary duties to act in the best interests of the company; those duties could evolve so as to incorporate obligations to take sufficient account of human rights and environmental concerns in making decisions on behalf of the company; Nolan, above n 63, at 17. Discussion of the potential human rights duties arising from the realm of corporate law is beyond the scope of this book.

[67] See CA Williams, 'The Securities Exchange Commission and Corporate Social Transparency' (1999) 112 *Harvard Law Review* 1197, advocating a similar requirement in US corporate law. See also the 'International Right to Know' campaign, at <http://www.irtk.org/> (13 January 2004), campaigning for separate legislation to compel US-listed companies to publish details of their human rights practices abroad.

notwithstanding the availability of a *Nike*-type consumer actions, or else companies will open themselves up to litigation by shareholders or regulators.

Improving the Quality of the Debate regarding Corporations and Human Rights

If TNCs are forced to take greater care in making factual statements about their human rights and environmental records, the outcome should be that TNC human rights statements are rendered more credible,[68] a good result for TNCs given the skepticism that commonly greets their announcements of human rights initiatives.

Furthermore, it must be remembered that the prohibition on misleading and deceptive conduct will not disadvantage commercial speakers with regard to each other. For example, Nike's competitors such as Adidas, Reebok and Puma are similarly bound by the Californian law so long as they advertise in California. The uniform imposition of such a duty on all commercial speakers should enhance the quality of the debate over the proper level of human rights responsibility for corporations and other commercial enterprises. Commercial speakers will be forced to seriously engage their critics, rather than be allowed to deflect criticism by wrongly denying the existence of a problem (there of course being no legal issue with truthful denial). The net result should be that a truthful picture of the real level of corporate human rights abuse, as well as of the difficulties faced by corporations in preventing human rights abuse, whether at home or abroad, is painted for consumers and investors, who can then make a more educated determination of the appropriate 'market' level of ethical commercial behaviour.

Finally, the *Nike* litigation could improve the human rights practices of TNCs, presumably the main motivation behind the suit. In order to maintain or attract customers and investors by making true statements about 'good' human rights practices, TNCs will have to improve those practices to reflect the human rights standards demanded by the market.[69] In any case, it appears that the human rights victims of TNCs would not suffer from the *Nike* litigation: false statements about a corporation's human rights practices do little to improve their lot, and are not likely to be missed.

---

[68] See Ward, above n 44, at 20.
[69] See *Nike v Kasky* 27 Cal 4th 939 (SCt Cal 2002) 969 on how labour practices influence the consumer choices of 'a significant segment of the buying public; see also Lu, above n 37, at 628.

6

Transnational Human Rights Litigation in Other Countries

THE VAST MAJORITY of transnational human rights cases against corporations have arisen in the United States. This is not surprising, given the juridical advantages for plaintiffs pursuing novel legal actions available in that country. However, transnational human rights litigation has arisen in three other common law countries, England, Australia and Canada. The features of that litigation in those countries are considered in this chapter.

ENGLAND

England is a largely untested forum for transnational civil claims based on international human rights norms against corporations or indeed any other entity.[1] However, a few recent transnational tort cases against TNCs in England have raised its profile as a potential forum for the imposition of corporate human rights accountability.

Extraterritorial Jurisdiction over Corporations

English courts can exercise jurisdiction over the extraterritorial acts of English companies, as well as foreign corporations that carry on business 'to a definite and, to some reasonable extent, permanent place' within jurisdiction;[2] the foreign corporation must have 'premises in England from which or at which its business is carried on'.[3] One of the more lenient (and early) applications of this standard was its satisfaction by the exhibition for nine days of the defendant

---

[1] See, generally, International Law Association Human Rights Committee (ILAHRC), 'Report on Civil Actions in the English Courts for Serious Human Rights Violations Abroad' [2001] *European Human Rights Law Review* 129.
[2] *Littauer Glove Corp v F W Millington (1920) Ltd* (1928) 44 TLR 746 (KB Div) 747, quoted in *Adams v Cape Industries* [1990] Ch 433 (CA) 467.
[3] *Adams v Cape Industries* [1990] Ch 433 (CA) 468.

company's product (a motor car) at a London exhibition.[4] The existence of a branch office, or another place of business, suffices to attract jurisdiction.[5] In such cases, the litigation must in some way involve the business of the branch, though not necessarily to a significant extent. A foreign corporation may also be vulnerable to English jurisdiction if its agent, including a subsidiary, is present within jurisdiction. In numerous cases, it has been held that the putative agent must have independent authority to enter into contracts on behalf of the corporation in order for its existence to attract jurisdiction.[6]

English courts in fact have more extraterritorial power than those in the US due to a lack of strict constitutional due process restrictions. For example, service out of jurisdiction is permitted, so long as the case has 'a sufficiently close connection with England so as to make it reasonable for the prospective defendant . . . to be required to defend the allegations' in England.[7] Such service is allowed when 'a claim is made in tort where . . . damage is sustained within jurisdiction'.[8] In *Al-Adsani v Government of Kuwait*, the Court of Appeal appeared to accept the proposition that the plaintiff had sustained damage within England for the extraterritorial commission of torture, due to his continuing mental health problems arising from that torture.[9] Thus, a human rights victim resident in England, who suffers continuing damage from violations of his/her rights, such as nervous shock or physical deterioration, should be able to serve an overseas company.[10] Even a non-resident victim in England for medical treatment related to the human rights violations could perhaps take advantage of such provisions.[11]

---

[4] *Dunlop Pneumatic Tyre Co Ltd v Actien-Gesellschaft für Motor und Motorfahrzeugbau Vorm Cudell & Co* [1902] 1 KB 342 (CA).

[5] See *Companies Act* 1985, ss 690 A, 694A, 695, and Schedule 21A, and also *Civil Procedure Rules*, rr 6.2(2) and 6.5(6). See also *Saab v Saudi American Bank* [1998] 1 WLR 937 (QB Div), and [1999] 1 WLR 1861 (CA).

[6] *Adams v Cape Industries* [1990] Ch 433 (CA) 539–49; *Saccharin Corporation Ltd v Chemische Fabrik Von Heyden Aktiengesellschaft* [1911] 2 KB 516 (CA); *Thames and Mersey Marine Insurance Co v Societa di Navigazione a Vapore del Lloyd Austriaco* (1914) 111 LT 97 (CA); *The World Harmony* [1967] P 341 (Probate, Divorce and Admiralty Division); *F and K Jabbour v Custodian of Israeli Absentee Property* [1954] 1 WLR 139 (QB Div). See also *Okura & Co Ltd v Forsbacka Jernverks Aktiebolag* [1914] 1 KB 715 (CA), and *The Lalandia* [1933] P 56 (Probate, Divorce and Admiralty Division), where the putative agent did not have such contractual authority, so no general jurisdiction was found to exist over the relevant foreign corporations.

[7] ILAHRC, above n 1, at 141.

[8] See Civil Procedure Rules, United Kingdom Statutory Instrument 1998/3132, Rule 6.20(8)(a).

[9] (1994) 100 ILR 465 (CA) 469. See below, text at n 14, on the facts in *Al-Adsani*.

[10] ILAHRC, above n 1, at 143.

[11] M Byers, 'English Courts and Serious Human Rights Violations Abroad: A Preliminary Assessment' in M Kamminga and S Zia-Zarifi (eds) *Liability of Multinational Corporations under International Law* (The Hague, Kluwer Law International, 2000) 241, 245. Of course, it may be very difficult to enforce a judgment against a body that has no presence in the UK.

Subject Matter Jurisdiction

The UK has no statute which equates with the ATCA or the TVPA. However, civil 'human rights' claims may lie via customary international law, which is accepted as being part of English common law.[12] It seems possible to make claims of breaches of custom in an English court so long as English law is the 'applicable law'.[13] Indeed, a civil claim for torture was made against a foreign government in *Al-Adsani*, though the claim was dismissed due to the defendant's sovereign immunity.[14] Most breaches of customary human rights law require an element of State action, though certain human rights violations, such as genocide, are prohibited by custom regardless of the status of the perpetrator.[15] Therefore, in most cases, a customary human rights claim against a corporation would have to allege collusion by the corporation with a State actor.[16]

English courts also have jurisdiction over torts committed overseas under the *Private International Law Miscellaneous Provisions Act* 1995 (the PILMPA). Indeed, a number of transnational tort cases have been brought against British TNCs.[17] These English cases have, like their US counterparts, focused on preliminary issues, rather than the actual merits of the complaint. The key development in the litigation so far has been an apparent relaxation of the doctrine of *forum non conveniens* (FNC) in favour of plaintiffs, discussed directly below.

Forum non Conveniens in England

The seminal case on FNC in England is *Spiliada Maritime Corp v Cansulex*.[18] Dismissal for FNC will arise under *Spiliada* when there exists 'another available forum, having competent jurisdiction, which is the more appropriate forum for the trial of the action'.[19] In determining 'the more appropriate forum', the courts adopt a two-part test. First, taking into account the interests of the parties and the nature of the subject matter, a determination is made as to whether

---

[12] See *Trendtex Trading Corp v Central Bank of Nigeria* [1977] 2 WLR 356 (CA). Treaties are not part of English law unless they are incorporated by legislation.
[13] ILAHRC, above n 1, at 159; see below, text at nn 46–54, on choice of law.
[14] *Al-Adsani v Government of Kuwait* [1996] TLR 192 (CA). See below, on foreign sovereign immunity, text at nn 58–60.
[15] See ch 2, pp 33–39, discussing the 'state action' requirement for breaches of customary international law for the purposes of the ATCA in the US. See also *ibid*, pp 48–49, for a discussion of the small number of human rights abuses that US courts have found to be actionable under ATCA (and therefore breaches of customary international law according to US courts) without state action.
[16] Given the breadth of foreign sovereign immunity in England, it may be that the direct effect of customary international law in English law will not be capable of generating many viable transnational human rights cases. See below, text at nn 58–60.
[17] See ch 7, pp 134–36 however, on why these cases may not actually involve extraterritorial jurisdiction, as the claims target decisions made locally in corporate boardrooms.
[18] [1987] AC 460 (HL).
[19] *Ibid* at 476.

another forum is more appropriate than England. Second, the courts inquire as to whether 'substantive justice' will be achieved in that other forum.[20] This second limb distinguishes the English test from the US test, where 'justice' is not such an explicit part of the FNC test for determining the adequacy of a foreign forum.[21] The significance of this 'justice' limb has been highlighted in two recent transnational tort cases, *Connelly v RTZ*[22] and *Lubbe et al v Cape plc*.[23]

Connelly concerned an action against RTZ by a former employee of RTZ's subsidiary, Rossing Uranium Ltd, which ran a uranium mine in Namibia. The plaintiff Connelly claimed that the British parent company, RTZ, had failed in its duty of care to ensure that its subsidiary provided adequate work safety systems so as to protect him as an employee from the effects of uranium ore dust. Connelly claimed that this negligence contributed to his contraction of throat cancer. The defendant applied to have the claim dismissed for FNC. The FNC motion was granted by the trial judge, but reversed by the Court of Appeal. The Court of Appeal's decision was ultimately upheld by the House of Lords, so the case stayed within jurisdiction.[24]

Even though the plaintiff's case was cast so as to directly target RTZ's decisions within jurisdiction, all judges agreed that Namibia, the site of most of the witnesses, and the site of a potentially necessary mine inspection, was the more appropriate forum. However, the Court of Appeal and the House of Lords found that justice was not likely to be achieved in Namibia, due to the non-availability of legal aid for the plaintiff. In the House of Lords, Lord Goff, speaking for the majority, noted that normally, a plaintiff must take a more appropriate overseas forum as he/she finds it.[25] Thus, lower damages, more stringent discovery rules, different rules of evidence, and even the non-availability of legal aid per se were not reasons to assume that justice would not be served in an overseas forum.[26] Nonetheless, the House of Lords found that

---

[20] *Ibid*; see also P Muchlinski, 'Holding Multinationals to Account: Recent Developments in English Litigation and the Company Law Review' 23(6) *The Company Lawyer* 168 (2002).

[21] However, the interests of justice have been one of the factors considered by judges in exercising their decision to grant or not grant FNC applications in the US, as in cases where an FNC application has been refused because the putative alternative forum is considered too corrupt to be able to properly decide the case. See ch 4, pp 90–92.

[22] [1998] AC 854 (HL).

[23] [2000] 4 All ER 268 (HL). See, on *Cape*, H Ward, 'Towards a New Convention on Corporate Accountability? Some Lessons from the Thor Chemicals and Cape Plc cases' [2002] *Yearbook of International Environmental Law* 105, 122–33. See also *Ngcobo v Thor and Sithole v Thor*, unreported decisions of the Queen's Bench, discussed in R Meeran, 'Liability of Multinational Corporations: A critical stage in the UK' in Kamminga and Zia-Zarifi, above n 11, at 251, 255–56; and in Ward, *ibid*, at pp 113–22.

[24] The case was ultimately dismissed for being filed outside the applicable statute of limitations in *Connelly v RTZ*, Queen's Bench Division (Judge Wright), 4 December 1998, transcript available via LEXIS <http://web.lexis-nexis.com/universe/document?_m=292bf92712aa9cc4c4b2c328 e690af2b&_docnum=10&wchp=dGLbVlz-zSkVA&_md5=a09ce5706fe28bc8704c1e785a8c7a4d> (16 January 2004).

[25] *Connelly v RTZ* [1998] AC 854 (HL) 872.

[26] *Ibid* at 872; see also *Spiliada Maritime Corp v Cansulex* [1987] AC 460 (HL) 482.

'the nature and complexity of the case', which required expert evidence, 'is such that it cannot be tried at all without the benefit of legal assistance'.[27] The majority essentially upheld the sentiments expressed in *Connelly* in the Court of Appeal by Sir Thomas Bingham MR:

> [F]aced with a stark choice between one jurisdiction, albeit not the most appropriate in which there could in fact be a trial, and another jurisdiction, the most appropriate in which there never could, in my judgment, the interests of justice would tend to weigh, and weigh strongly in favour of that forum in which the plaintiff could assert his rights.[28]

A similar case arose in *Lubbe v Cape plc*. A class action with over 3000 claimants was launched against Cape for its negligent failure to ensure that its South African subsidiary adopted safe working practices to prevent the occurrence of illnesses caused by asbestos exposure. The House of Lords unanimously refused the defendant's application for a stay on the basis of FNC. As in *Connelly*, the *Lubbe* Court agreed that the defendants had satisfied the first part of the FNC test, in that South Africa was the more appropriate forum.[29] The crux of the case was again the second 'justice' limb of the test. The House of Lords found first that the issues in the case would be complex, so litigants would require professional legal assistance and expert witnesses and evidence. Second, it was extremely unlikely that legal aid would be made available to the claimants in South Africa. Third, the claimants were unlikely to obtain counsel in South Africa on a contingency basis. Finally, the claim could only be efficiently handled as a group or class action: it was desirable 'to avoid determination of the claims on a claimant by claimant basis'. Though the situation 'involve[d] the kind of procedural comparison which the English court should be careful to eschew',[30] the House of Lords nonetheless attributed some significance to the lack of developed class action procedures in South Africa. For example, such 'procedural novelty' would act as a 'disincentive to any person or body considering whether or not to finance the proceedings'.[31] Taking into account all of these factors, the Court found that it was likely that 'the claimants would have no means of obtaining the professional representation and expert evidence [in South Africa] which would be essential if these claims were to be justly decided'.[32] Thus, *Lubbe* followed *Connelly* in denying the defendant's application for a stay based on FNC. The key factor in both cases was that the case could not go ahead at all in the alternative forum, due to the lack of legal aid and/or a contingency arrangement.[33] The decisions exhibit a greater focus on

---

[27] *Connelly v RTZ* [1998] AC 854 (HL) 872.
[28] *Ibid* at 866.
[29] *Lubbe v Cape Plc* [2000] 4 All ER 268 (HL) 277.
[30] *Ibid* at 280.
[31] *Ibid*.
[32] *Ibid* at 279.
[33] See Ward, above n 23, at 135, on the legal aid crisis in South Africa.

the 'substantive justice' limb of *Spiliada* away from mere corporeal concerns such as site of the harms.[34]

Two more important points were made in *Lubbe*. In the proceedings before the Court of Appeal, which had granted the FNC motion, *Union Carbide Bhopal* had been cited with approval, particularly with regard to its balancing of public interests.[35] The House of Lords however denied that the English test of FNC involves a balancing of public interests unrelated to the interests of the specific parties. Thus, court congestion concerns are now irrelevant to an English FNC determination. Similarly, concerns that the 'legal aid' test favours poor claimants over rich claimants, and that it encourages 'home' litigation against British TNCs (both cited as relevant considerations by Lord Hoffman in a dissenting opinion in *Connelly*)[36] are irrelevant.[37] This rejection of the relevance of public interest factors is quite different from the FNC test in the US, and limits the reasons for which an FNC motion can be granted in the UK.

Second, the claimants submitted that the grant of a stay for FNC would contravene article 6 of the European Convention on Human Rights (ECHR), denying them a fair trial. The court in *Lubbe* suggested that the *Spiliada* principles were in fact fully compatible with article 6; indeed those principles dictated against a stay in the *Lubbe* case.[38] The ECHR has now been incorporated into UK law by the Human Rights Act 1998, which can only enhance the developing 'due process' approach to the second limb of the FNC test.[39]

Practical inability to access the courts of alternative forums, particularly in developing countries which, for example, cannot afford legal aid systems, is quite common in transnational human rights cases, as indicated by the frequency with which an FNC dismissal has resulted in the effective end of the litigation. The *Connelly* and *Lubbe* precedents indicate that such cases, when instigated in English courts, are now likely to stay within that forum.[40]

Even more significant could be a recent decision by the European Court of Justice (ECJ) in *Societe Group Josi Reinsurance Co SA v Universal Group*

---

[34] S Joseph, 'Taming the Leviathans: Multinational Enterprises and Human Rights' (1999) 46 *Netherlands International Law Review* 171, 179.

[35] *Lubbe v Cape plc* [2000] 1 Lloyd's Rep 139 (CA) 155.

[36] *Connelly v RTZ* [1998] AC 854 (HL) 876. See also N Pengelley, 'Judicial Chauvinism or Respect for Comity: Is it Time to Bury the Anti-Suit Injunction' (unpublished PhD thesis, Monash University) 55.

[37] Lord Hoffman joined in the House of Lords' unanimous decision in *Lubbe*.

[38] *Lubbe v Cape Plc* [2000] 4 All ER 268 (HL) 281.

[39] Muchlinski, above n 20, at 172; see also M Anderson, 'Transnational Corporations and Environmental Damage: Is Tort Law the Answer?' (2002) 41 *Washburn Law Journal* 399, 413–14; G Virgo, 'Characterisation, Choice of Law and Human Rights' in C Scott (ed) *Torture as Tort* (Oxford, Hart Publishing, 2001) 325, 339–42; C Scott, 'Multinational Enterprises and Emergent Jurisprudence on Violations of Economic Social and Cultural Rights' in A Eide, C Krause and A Rosas (eds) *Economic Social and Cultural Rights* 2nd edn (The Hague, Kluwer Law International, 2001) 593.

[40] See also Meeran, above n 23, at 254–55. In *Carlson v Rio Tinto* [1999] CLC 551 (QB) Judge Wright followed *Connelly* on the FNC issue in a case with substantially similar facts.

Insurance.⁴¹ The Judges therein state that the general rule under Article 2 of the Brussels Convention on Jurisdiction and Enforcement of Judgments in Civil and Commercial Matters is that the courts of States members of the European Union (EU) must exercise jurisdiction whenever a defendant is *domiciled* within jurisdiction, *regardless* of the domicile of the claimant.⁴² As the UK is bound, as a member of the EU, by ECJ rulings, the case could 'spell the death of the forum non conveniens principle in foreign direct liability cases involving defendant companies domiciled' in the UK.⁴³ Recently, *Group Josi's* relevance to FNC questions where the relevant alternative forum lies outside the EU was denied by an English court.⁴⁴ The issue of the applicability of Article 2 in a case where a defendant argues for FNC in favour of a non-EU forum has now been referred to the ECJ by the English Court of Appeal in *Owusu v Jackson*.⁴⁵ The ECJ opinion will be of great importance to potential transnational human rights litigants against British companies. No decision had been issued at the time of writing.

Choice of Law

Under s 11 of the PILMPA, English courts in transnational tort cases must apply 'the law of the country in which the events constituting the tort or delict took place'. Where elements of the tort occur in more than one country (as is the case where decisions are made in one State and the harm occurs in another), s 11(c) dictates that the court apply 'the law of the country in which the most significant element or elements of the events occurred'. Section 12 permits departure from s 11 in cases where it is deemed appropriate to apply the law of another country, due to the significant links between that second country (which could be the UK itself) and the tort.⁴⁶

Thus, problems for claimants may arise in transnational human rights litigation in England if the law of the site of the human rights abuse somehow exempts perpetrators of the impugned conduct from liability. However, this will rarely be the case with regard to extreme human rights abuses, such as torture.⁴⁷ Though perpetrators of such abuses may have de facto impunity in a foreign State, rarely will they have de jure impunity.⁴⁸ On the other hand,

---

⁴¹ [2000] All ER (EC) 653.
⁴² *Ibid*, § 61, emphasis added.
⁴³ H Ward, 'Securing Transnational Corporate Accountability through National Courts: Implications and Policy Options' (2001) 24 *Hastings International and Comparative Law Review* 451, 461–62.
⁴⁴ See, eg, *Ace Insurance SA-NV v Zurich Insurance Co* [2001] 1 Lloyd's Rep 618 (CA), following *Harrods (Buenos Aires) Ltd (No 2)* [1992] Ch 72 (HL), which predates *Group Josi*. The House of Lords in *Lubbe v Cape Plc* [2000] 4 All ER 268 (HL) 282 found it unnecessary to decide if an FNC dismissal in that case would contravene the Brussels Convention.
⁴⁵ [2002] IL Pr 45 (CA), Civil Division, 19 June 2002.
⁴⁶ See, eg, *Edmunds v Simmonds* [2001] 1 WLR 1003 (QB).
⁴⁷ Byers, above n 11, at 244.
⁴⁸ J Terry, 'Taking Filartiga on the Road: Why Courts outside the United States should accept Jurisdiction over Actions involving Torture Committed Abroad' in Scott, above n 39, at 124.

amnesty laws have been passed in numerous States which do exempt human rights violators from liability, including corporations.[49]

Section 14(3) of the 1995 Act provides that application of a foreign law may not lie where its application would conflict with principles of English public policy. Certainly, it seems likely that the application of foreign law to an extraterritorial tort litigated in a British court in such a way as to exempt perpetrators of liability for egregious human rights abuses breaches English public policy.[50] Such 'public policy' considerations may not however assist claimants in tort cases involving occupational health and safety such as *Connelly* and *Lubbe*. In such cases, the law of the foreign country where the tort arose is often much more lenient to the defendant when that country is a developing nation,[51] but such leniency may not be deemed to effectively excuse behavior so egregious and heinous (such as deliberate torture) as to activate the 'public policy' exception.

However, *Connelly* and *Lubbe* also demonstrate that the identification of the site of the tort may not be easy. In both cases, the claimants' arguments largely targeted the policy decisions regarding work practices made in boardrooms in England, rather than the actual implementation of the work practices in southern Africa.[52] Neither case reached the stage where the Court had to determine choice of law, with *Connelly* eventually dismissed on statute of limitations grounds[53] and *Lubbe* settling in early 2002.[54]

Advantages and Disadvantages of Litigation in England

As noted in Chapter 1, there are a number of important advantages in pursuing transnational human rights litigation in the United States, and corresponding disadvantages in non-US forums like England.[55] Perhaps most important is the 'loser pays' principle, under which an unsuccessful litigant is commonly required to pay the costs of his/her opponent, which is probably the most significant deterrent to international human rights litigation in England,[56] especially considering the risky nature of uncharted arguments.[57]

---

[49] For example, the *Ok Tedi Mine Continuation (Ninth Supplemental) Act* 2001 in PNG purports to exempt Australian mining company BHP from environmental claims regarding pollution of the Ok Tedi river. See Slater & Gordon Solicitors *BHP's Ok Tedi exit plans face challenge* Press Release (12 December 2001).
[50] ILAHRC, above n 1, at 162.
[51] Anderson, above n 39, at 417–18.
[52] This was the crux of the *Lubbe v Cape Plc* [2000] 4 All ER 268 (HL) case. In *Connelly*, some of the allegations related to improper actions on site in Namibia.
[53] As Namibian and English law dictated the same limitations periods, nothing turned on the choice of law point in the case.
[54] Muchlinski, above n 20, at 169. Payment was completed in 2003.
[55] See ch 1, pp 16–17.
[56] Byers, above n 11, at 244.
[57] ILAHRC, above n 1, at 158–59.

Furthermore, the British doctrine of sovereign immunity is more extensive than that applied in the US, particularly in its application to individuals.[58] In *Propend Finance Pty v Alan Sing and the Commissioner of the Australian Federal Police*,[59] it was held that the sovereign immunity granted to a state government extended to all State employees and agents of foreign States. Therefore, it is possible that corporations operating in close proximity with governments, such as perhaps Unocal in Myanmar, might benefit from that government's immunity.[60]

On the other hand, the 'act of State' doctrine appears to have significantly smaller scope in England. As noted, the paramount issue regarding 'act of state' under US law is a prevention of litigation that would interfere with the executive's conduct of foreign affairs. In the US, the fact that an impugned act of state constitutes a breach of international law is merely 'one policy informing application of the doctrine'.[61] As seen in *Sarei v Rio Tinto*, breaches of the law of nations can still be classed as 'acts of state' in the US.[62] In England, the *raison d'etre* behind the doctrine is a desire to respect the legitimate acts of foreign nations, rather than a desire to avoid clashes with the foreign policy of the British government.[63] The focus on legitimacy means that English courts are less likely to characterise breaches of international human rights law as 'acts of state'.[64] The position may be summarised by paraphrasing Lord Cross in *Oppenheimer v Cattermole*:

> [I]t is part of the public policy of this country that our courts should give effect to clearly established rules of international law.... To my mind a law [that] constitutes [a] grave ... infringement of human rights [is one] that the courts of this country ought to refuse to recognise it as a law at all.'[65]

Similarly, the principle of non-justiciability enunciated in *Buttes Gas v Hammer*[66] is much narrower than its American counterpart, the political question doctrine. The US doctrine seeks to remove overly political issues from the

---

[58] See *ibid* at 155, n 14.

[59] [1997] TLR 238; see also M Byers, 'Decisions of British Courts during 1997 involving Questions of International Law' (1997) 68 *British Yearbook of International Law* 301, 316–18.

[60] Byers, above n 11, at 245. Britain's state immunity laws have recently survived challenges in the European Court of Human Rights in *Al-Adsani v United Kingdom (No 2)* (2002) 34 EHRR 11 (ECHR), *McElhinney v Ireland and United Kingdom* (2000) 29 EHRR CD 214 (ECHR), and *Fogarty v United Kingdom* (2000) 29 EHRR CD 157 (ECHR).

[61] M Bühler, 'The Emperor's New Clothes: Defabricating the Myth of "Act of State" in Anglo-Canadian Law' in Scott, above n 39, at 364.

[62] See ch 2, p 42.

[63] See Bühler, above n 61, at 352–53, 364–65.

[64] Byers, above n 11, at 247. See also *Kuwait Airways Corp v Iraqi Airways Co* [2002] 2 AC 883 (HL) 970–77.

[65] [1976] AC 249 (HL) 278; in *Oppenheimer* the House of Lords refused to give effect to a Nazi nationality law that deprived Jews outside Germany of their nationality. However, note Bühler's concern, above n 61, at 366–71 that obiter in *R v Bow Street Metropolitan Stipendiary Magistrate, ex parte Pinochet Ugarte (No 3)* [1999] 2 All ER 97 (HL) incorrectly applied the act of state doctrine in a manner that resembled the American doctrine.

[66] [1981] 3 All ER 616 (HL).

arena of the courts, as such matters are best dealt with by the legislature and/or the executive.[67] The resolution of the issue in *Buttes* would have required the House of Lords to determine an international boundary disputed by four countries. Lord Wilberforce, speaking for the court, held that the matter was non-justiciable as it related to a matter wholly within the domain of *unresolved* international law,[68] devoid of manageable standards that could be applied by a domestic court.[69] Thus, non-justiciability was based on an absence of *any* applicable law, rather than the possibility of encroaching upon the domain of, and possibly embarrassing, the executive government.[70] 'Embarrassing' situations may easily arise in disputes that are capable of domestic judicial resolution; such disputes would appear to be justiciable in English law.[71]

A final important advantage to the claimants in English litigation is that, as noted above, English courts have recently adopted a 'refreshingly liberal approach to the issue of *forum non conveniens*'.[72]

AUSTRALIA

Commonwealth countries such as Australia and Canada are, like England, largely untested forums for transnational human rights litigation. The law in these jurisdictions is likely to be the same in many respects as English law. In this section, jurisdictional features in Australia are examined to the extent that they are likely to differ from those in the UK. At the outset, it must be noted that many salient issues, such as the extent of sovereign immunity, the act of state doctrine, and political question non-justiciability, have not been litigated in a relevant sense in Australia.[73]

Australian federal courts do not have jurisdiction at all unless granted by federal statute or the Constitution, which has not occurred with regard to extraterritorial corporate human rights abuses. Australian States are constrained by constitutional limitations on their extraterritorial power: there must be a nexus between the impugned extraterritorial act and the jurisdiction.[74] As in England,

---

[67] See ch 2, pp 44–46.
[68] *Buttes Gas v Hammer* [1981] 3 All ER 616 (HL) 633.
[69] Ibid.
[70] See also Bühler, above n 61, at 356–58.
[71] See also ILAHRC, above n 1, at 164, and M Davies, 'Kuwaiti Airways Corp v Iraqi Airways Co: The Effect In Private International Law of a Breach of Public International Law by a State Actor' (2001) 2 *Melbourne Journal of International Law* 523, 529, 534.
[72] Byers, above n 11, at 246.
[73] See, on the likely extent of act of state in Australia, B Wells and M Burnett, 'When Cultures Collide: An Australian Citizen's Power to Demand the Death Penalty under Islamic Law' (2000) 22 *Sydney Law Review* 5, 29–30, 44. See G Lindell, 'The Justiciability of Political Questions: Recent Developments' in HP Lee and G Winterton (eds) *Australian Constitutional Perspectives* (Sydney, Lawbook Co, 1992) 180, for an overview of the likely role of non-justiciability in Australia. See also *Re Ditfort, ex parte Deputy Commissioner of Taxation* (1988) 83 ALR 265 (FCA) 284–9 per Gummow J.
[74] S Joseph and M Castan, *Federal Constitutional Law: A Contemporary View* (Sydney, Lawbook Co, 2001) 82.

superior Courts within the Australian states are authorised under their rules to hear cases involving damage suffered partly within jurisdiction.[75] Service outside jurisdiction is also permitted.[76] Thus, a resident victim receiving medical treatment in New South Wales for injuries suffered in a New Caledonian car accident was able to proceed against a French car manufacturer with no presence in Australia in the Supreme Court of New South Wales in *Regie Nationale des Usines Renault SA v Zhang*.[77] The *Renault* case indicates that Australian courts interpret the constitutional and regulatory nexus requirements extremely leniently.[78]

As in the US and the UK, foreign corporations are susceptible to the exercise of personal jurisdiction on a general basis in an Australian State if they conduct business in that State. Indeed, it seems that a relatively lenient approach is taken to the 'doing business' standard. In *BHP v Oil Basins Ltd*,[79] a foreign corporation's presence within Victoria was established by agents and solicitors who collected investment cheques on its behalf.[80]

Unlike England, customary international law is not accepted as part of common law in Australia, so there is apparently no scope for a tort action based simply on custom. For example, in *Nulyarimma v Thompson*,[81] a Federal Court majority denied that the customary prohibition on genocide is part of Australian law. Custom does not become part of Australian law unless it is specifically incorporated by statute.

The FNC test in Australia is more favourable to plaintiffs than the tests in England and the US. In *Voth v Manildra Flour Mill*,[82] the High Court of Australia adopted a test whereby cases will only be dismissed for FNC if the relevant Australian jurisdiction is 'a clearly inappropriate forum'. In contrast, the standard for dismissal in England is that there exists a 'more appropriate forum', or, in the US, a more convenient forum. Clearly, a more appropriate or convenient forum may exist in many circumstances where Australia or a constituent State is not 'clearly inappropriate' as a site for the litigation.[83] In *Renault*, the High Court majority arguably tightened the *Voth* test by requiring that FNC only be granted when trial within the Australian forum 'would be productive of injustice, . . . oppressive in the sense of seriously and unfairly

---

[75] See, eg, Rules of the Supreme Court of NSW, Part 10, rule 1A(1)(e); Rules of the Supreme Court of Victoria, Rule 7.01(1)(j).
[76] See eg, Part 10 of the Rules of the Supreme Court of NSW.
[77] (2002) 210 CLR 491 (HCA).
[78] Indeed, the case did not even focus on the constitutionality of the exercise of jurisdiction, focusing instead on FNC and choice of law issues. These aspects of the case are discussed below in the text at nn 92–96.
[79] [1985] VR 725 (SCt Vic) 730–5; see also *Amalgamated Wireless (Australasia) Ltd v McDonnell Douglas Corporation* (1987) 77 ALR 537 (FCA) 540.
[80] See also P Nygh, 'The Common Law Approach' in C McLachlan and P Nygh (eds), *Transnational Tort Litigation: Jurisdictional Principles* (Oxford, Clarendon Press, 1996) 28.
[81] *Nulyarimma v Thompson* (1999) 96 FCR 153 (FCA).
[82] (1990) 171 CLR 538 (HCA).
[83] See *ibid* at 556–57.

burdensome, prejudicial and damaging, or vexatious, in the sense of productive of serious and unjustified trouble and harassment'.[84] The majority dismissed the foreign defendants' FNC application in *Renault* as this strict test had not been satisfied. Given the tenuous connection between the relevant tort and the forum of New South Wales,[85] *Renault* indicates that FNC stays in Australia are virtually impossible to attain for Australian-based defendants.

In 1997, an Australian company, BHP, was sued in Victoria over environmental damage allegedly caused by its mining operations in Papua New Guinea in *Dagi v BHP*.[86] BHP was sued in tort for intentionally or otherwise polluting the Ok Tedi River and adjacent land, thus prejudicing the plaintiffs' enjoyment of the relevant land and waters. Interestingly, the defendants did not seek dismissal on the ground of FNC, perhaps because they felt such an argument would be unsuccessful due to the *Voth* principle.[87] The matter subsequently settled after a preliminary hearing. It is likely that the absence of FNC arguments sped up the *Dagi* proceedings and facilitated the original settlement. Furthermore, Prince has argued that the availability of an Australian forum in *Dagi* facilitated the peaceful Ok Tedi settlement.[88] In contrast, violence erupted on the PNG island of Bougainville, partly due to grievances felt by the local people against Rio Tinto's local mining operations. In the latter case, the Bougainvilleans may have perceived that they had no access to meaningful legal recourse.[89]

The parties in the Ok Tedi dispute returned to court in *Gagarimabu v BHP* to address disputes arising from the original settlement.[90] These new proceedings were dismissed in early 2004.[91]

The flipside of Australia's generosity to plaintiffs regarding FNC is its strictness regarding the issue of choice of law. In *Renault*, the majority stated that the substantive law of the site of the tort would be the applicable law in all foreign tort cases. The Court made clear that there was no room for a so-called flexible exception, to be applied in cases where the forum State for some reason has a closer connection to the events giving rise to the case than the situs State.[92] The High Court does concede that 'public policy' could continue to play a role so as

---

[84] *Regie Nationale des Usines Renault SA v Zhang* (2002) 210 CLR 491 (HCA) 521.

[85] In dissent, Callinan J noted at para 202 that the alleged wrong had no connection with New South Wales. *Ibid* at 567.

[86] [1995] 1 VR 428 (SCt Vic).

[87] See P Prince, 'Bhopal, Bougainville and Ok Tedi: Why Australia's *Forum non Conveniens* Approach is Better' (1998) 47 *International and Comparative Law Quarterly* 573, 594.

[88] *Ibid* at 594–95, 597.

[89] *Ibid* at 594; see R Hawes, 'Politicians turn talk into intimidation' *The Australian* (New South Wales, Australia, 25 March 1997) 6, quoting plaintiffs' lawyer Nick Styant-Browne. Proceedings regarding Rio Tinto's actions in Bougainville were eventually commenced in the US in 2000, where they were dismissed for reasons other than FNC. See above, ch 2, pp 42, 45–47.

[90] [2001] VSC 517 (SCt Vic), interim decision of Bongiorno J, Supreme Court of Victoria, 21 December 2001.

[91] 'Court dismissed Ok Tedi proceedings', *The Age*, 16 January 2004.

[92] *Regie Nationale des Usines Renault SA v Zhang* (2002) 210 CLR 491 (HCA) 520. See generally, R Anderson, 'Case notes: International Torts in the High Court of Australia' (2002) 10 *Torts Law Journal* 1. By way of contrast, the flexible exception is permitted in the UK under s 12 of PILMPA.

to prevent 'the admission of foreign laws that offend local social and moral values'.[93] However, it seems that such considerations will be used by courts to close the door on litigation in the forum, rather than open the door to the application of local law.[94] One unresolved issue, explicitly left undecided in *Renault*, was whether procedural matters such as quantum of damages fell within this strict 'choice of law' rule.[95] It may be added that the *Renault* rule may simplify the choice of law rules in Australia, but does not simplify the process of identifying the site of the tort in cases with transnational elements.[96]

CANADA

There have been two relevant cases in Canada. Canada, like Australia, is likely to be similar to England in terms of advantages and disadvantages as a forum for transnational human rights jurisdiction. For example, like England (but unlike Australia), customary international law is accepted as being part of the common law of the Canadian provinces, and thus could provide a basis for an extraterritorial human rights tort action.[97]

As in Australia, Canada is ostensibly restricted in its extraterritorial jurisdiction to cases which have a 'real and substantial' connection with the forum.[98] The recent Supreme Court decision in *Spar Aerospace Ltd v American Mobile Satellite Corp*[99] evinced a broad definition of the 'real and substantial' requirement, perhaps akin to the lenient approach in Australia.[100]

In *Bouzari v Islamic Republic of Iran*,[101] the plaintiff Bouzari attempted to sue the government of Iran, as well as a company wholly owned by the Iranian government, for torture committed in Iran. The Ontario Superior Court noted that

---

[93] R Garnett, '*Renault v Zhang*: A Job Half Done' (2002) 10 *Tort Law Review* 145, 147.

[94] *Regie Nationale des Usines Renault SA v Zhang* (2002) 210 CLR 491 (HCA) 515; cf Garnett, *ibid* at 150.

[95] *Regie Nationale des Usines Renault SA v Zhang* (2002) 210 CLR 491 (HCA) 520; see also Garnett, *ibid* at 151.

[96] See, for a discussion of such principles with in the context of internet defamation, *Dow Jones & Company Inc v Gutnick* (2002) 210 CLR 757 (HCA). The High Court of Australia controversially decided that the site of an act of internet defamation takes place in the place where the defamatory material is downloaded, rather than where it is placed on the internet.

[97] *Suresh v Canada (Minister for Citizenship and Immigration)* (2000) 183 DLR (4th) 629 (Fed Canada) 659; see also EM Hyland, 'International Human Rights Law and the Tort of Torture: What Possibility for Canada?' in Scott, above n 39, at 419–20.

[98] *Tolofson v Jensen* [1994] 3 SCR 1022 (SCt Canada) 1049. See AC McConville, 'Taking Jurisdiction in Transnational Human Rights Tort Litigation: Universality Jurisdiction's Relationship to *Ex Juris Service, Forum non Conveniens* and the Presumption of Territoriality' in Scott, above n 39, at 161–66.

[99] [2002] Carswell Queb 2593 (SCt Canada). A real and substantial connection was established by the damage allegedly suffered by the plaintiff to its business reputation in Quebec.

[100] The case actually concerned the interpretation of a Quebec statute permitting the exercise of jurisdiction where some 'damage' was suffered within the province (see *Civil Code of Quebec*, s 3148(3). The Supreme Court found that these statutory provisions most likely incorporated the constitutional requirement of a real and substantial connection at para 56.

[101] [2002] Carswell Ont 1469 (Ontario Superior Court of Justice).

the impugned acts occurred in Iran many years before the plaintiff settled in Canada. Though Bouzari 'suffers ongoing effects from those injuries . . . the logical conclusion would be that there is no real and substantial connection between the wrongdoing that gave rise to the litigation and Ontario'.[102] However, given the fact that Bouzari could 'not bring such an action in Iran, given the facts alleged',[103] the judge did 'not feel it appropriate to decide [the] case on conflicts rules alone'. Indeed, Swinton J added that '[i]t may be that the Canadian courts will modify the rules on jurisdiction . . . where an action for damages for torture is brought with respect to events outside the forum'.[104] Thus, Swinton J seemed to moot the idea that Canadian courts might exercise jurisdiction over torture, and presumably other severe breaches of human rights, in circumstances where no real connection exists between the Canadian forum and the cause of action. Such a move however would seem unconstitutional,[105] unless a breach of a *jus cogens* norm was held to per se constitute a nexus with the Canadian forum. Ultimately, the case was dismissed on the basis of sovereign immunity.

The application of FNC in Canada resembles that of England, being based on a test of 'more appropriate forum'.[106] A case against a Quebec mining company Cambior regarding alleged environmental harms in Guyana was dismissed for FNC in 1998 because Guyana was deemed to be a more appropriate forum.[107] The following factors weighed in favour of Guyana as the appropriate forum:

> 'the place of residence of the parties and witnesses, the location of the evidence, the place where the fault occurred, the existence of court proceedings in another forum,[108] the location of property owned by the defendant,[109] the law applicable to the case, juridical advantage to the plaintiff in the chosen forum,[110] and the interests of justice'.[111]

As in the US, the FNC hurdle was not cleared by plaintiffs in an environmental case, where evidence is probably more site-specific than in other human rights/personal injury cases. Regarding 'the interests of justice', the Quebec Superior Court

---

[102] *Ibid* at para 16.
[103] *Ibid* at para 17.
[104] *Ibid*.
[105] In *Bouzari*, the test of 'real and substantial connection' was described at para 15 as one arising from the common law, and therefore one which may be amenable to alteration or development to accommodate plaintiffs in the unusual situation of Mr Bouzari. On the other hand, the test was described as constitutional in *Spar Aeropace*, which would seem to leave Canadian courts little flexibility in its application: see also McConville, above n 98, at 161.
[106] McConville, *ibid* at 188–89.
[107] *Recherches Internationales Quebec v Cambior Inc* [1998] QJ No 2554, Quebec Superior Court, 14 August 1998, cited in Ward, above n 43, at 455–57. See also C Forcese, 'Deterring 'Militarized Commerce': The Prospect of Liability for 'Privatized' Human Rights Abuses' (2000) 31 *Ottawa Law Review* 171, 204–6.
[108] 900 victims had already filed similar claims in Guyana; see Forcese, *ibid* at 205.
[109] The court found that the value of the defendants' Guyanese assets was sufficient to satisfy any adverse judgment; see Forcese, *ibid*.
[110] As the plaintiffs had no real ties to Quebec, they had 'no legitimate claim' to the juridical advantage entailed in the availability of a class action, Furthermore, it was deemed important to discourage forum shopping; see Forcese, *ibid* at 205.
[111] Forcese, *ibid* at 205.

considered submissions that the plaintiffs would not receive a fair trial in Guyana, but ultimately concluded that Guyana was an adequate alternative forum.[112]

The recent English focus on the 'justice' limb of the *Spiliada* test was recently upheld in Canada in *Wilson v Servier Canada*,[113] where the House of Lords decision in *Lubbe v Cape Plc* was cited to support a denial of an FNC application. The Ontario court in *Wilson* determined that a products liability action against a Canadian pharmaceutical company for injuries suffered in France by French plaintiffs should remain in Ontario, where a class action procedure would facilitate the just resolution of their claims.

In *Bouzari*, Swinton J noted that the application of ordinary FNC rules in the case would lead a court to dismiss the case, given the lack of a connection between Canada and the alleged act of torture in Iran.[114] However, Swinton J indicated that it might be possible for Canadian courts to modify the FNC test in cases where the plaintiff alleges particularly egregious abuses of his/her human rights in another country where he/she cannot realistically seek legal redress.[115] As noted, the case was dismissed for sovereign immunity rather than FNC.

The recent decisions in *Wilson v Servier* and *Bouzari* indicate that FNC may now be a lesser obstacle for human rights plaintiffs in Canada than was evinced in the *Cambior* case.

In *Tolofson v Jensen*,[116] the Supreme Court of Canada purported to formulate a strict choice of law rule that the law of the site of a tort be the governing law in a case litigated in Canada. The case was decided in an inter-provincial rather than international context. La Forest J, speaking for the Court, explicitly noted that exceptions may be required at the international level so as to avoid 'injustice', but added that such an exception would be necessary in 'few cases'.[117] An exception would probably lie in a case where the law of the forum exempted a defendant for gross, egregious human rights abuses recognised by customary international law.[118] However, it is unlikely that an exception would arise with regard to the lesser abuses which might arise under ordinary transnational tort jurisdiction (eg negligence claims such as that in *Connelly* and *Lubbe*), given the clear preference for a narrow zone of exception exhibited in *Tolofson*.[119]

---

[112] *Ibid* at 206; see also McConville, above n 98, at 194–95.
[113] 50 OR (3d) 219 (2000), Ontario Superior Court of Justice.
[114] *Bouzari v Islamic Republic of Iran* [2002] Carswell Ont 1469 (Ontario Superior Court of Justice) para 16.
[115] *Ibid* at para 17.
[116] [1994] 3 SCR 1022 (SCt Canada).
[117] *Ibid* at 307.
[118] See JA Orange, 'Torture, Tort Choice of Law, and *Tolofson*' in Scott, above n 39, at 321–22. See also Forcese, above n 107, at 208
[119] An exception was applied in *Wong v Wei* (1999) 65 BCLR (3d) 222 (SCt BC) regarding a torts claim between two residents of British Columbia regarding a car accident occurring while they vacationed together in California.

CONCLUSION

Subject matter jurisdiction in non-US jurisdictions has been based on tort law, though there is the possibility of suits in England and Canada being based in the future upon allegations of breaches of customary international law. As in the United States, transnational human rights litigation against companies has focused on preliminary matters, such as FNC and choice of law. Recent decisions indicate that England, Australia, and Canada may be more amenable jurisdictions for plaintiffs regarding FNC, personal jurisdiction over defendants, and the application of doctrines of abstention, such as the 'act of state' doctrine. These countries have more rigid and predictable rules regarding choice of law than the United States, but the 'public policy' exception applies so as to preclude the application of foreign laws that exempt defendants from liability for gross violations of human rights. Finally, foreign sovereign immunity is broader in these non-US jurisdiction compared to the US, and could operate to exclude cases against corporations who are accused of acting jointly with governments.

7

Parent Corporation Liability in Transnational Human Rights Cases

MOST OF THE litigants in the current transnational human rights cases concerning corporations are attempting to attribute blame to a corporate parent for the actions of its subsidiary in a developing State. There are a number of reasons for targeting the parent rather than the subsidiary. First, a home State's court is more likely to have personal jurisdiction over the parent. This consideration is important if, as is the case with most of the litigation discussed in this book, the plaintiff feels that litigation in the subsidiary's jurisdiction is not feasible. Second, the parent will be more asset-rich than the subsidiary, and therefore more capable of satisfying any damages award.[1] As none of the salient cases have been decided on the merits, few of the cases in any of the jurisdictions have seriously confronted the crucial issue of the extent of liability of parent corporations for the human rights-abusing actions of their subsidiaries.[2] This issue is therefore addressed in this chapter at a general level, rather than on a jurisdiction-by-jurisdiction basis.

THE CORPORATE VEIL

It is generally difficult to hold a parent legally liable for the actions of its subsidiary companies.[3] The most obvious problem is that corporations are legally separated from their shareholders (including corporate shareholders) by a 'corporate veil'. The veil serves to establish a separate juridical personality for a

---

[1] J Cassels, 'Outlaws: Multinational Corporations and Catastrophic Law' (2000) 31 *Cumberland Law Review* 311, 323. Indeed, note that the operations of Cape plc's subsidiary in South Africa had ceased, so pursuance of the subsidiary was impossible in the litigation in *Lubbe v Cape plc*; H Ward, 'Securing Transnational Corporate Accountability through National Courts: Implications and Policy Options' (2001) 24 *Hastings International and Comparative Law Review* 451, 463.

[2] The issue has been decisive in cases at a preliminary stage, such as *Alomang v Freeport-McMoran* 811 So 2d 98 (La App 2002) in a jurisdictional context, and has been influential in other preliminary outcomes (see below, text at n 23).

[3] W Loomis, 'The Responsibility of Parent Corporations for the Human Rights Violations of their Subsidiaries' in M Addo (ed), *Human Rights Standards and the Responsibility of Transnational Corporations* (The Hague, Kluwer Law International, 1999) 145.

corporation, and therefore to protect shareholders (natural and artificial) from liability for the actions of the corporation beyond the extent of their investment.[4]

The corporate veil is not impregnable; courts are willing in exceptional instances to 'pierce the veil' and expose shareholders to liability for the acts of the corporation. Unfortunately, there is no precise ascertainable test for veil-piercing. Veil-piercing in the US has been accurately described as 'characterised by ambiguity, unpredictability, and even a seeming degree of randomness'.[5] Veil-piercing jurisprudence in the UK is 'a wilderness of isolated precedents'.[6] Similarly, courts in Australia 'tend to take a fact-based approach to questions of piercing the corporate veil, and no particular trend is readily discernible from an overview of the cases'.[7] A number of factors, of varying degrees of importance in a given situation, may be cited to justify piercing. The 'laundry list'[8] of considerations that have historically lead to the piercing of a company includes undercapitalisation of that company, a failure to observe legal formalities, or that the level of control exercised by a shareholder may be so extreme as to render the corporation an alter ego or a sham.[9] To the extent that it is possible to generalise, it seems that a court will often be willing to pierce the corporate veil in circumstances where the shareholder/s exercise extreme control over the relevant company, and the considerations of justice and policy mandate that the shareholder/s should bear the burden of a wrong perpetrated by the company, rather than the person/s who have suffered from that wrong. Of course, within that proposed 'test' lie many ambiguities. For example, when does the level of control reach an extreme point? 'Considerations of justice and public policy' are value judgments which will differ from person to person, and judge to judge, and of course will vary according to each particular fact situation.

---

[4] See also International Council on Human Rights Policy [ICHRP], *Beyond Voluntarism: Human Rights and Developing International Legal Obligations of Companies* (ICHRP, Versoix, 2002) 81 (also available via <http://www.ichrp.org/>) (5 January 2004).

[5] SM Bainbridge, 'Abolishing Veil Piercing' (2001) 26 *Journal of Corporate Law* 479, 507.

[6] D Prentice, 'Veil Piercing and Successor Liability in the United Kingdom' (1996) 10 *Florida Journal of International Law* 469, 474.

[7] I Ramsay and D Noakes, 'Piercing the Corporate Veil in Australia' (2001) 19 *Company and Securities Law Journal* 250, 252.

[8] Bainbridge, above n 5, at 510.

[9] For example, in *John Doe I v Unocal Corp* 2002 US App LEXIS 19263 (9th Cir 2002) 14222–23, n 30, and 14259 (*Unocal 2002*) and *Wiwa v Royal Dutch Petroleum Co* No 96 Civ 8386, 2002 US Dist LEXIS 3293 (SDNY Feb 22, 2002) 41, n 14, the respective federal courts indicated that Unocal's Myanmar subsidiaries and Shell Nigeria were the alter egos of the defendant parent companies. Of course, these were preliminary decisions, and the issues have not been finally determined at trial. FA Gevurtz, 'Piercing Piercing: An attempt to lift the veil of confusion surrounding the doctrine of piercing the corporate veil' (1997) 76 *Oregon Law Review* 853, 855 has described such terms as 'sham' and 'alter ego' in the context of veil-piercing as 'pejorative' and 'unhelpful'. On the other hand, Chaney J in the California Superior Court has recently ruled that Unocal's Myanmar subsidiaries cannot be characterised as its alter egos: see http://www.earthrights.org/news/unocalupdate.shtml (14 April 2004).

The corporate veil is essentially a device designed to protect shareholders so as to encourage entrepreneurial risk-taking and innovation.[10] Limited liability arose at a time when corporations were generally prohibited from holding shares in other corporations, so corporate groups were unknown.[11] Nonetheless, courts have automatically applied the limited liability doctrine to corporate groups so as to shield parent companies from the debts of subsidiaries, without questioning whether extension of limited liability from natural to artificial persons was warranted.[12] Indeed, serious questions can perhaps be raised over whether the *raison d'etre* of limited liability justifies its application to TNCs.[13] For example, TNCs, with all of their economic wealth and power, are hardly the 'entrepreneurial upstarts' for whom the protection of limited liability was originally designed.[14] Furthermore, limited liability for shareholders within corporate groups 'opens the door to multiple layers of insulation [from liability], a consequence unforeseen when limited liability was adopted long before the emergence of corporate groups'.[15] The corporate veil can be abused by TNCs to shed responsibility and 'manipulate the amount of their business liabilities'.[16] Moreover, the legal fiction of the corporate veil is particularly unrealistic in the case of corporate groups, which are often viewed economically and politically as a single 'firm', but are viewed in law as unconnected entities.[17]

Nevertheless, the corporate veil poses a formidable obstacle to transnational human rights claimants seeking redress from corporate parents for the actions of their subsidiaries. Empirical studies have found that courts in the US, England, and Australia were *less* likely to pierce the veil to expose corporate shareholders in a corporate group, as opposed to individual shareholders.[18] For example, US '[c]ourts appear much more willing to permit shareholder

---

[10] See generally, PI Blumberg, 'Accountability of Multinational Corporations: The Barriers Presented by Concepts of the Corporate Juridical Entity' (2001) 24 *Hastings International and Comparative Law Review* 297, 300–4.

[11] *Ibid* at 302.

[12] *Ibid* at 302–3. See also *Briggs v James Hardie* (1989) 16 NSWLR 549 (CA NSW) 577 per Rogers AJ; *Qintex Australia Finance Ltd v Schroders Australia Ltd* (1990) 3 ACSR 267 (SCt NSW) 268–69 per Rogers CJ.

[13] See Ramsay and Noakes, above n 7, at 263–64.

[14] E Marcks, 'Avoiding Liability for Human Rights Violations in Project Finance' (2001) 22 *Energy Law Journal* 301, 323; see also JL Westbrook, 'Theories of Parent Company Liability and the Prospects for an International Settlement' (1985) 20 *Texas International Law Journal* 321, 324. See also generally, RB Thompson, 'Piercing the Veil within Corporate Groups: Corporate Shareholders as Mere Investors' (1999) 13 *Connecticut Journal of International Law* 379, 379–83.

[15] PI Blumberg, *The Multinational Challenge to Corporation Law: The Search for a New Corporate Personality* (New York, Oxford University Press, 1993) 139 and see ch 6, for a comprehensive overview of the policy reasons behind limited liability, and their inapplicability to corporate groups. See also Thompson, *ibid* at 384.

[16] LM LoPucki, 'Virtual Judgment Proofing: A Rejoinder' (1998) 107 *Yale Law Journal* 1413, 1422.

[17] Blumberg, above n 10, at 303.

[18] See, See RB Thompson, 'Piercing the Corporate Veil: An Empirical Study' (1991) 76 *Cornell Law Review* 1036, 1038; C Mitchell, 'Lifting the Corporate Veil in the English Courts: An Empirical Study' (1999) 3 *Company Financial and Insolvency Law Review* 15, 22; Ramsay and Noakes, above n 7.

domination when the shareholder is another corporation as opposed to individuals'.[19] Further bad news for transnational human rights litigants is that the studies strongly indicated that US, English, and Australian courts are less willing to pierce the veil in tort cases than in non-tort cases.[20]

JOINT LIABILITY

Given that a parent corporation and its subsidiary are recognised in law as two separate entities, they can in certain circumstances be held jointly liable under ordinary tort principles, as discussed in chapter 3.[21]

For example, in *Bowoto v Chevron Texaco*,[22] Illston J recently held that there was sufficient evidence to permit a jury to hold Chevron liable for the acts of its Nigerian subsidiary, Chevron Nigeria Ltd (CNL). The case concerns ATCA claims regarding the deaths and injuries of protesters against CNL's operations at the hands of the Nigerian military, allegedly acting in concert with CNL as its hired security. Though Illston J was not prepared to pierce the veil and deem CNL to be Chevron's 'alter ego',[23] she found that there was enough evidence to conclude that CNL was Chevron's agent. In particular, Illston J was influenced by the volume, content and timing of certain communications between Chevron and CNL;[24] the degree to which Chevron actively participated in the security policy of CNL; the large number of common officers

---

[19] Thompson, above n 14, at 387–88 and see p 391, for an explanation of how the focus on formal indicators of control favours corporate over individual shareholders: 'This focus on shareholders acting as mere investors and the normal shareholder role makes it too easy for corporate shareholders to avoid liability. This framing of the issues emphasises the separate roles of shareholders and managers that is inherent in the corporate form. The use of this distinction to determine liability serves corporations well because, as artificial entities, they are recognised in the law as capable of holding shares and being shareholders but they are not capable of being an officer or director which requires a natural person. When a corporate shareholder names a real person, perhaps one of its employees, as a director or officer of the subsidiary, it is only doing what shareholders normally do. If an individual shareholder names himself as a director or officer it seems more nefarious and is a factor more likely to lead to piercing. Lawyers for corporate shareholder-defendants can portray everything the corporate shareholder does directly as within the normal shareholder role of a mere investor. When the corporate shareholder gets a report from its employee, who is a director of the subsidiary, it is merely checking on its investment. If it advances funds or guarantees the subsidiary's debt, it is merely providing financing which is what shareholders are supposed to do. The corporation only exposes itself to liability when it completely ignores or circumvents the corporate formalities of the subsidiary. Corporations with sufficient planning and legal counsel can avoid such liability.' See also Ramsay and Noakes, *ibid* at 264.

[20] See Thompson, above n 18, at 1058; Mitchell, above n 18, at 23; Ramsay and Noakes, *ibid* at 265.

[21] See generally, ch 3, pp 67–68.

[22] No C 99-2506 SI, 2004 US Dist LEXIS 4603 (ND, Cal 2004).

[23] *Ibid*,*45–*47.

[24] These communications exhibited 'an extraordinarily close relationship between' the companies (ibid, *36). Furthermore, there was a particularly high volume of communications on the day of a protest during which 'an oil platform was taken over by local people' (*ibid*, *37).

between the companies;[25] the importance of CNL for the overall success of Chevron's operations;[26] and evidence that CNL was acting within the scope of its purported agency. Illston J concluded that:

> a reasonable juror could find that [Chevron] exercised more than the usual degree of direction and control which a parent exercises over its subsidiary. The agency relationship alleged by plaintiffs is directly related to the plaintiffs' cause of action, in that plaintiffs allege that defendants were significantly involved in security matters and benefited directly from CNL's oil production, which was made possible or at least protected by the military's wrongful use of force to quell unrest among Nigerians.[27]

Illston J also found that the same facts could establish Chevron's liability as an aider and abettor of the actions of CNL.[28] Finally, and most interestingly, Illston J found that Chevron could be liable under a theory of 'ratification'. 'An agency may be created, and an authority may be conferred by a precedent authorization, or by subsequent ratification.'[29] Thus, an agency can be created even if the purported agent operates outside authority, if the principal expressly or implicitly adopts the agent's acts after the fact.[30] Implicit adoption may be entailed by a failure to 'disavow' the impugned acts.[31] Illston J found that CNL's agency could be implied by Chevron's alleged 'dissembling' and 'covering up' of CNL's misdeeds.[32]

Chevron indicates that it may be easier to establish TNC liability under an agency theory than under an alter ego theory. Agency will nevertheless only lie in situations where an extreme level of control by the parent over the subsidiary is demonstrable on the facts. On the other hand, the decision regarding ratification may pose a great threat to TNCs who believe that they are quarantined legally from their subsidiary's actions. Most TNCs would probably be tempted to dissemble before the media if an offshore subsidiary is accused of human rights abuses, especially where those abuses are particularly egregious as in the *Chevron* case. Intriguingly, Illston J indicates that such cover-ups may give rise to an after-the-fact implication of agency, rendering the parent company liable as principal. However, it would still be necessary to establish the other essential features of agency, such as a great degree of control exercised by purported principal over the purported agent.

---

[25] 'The revolving door of managers and directors at the highest levels between CNL and defendants is dramatic evidence of . . . an agency relationship' (*ibid*, *39–*40). Without more, however, it is unlikely that common personnel could of itself establish agency; see *ibid*, *39, and *US v Bestfoods* US v Bestfoods 118 SCt 1876 (SCt 1998) 1888–89.
[26] For example, 'CNL's profits were used to fund other Chevron subsidiary corporations'; *ibid*, *41.
[27] Ibid, *44.
[28] See, on 'aiding and abetting' in the context of finding a TNC jointly liable with a government, ch 2, pp 33–39.
[29] Ibid, *48, quoting *Rakestraw v Rodrigues* 8 Cal 3d 67, 73 (1977).
[30] Ibid* 49.
[31] Ibid.
[32] Ibid, *49–*52.

DIRECT PARENT LIABILITY

An increasingly common argument in the salient cases is to *directly* target the actions or omissions that arise in boardrooms at corporate headquarters as causes of a plaintiff's harm, rather than the harmful behavior of a subsidiary corporation in another State. This argument has a number of possible advantages. First, the site of the tortious act will be the corporation's home State, often the place where the plaintiff wishes to commence litigation. Hence, the action is more likely to survive a motion for FNC, due to the greater connections between the impugned behaviour and the forum.[33] Second, in focusing on a parent's own actions, the plaintiff can avoid arguments regarding the corporate veil.[34]

Such arguments failed to stave off FNC dismissals in the *Union Carbide (Bhopal)* litigation in New York (discussed below) and in *Aguinda v Texaco*. In *Aguinda*, the plaintiffs unsuccessfully argued that the true site of the alleged environmental torts was the US, as the salient policy decisions had been made at Texaco's US headquarters. Rakoff J however found that the evidence did not establish 'a meaningful nexus between the United States and the decisions and practices' complained of.[35]

An instructive case in this regard, even though it is not a transnational human rights decision, is *CSR v Wren*, a decision of the Court of Appeal of New South Wales.[36] The plaintiff Wren was a former employee of CSR's subsidiary, Asbestos Products (AP), and alleged that the negligence of both CSR and AP contributed to his contraction of mesothelioma from asbestos exposure. The Court unanimously held that CSR could be held liable to Wren for negligence. First, the evidence demonstrated that Wren's injury was foreseeable for CSR. For example, it knew at the relevant time that asbestos was a carcinogen. Second, CSR had a reasonably proximate relationship with Wren so as to owe

---

[33] Mr James Stewart QC, sitting as a Deputy Judge of the High Court, in *Ngcobo v Thor Chemicals Holdings Ltd*, unreported judgment of 11 April 1995, implicitly accepted that the alleged tort arose in England with the decisions of the parent company rather than in South Africa with the implementation of those decisions (transcript at 20). The *Thor* case ultimately settled; see H Ward, 'Towards a New Convention on Corporate Accountability? Some Lessons from the Thor Chemicals and Cape Plc cases' [2002] *Yearbook of International Environmental Law* 105, 120–21.

[34] MJ Rogge, 'Towards Transnational Corporate Liability in the Global Economy: Challenging the Doctrine of Forum non Conveniens in *Re: Union Carbide, Alfaro, Sequihua, and Aguinda*' (2001) 26 *Texas International Law Journal* 299, 313–14; S Zia-Zarifi, 'Suing Multinational Corporations in the US for Violating International Law' (1999) 4 *University of California at Los Angeles Journal International Law and Foreign Affairs* 81, 142–43; see also H Ward, 'Securing Transnational Corporate Accountability through National Courts: Implications and Policy Options' (2001) 24 *Hastings International and Comparative Law Review* 451, 470; B Stephens, 'Accountability: International Human Rights Violations Against Corporations in US Courts' in M Kamminga and S Zia-Zarifi (eds), *Liability of Multinational Corporations under International Law* (The Hague, Kluwer Law International, 2000) 223.

[35] *Aguinda v Texaco* 142 F Supp 2d 534 (SDNY 2001) 548–50.

[36] *CSR Ltd v Wren* (1997) 44 NSWLR 463 (CA NSW).

him a duty of care even though it was not his direct employer. Proximity was established by CSR's 'direction, control and involvement' in AP's operations,[37] including the fact that the whole of AP's management staff were also CSR staff. CSR created this de facto employer/employee relationship by its choice to use its staff to 'assume responsibility for the working conditions' at AP.[38] The Court noted that policy considerations were relevant in deciding whether a person owed a duty of care to another.[39] First, a duty of care should not be so onerous as to expose one to liability to an indeterminate class of people for an unlimited amount of time. Second, a tortfeasor should not be subject to a liability which is totally disproportionate to the negligent act. Furthermore, tort law should not be used so as to supplant other areas of the law, such as contract. None of these policy reasons applied so as to deny the creation of a duty of care owed by CSR to Wren. In particular, CSR was not exposed to potential indeterminate liability, as the case simply exposed it to liability to AP's employees.

The District Court of Illinois in *The Amoco Cadiz*[40] reached a similar decision, though the Court did not engage in a comprehensive evaluation of the parent company's duty of care. Standard, the parent corporation in a multinational conglomerate, was held liable for environmental damage caused by an oil spill by a tanker off the coast of France, despite its legal insulation from the vessel via a number of subsidiary companies. The evidence demonstrated that Standard exercised such dominant control over those subsidiaries, including the maintenance of the relevant vessel, that it was liable for its own negligence in failing to adequately maintain the vessel.[41]

The merits of such 'parent liability' arguments were briefly addressed in *Connelly v Rio Tinto plc*, upon its remission to Wright J of the Queen's Bench after the failed FNC challenge.[42] In *Connelly*, the defendants sought to have the claim struck out on a number of grounds. One ground was that the defendants owed no duty of care to the employees of Rossing, which was the defendant's subsidiary company.[43] Wright J disagreed, and noted that in certain circumstances, third parties could owe duties of care to employees which resembled those owed by employers. It had been alleged that the defendants had taken responsibility for 'devising an appropriate policy for health and safety to be operated at the Rossing mine', and actually implemented the policy through its

---

[37] *Ibid* at 484.
[38] *Ibid* at 486. Cf *US v Bestfoods* 118 SCt 1876 (SCt US 1998) 1888–89 where the presence of numerous joint officers and directors did not necessarily give rise to direct liability by a parent for negligence in the subsidiary's facility. The US Supreme Court accepted that joint officers usually wear two 'hats' depending on which corporation they are acting for at a given time. See also above, n 25.
[39] *CSR Ltd v Wren* (1997) 44 NSWLR 463 (CA NSW) 477–83.
[40] [1984] 2 Lloyd's Rep 304 (ND Ill 1984).
[41] See also *Anglo Eastern Bulkships v Ameron* 556 F Supp 1198 (DCNY 1982).
[42] Decision of 4 December 1998, transcript available via LEXIS <http://web.lexis-nexis.com/universe/document?_m=292bf92712aa9cc4e4b2c328e690af2b&_docnum=10&wchp=dGLbVlz-zSkVA&_md5=a09ce5706fe28bc8704c1e785a8c7a4d> (16 January 2004).
[43] Counsel for the plaintiff had not attempted to argue that Rossing was the alter ego of the defendants, and therefore not a separate entity at all.

own employees. If true, the allegations gave rise to 'a duty of care upon those Defendants who undertook those responsibilities, whatever contribution Rossing itself may have made towards the safety procedures at the mine'.[44]

The courts in *CSR*, *The Amoco Cadiz*, and *Connelly* all identified the degree of actual control assumed by parents over the subsidiaries' relevant actions as an important factor in establishing that the parent owed a duty of care to the plaintiffs. This emphasis on control seems to echo the criteria for piercing the veil.[45] However, the control test is quite different in the 'direct liability' context. The issue is *not* control by the parent over the subsidiary. Rather, the relevant control is that exercised by the parent over the conduct which gave rise to the tort at issue.[46] Thus, the relevant 'control test' focuses on the extent to which a parent is somehow in control of the causes of the tort, which will be linked to, but will not be the same as, the issue of a parent's control over its subsidiary.[47]

Similarly, a parent corporation may attract direct liability if it undertakes to perform services for a subsidiary; it then owes a duty of care to take reasonable care in performing those services to third parties to whom the subsidiary owed a duty in respect of those services.[48] For example, employees of subsidiaries have successfully sued parent companies on the basis that the parent undertook but failed to provide a safe workplace on behalf of the subsidiary.[49] Indeed, this was the situation alleged in *Connelly*. Thus, if a corporation chooses to become involved in a subsidiary's work, the parent will be directly liable for the tortious outcomes of that involvement.

The 'direct liability' cases above focus on the affirmative actions of a parent corporation. What of the situation where a TNC is alleged to commit negligence by *omission* rather than action, in that it fails to exercise appropriate control over its subsidiary? For example, can a parent corporation be held liable for failing to ensure that its subsidiaries adopt health and safety policies in developing countries which the parent knows are necessary to ensure worker safety? It is one thing to hold a parent liable for negligence in its positive engagement with a subsidiary's operations; it is another to hold it liable for its *failure to control*

---

[44] Decision of 4 December 1998, transcript available via LEXIS <http://web.lexis-nexis.com/universe/document?_m=292bf92712aa9cc4c4b2c328e690af2b&_docnum=10&wchp=dGLbVlz-zSkVA&_md5=a09ce5706fe28bc8704c1e785a8c7a4d> (16 January 2004) 5.

[45] Indeed, JW Bartlett III argues in 'In re Oil Spill by the Amoco Cadiz: Choice of Law and a Pierced Corporate Veil defeat the 1969 Civil Liability Convention' (1985) 10 *The Maritime Lawyer* 1, 14–19, that the *Amoco Cadiz* was an example of veil piercing, rather than of direct liability.

[46] See, eg, *US v Bestfoods* 118 SCt 1876 (SCt US 1998) 1187; see also LJ Oswald, 'Bifurcation of Owner and Operator Analysis under CERCLA: Finding order in the chaos of pervasive control' (1994) 72 *Washington University Law Quarterly* 223, 269, 272.

[47] See N Rosenkrantz, 'The Parent Trap: Using the Good Samaritan Doctrine to hold Parent Corporations directly liable for their negligence' (1996) 37 *Boston College Law Review* 1061, 1086–7.

[48] See RESTATEMENT (SECOND) OF TORTS § 324A (1965).

[49] See, generally, AJ Natale, 'Expansion of Parent Corporate Shareholder Liability through the Good Samaritan Doctrine: A Parent Corporation's Duty to Provide a Safe Workplace for Employees of its Subsidiary' (1988) 57 *University of Cincinnati Law Review* 717, 729–36.

or prevent injurious actions by its subsidiary. Such claims pose a greater 'challenge [to] the advantage of limited liability implicit in the corporate separation between parent and subsidiary'.[50] The claims are also more problematic from a tort law point of view: it is more difficult to establish a duty to act to prevent harm than a duty to take care to refrain from harm when engaged in affirmative actions.[51] There is also generally no duty upon a person to prevent others from causing harm.[52] An unfortunate result of direct liability attaching to parent companies only in cases of actions rather than omissions (if this is indeed the case) is that parents will be discouraged from intervening in their subsidiary's operations, even though they may have superior knowledge and technical expertise.[53] Alternatively, parent companies might maintain 'strategic control' but avoid responsibility by delegating operational matters, which are more likely to give rise to tortious consequences.[54] On the other hand, it may be doubted that parent corporations would regularly risk revenue losses and other consequences by deliberately neglecting to oversee subsidiary operations.

In *Doe v Unocal* before the Superior Court of California, Chaney J summarily dismissed an argument that Unocal owed the plaintiffs a duty of care to prevent the Myanmar military from harming them.[55] Chaney J confirmed that, under Californian tort law, a person generally owes no duty to prevent a third party from harming another. However, an exception lay if the defendant was able to control the third party.[56] Furthermore, a defendant owes a duty to a person not to create a foreseeable risk posed by a third party to that person, or to increase or exacerbate such a risk.[57] Chaney J decided that Unocal did not owe a relevant duty to the plaintiffs.[58] This decision of course did not concern a parent's possible duty to control the acts of a subsidiary.[59] It may be possible to

---

[50] P Muchlinski, 'Holding Multinationals to Account: Recent Developments in English Litigation and the Company Law Review' 23(6) *The Company Lawyer* 168 (2002) 171. See also Oswald, above n 46, at 260–65.

[51] See, eg, DB Dobbs, *The Law of Torts: Volume 2* (West Group, St Paul, 2001) § 314. However, the distinction between an act and an omission is not always easy to establish. For example, a failure to apply the brakes while driving a car is classified as tortious misfeasance rather than an omission. Indeed, there are no concrete rules for identifying misfeasance from nonfeasance; § 315. See also M Brazier and J Murphy (eds), *The Law of Torts* 10th edn, (London, Butterworths, 1999) 182 and CD Baker et al (ed), *Torts Law in Principle* 3rd edn, (Sydney, Lawbook Co, 2002) ch 8, pp 49–50.

[52] Dobbs, *ibid* at § 322; see also P Giliker and S Beckwith, *Tort* (Sweet & Maxwell, London, 2000) 35–38, and ICHRP, above n 4, at 81.

[53] Natale, above n 49, at 736.

[54] Cassels, above n 1, at 326.

[55] 'Ruling on Defendants' Motion for Summary Judgment, or in the Alternative, Summary Adjudication on each of the Plaintiffs' Tort Claims' [Tort Ruling], Decision of the Superior Court of California, County of Los Angeles, 7 June 2003, available via <http://www.earthrights.org/unocal/index.shtml> (11 September 2003).

[56] *Lopez v McDonald's Corp* 193 Cal App 3d 495 (1987) 515. See also ch 3, n 35.

[57] *Lugtu v California Highway Patrol* 26 Cal 4th 703 (SCt Cal 2001) 716.

[58] See above, ch 2, p 71.

[59] Chaney J recently ruled that Unocal's Mynamar subsidiaries were not its alter egos. However, she 'left the door open for plaintiffs to continue the trial under other theories of liability', such as agency. See, on this latest decision in the State litigation, http://www.earthrights.org/news/unocalupdate.shtml (14 April 2004).

argue in numerous fact situations that a parent's strategic decision to distance itself from its subsidiary and fail to advise it in regard to certain operational matters creates or exacerbates a risk posed by that subsidiary to another person.

The above analysis has focused on parent liability under the tort of negligence for acts perpetrated by their subsidiaries. Many human rights cases against TNCs have involved potentially intentional or at least reckless behaviour. For example, in *Unocal 2002*, recklessness was one basis upon which Reinhardt J determined that Unocal could be liable for the actions of the Myanmar army. The Court was willing at the preliminary stage to conclude that Unocal's subsidiaries in Myanmar were in fact Unocal's alter egos.[60] However, let us assume that Unocal's *legitimate* subsidiary recklessly hired the Myanmar army to perform project tasks. Certainly, it seems in such a situation that Unocal could be held liable for its *actions in promoting* its subsidiary's relationship with the Myanmar military, in reckless disregard of the likely human rights consequences of that relationship. However, it is unlikely that Unocal could be held liable for recklessly *allowing* its subsidiary to engage with the Myanmar government. Again, the difference between actions and omissions could prove crucial to an analysis of direct liability via alleged reckless behaviour.

It will normally be difficult to prove that a corporation has *intended* to cause human rights harm. However, Reinhardt J in *Unocal 2002* indicated that a corporation (Unocal) could be held liable as a joint venturer for torts intentionally committed by its joint venture partner (the Myanmar army) or its agent (again the Myanmar army).[61] However, a court might baulk at holding Unocal so liable if it is found to be insulated from such intentional torts through a legitimate subsidiary.

MULTINATIONAL GROUP LIABILITY

As seen above, the legal principle of corporate separation and consequent limited liability makes it difficult to hold a parent liable for damage caused by its subsidiary's actions. Indirect liability will only be established in the exceptional circumstances where the corporate veil may be pierced, or where agency or another form of joint liability may be established. It seems likely that the veil will also cause courts to hesitate in attributing direct liability to parent corporations, especially with regard to allegations of tortious failures to control their subsidiaries' actions.

Bearing in mind arguments regarding the appropriateness of the extension of limited liability to corporate groups,[62] it seems arguable that limited liability

---

[60] The legitimacy of the corporate separation between Unocal and its subsidiaries will undoubtedly arise as an issue at trial should federal proceedings go that far. See above, n 59, on Chaney J's recent decision in this regard in State proceedings.
[61] *Unocal 2002*, above n 9, at 14258.
[62] See above, text at nn 13–17.

within corporate groups should give way in tort cases (including human rights cases), where the victims are in the position of an 'involuntary creditor'[63] as they have not willingly engaged the corporation in full awareness of its limited liability.[64] From a policy point of view, one might wonder why an involuntary tort (or human rights) victim should bear the cost of his/her injury, rather than a corporate parent who has profited from the actions of its overseas tortfeasor subsidiaries.[65] Perhaps a form of 'multinational group liability' should apply to compensate tort victims in cases where the tortfeasor subsidiary is unable to supply adequate recompense.[66]

The term 'enterprise liability' has been used to describe veil-piercing in the context of holding a corporate parent liable for the acts of its subsidiary. Indeed, it has been argued that the terms are inappropriately confused, and that 'veil piercing' should only apply in the context of holding natural persons accountable for the liabilities of companies in which they are shareholders, with 'enterprise liability' being the appropriate and exclusive term for the situation of exposing a corporate group behind a subsidiary.[67] Enterprise liability is certainly conceptually separate from veil-piercing when an affiliated corporation within a corporate group, rather than an actual parent corporation, is held liable for the acts of another company within the group.[68] Nevertheless, the current principles governing the judicial imposition of enterprise liability are similar, and are similarly vague, to the principles underlying veil-piercing.[69] Therefore, the imposition of enterprise liability is rare, so related corporations are generally protected from liability for each other's acts.[70]

Arguments have been put forward for a more radical concept of enterprise liability, or multinational group liability, whereby limited liability within highly integrated corporate groups is removed, at least in some circumstances such as in imposing tort liability. Such a concept has been supported by Richard Meeran, solicitor in the English cases of *Connelly* and *Lubbe v Cape plc*, who has argued:

> Another way of viewing the issue is to regard the TNC as a conglomeration of units of a single entity, each unit performing a specific function, the function of the parent company being to provide expertise, technology, supervision and finance. Insofar as

---

[63] Muchlinski, above n 50, at 172.
[64] Thompson, above n 18, at 1058–59. See also *Briggs v James Hardie* (1989) 7 ACLC 841 (CA NSW, 28 June 1989) 862–65 per Rogers AJ. See also H Hansmann and R Kraakman, 'Toward Unlimited Shareholder Liability for Corporate Torts' (1991) 100 *Yale Law Journal* 1879, even arguing for the unlimited liability of passive shareholders of public companies for corporate torts.
[65] Muchlinski, above n 50 at 172. See also Blumberg, above n 15, at 135.
[66] Muchlinski, *ibid*; Muchlinski laments that this issue was basically ignored in a recent report on company law reform in the UK by a Company Law Review Steering Group.
[67] Bainbridge, above n 5, at 527–28.
[68] *Ibid* at 526.
[69] *Ibid* at 530–31.
[70] See also Ramsay and Noakes, above n 7, at 257–59.

injuries result from negligence in respect of any of the parent company functions, then the parent should be liable.[71]

Such a concept has also been supported in Argentinian legislation. Article 10 of the Argentinian Draft Code of Private International Law clarifies that TNCs will be regulated 'on the basis of their economic unity and regardless of the legal separation between the various companies within the group'.[72]

A more conservative alternative is that the burden of proof could lie with the corporate group to demonstrate why group liability should not be imposed.[73]

So far, judicial support for such a concept is rare. Multinational group liability was pleaded in the *Union Carbide (Bhopal)* case in both New York and India:

> The complex corporate structure of the multinational, with networks of subsidiaries and divisions, makes it exceedingly difficult or even impossible to pinpoint responsibility for the damage caused by the enterprise to discrete corporate units or individuals. In reality there is but one entity, the monolithic multinational, which is responsible for the design development and dissemination of information and technology worldwide, acting through a neatly designed network of interlocking directors, common operating systems, global distribution and marketing systems, financial and other controls. In this manner, the multinational carries out its global purpose through thousands of daily actions, by a multitude of employees and agents. Persons harmed by the acts of multinational corporation are not in a position to isolate which unit of the enterprise caused the harm, yet it is evident that the multinational enterprise that caused the harm is liable for such harm. *The defendant multinational corporation has to bear this responsibility for it alone had at all material times the means to know and guard against hazards likely to be caused by the operation of the said plant, designed and installed or caused to be installed by it and to provide warnings of potential hazards. The inherent duty of the defendant multinational corporation is to exercise reasonable and effective means to promote safety and assure that information is shared with all sectors of its organisation and with the authorities in the country in which it operates.*[74]

This argument evidently failed in proceedings before Keenan J in New York, who was influenced in his decision to dismiss the case for FNC by the legal distance between the US parent company and its Indian plant.[75] However, Judge Seth of the Madhya Pradesh High Court in India in the *Union Carbide* litigation seemed to agree with the plaintiffs:

---

[71] R Meeran, 'The Unveiling of Transnational Corporations' in Addo, above n 3, at 161, 170. See also Ward, above n 33, at 136–37.

[72] P Muchlinski, *Multinational Enterprises and the Law*, 2nd edn, (Oxford, Blackwell, 1999) 139. The text of Article 10 is reproduced in Muchlinski, at pp 138–39. The text of the whole Draft Code is available at (1985) 24 *International Legal Materials* 269.

[73] See Muchlinski, *ibid* at p 331.

[74] See Union of India's Plaint in *Union of India v Union Carbide*, before the District Court, Bhopal, reprinted in U Baxi and A Dhanda, *Valiant Victims and Lethal Litigation: The Bhopal Case* (Bombay, NV Tripathi Pvt Ltd, 1990) 6, para 19, emphasis added.

[75] See *In re Union Carbide Corp Gas Plant Disaster at Bhopal* 634 F Supp 842 (SDNY 1986).

[T]here is no reason why ... the corporate veil ... cannot be lifted on purely equitable considerations in a case of tort which has resulted in a mass disaster and in which on the face of it the assets of the alleged subsidiary company are utterly insufficient to meet the just claims of multitude [sic] of disaster victims.[76]

Judge Seth endorsed *MC Mehta v Union of India*, where the Supreme Court of India held, in a case concerning a toxic gas emission in Delhi by an Indian public company, that an enterprise engaged in hazardous or inherently dangerous activities owed an 'absolute and non-delegable duty to the community' that no harm would arise from those activities.[77] The *Mehta* principle specifically concerns industries involving hazardous processes, where the consequences of malfeasance can be catastrophic, as in Bhopal, and where Cassels has argued that there is evidence of abuse of the corporate veil, as 'operations have been fragmented and segregated into smaller, thinly capitalised corporations in an effort to avoid liability'.[78]

The *Amoco Cadiz* is another rare example of a court apparently approving of a concept of multinational group liability. In that case, one of the grounds for Standard's direct liability was explained by McGarr J thus:

As an integrated multinational corporation which is engaged through a system of subsidiaries in the exploitation, production, refining, transportation and sale of petroleum products throughout the world, *Standard is responsible for the tortious acts of its wholly owned subsidiaries and instrumentalities* ... .[79]

However, this 'finding of liability against the parent on the basis of integrated management is . . . difficult to reconcile with [other US] authority'.[80] Unfortunately, the parameters of this 'integration liability' are totally unexplained in McGarr J's decision.

---

[76] *Union Carbide v Union of India*, Decision of the Madhya Pradesh High Court at Jabalpur, Civil Revision no 26 of 88, 4 April 1988, reprinted in Baxi and Dhanda, above n 74, at 378–79. It is however uncertain whether Judge Seth was basing his decision on a concept of strict multinational group liability, or on traditional notions of piercing the veil in cases where a parent exercises excessive control over a subsidiary; see Muchlinski, above n 72, at 325–27. The application of Judge Seth's principles in *Union Carbide* did not arise at trial however due to the case suddenly settling without, it must be noted, the consent of the plaintiffs. The Indian *Union Carbide* litigation ceased when the Supreme Court of India, on appeal from an interlocutory order for payment of interim compensation by the Madhya Pradesh High Court, ordered Union Carbide to pay $470 million as a final settlement in damages, due to the urgent need for immediate relief to the victims. This ruling has been severely criticised as grossly inadequate for the purposes of compensating the thousands of Bhopal victims; see, eg, Cassels, above n 1, at 330–31. Nonetheless, the settlement has precluded any further litigation arising out of the Bhopal disaster: see *Bano v Union Carbide Corp* 273 F 3d 120 (2d Cir 2001).

[77] AIR 1987 SC 975, at 1099; see also Cassels, *ibid* at 327.

[78] Cassels, *ibid* at 323. A corporation's undercapitalisation is of course a common reason for a court deciding to pierce its veil.

[79] [1984] 2 Lloyd's Rep 304 (ND Ill 1984) 338, emphasis added.

[80] Muchlinski, above n 72, at 325; see also n 12 therein, citing numerous US cases (eg *Moffat v Goodyear Tyre and Rubber Co* 652 SW 2d 609 (Tex Ct App 1983); *Grywczynski v Shasta Beverages Inc* 606 F Supp 61 (ND Cal 1984)) where the 'integrated nature' of a corporate group was insufficient to 'ground parent liability for the tortious acts of its subsidiary'. See also *Bowoto v Chevron Texaco Corp* No C 99–2506 SI, 2004 US Dist LEXIS 4603 (ND, Cal 2004), *17–*19.

It seems very likely that arguments regarding multinational group liability or enterprise liability will be further developed in arguments and judgments in transnational human rights litigation.

MULTINATIONAL ECONOMIC NETWORKS

Many allegations of human rights abusive behaviour by TNCs concern the direct actions of an entity with strong contractual links to a TNC, rather than those of a subsidiary. For example, the allegations by human rights activists against Nike and other garment companies have typically concerned working conditions in factories run by their suppliers.[81] Just as municipal laws tend to ignore the fact that subsidiaries and parent corporations are often part of the same 'firm', municipal laws tend to treat contractual partners as entities separated by a contractual veil, 'the "network" counterpart of . . . the corporate veil',[82] without necessarily inquiring into the level of control exercised by a dominant contract partner (eg a TNC) over a weaker partner (eg a supplier dependent upon the custom of that corporation). Contractual partners may in reality be an intrinsic part of a multination economic network.[83] As is the situation with the issue of parent liability for subsidiary activity, transnational human rights litigation against TNCs will likely in the future force the courts of a number of jurisdictions to confront the issue of whether the formation of principles beyond those which presuppose an ordinary degree of entity separation (eg. ordinary joint tortfeasor principles) is necessary to deal with the phenomenon of abuses caused within multinational economic networks, where such entity separation is often not the reality.[84]

In *Sinaltrainal v Coca Cola*,[85] the plaintiffs alleged that two companies, Coca Cola US and its subsidiary Coca Cola Colombia, were responsible for the actions of their contractual partner, a small bottling company Bebidas, which was run by Kirby and his son Kielland. It was further alleged that Kirby, Kielland, and Bebidas were liable for the murder of Isidro Segundo Gil, a trade union leader who had been attempting to organise employees at Bebidas' bottling plant in Carepa, Colombia, where Bebidas was performing contractual

---

[81] See M Davies, 'Just (don't) do it: Ethics and International Trade' (1997) 21 *Melbourne University Law Review* 601, 614–20.
[82] Muchlinski, above n 72, at 327.
[83] See also *ibid* at 62–65.
[84] See also *ibid*, at 327, n 24, citing Gunther Teubner, 'The Many-Headed Hydra: Networks as Higher-Order Collective Actors' in J McCahery, S Picciotto and C Scott (eds), *Corporate Control and Accountability* (Oxford, Clarendon Press, 1993) 41. See also International Restructuring Education Network Europe (IRENE), *Lawsuits against Multinational Corporations for Labor Rights Violations* (Amsterdam, copy on file with the author, September 2002) at 24.
[85] 256 F Supp 2d 1345 (SD Fla 2003).

work for the Coca Cola companies.[86] Thus, ATCA claims for the killing were brought against all three companies, as well as Kirby and Kielland. The court ultimately dismissed the case against the two Coca Cola companies after examining the Bottlers' Agreement between those two companies and Bebidas. The contract was a typical franchise agreement, which gave Coca Cola rights regarding the protection of its product in the marketplace (eg quality control, use of trademark, etc).[87] The Agreement did not impose upon Coca Cola 'a duty to monitor, enforce or control labour policies at' Bebidas.[88] Thus, the *Sinaltrainal* District Court was unwilling to look behind the contract to examine whether Coca Cola's control over Bebidas was more extreme than formally recorded in the contract. This case indicates that it will be difficult to hold TNCs liable for the actions of their private commercial contractual partners.[89]

CONCLUSION

The intersection between company law principles, which dictate corporate/shareholder separation even in the context of multinational groups, contract principles (regarding separation and allocation of responsibilities within multinational economic networks), and tort principles, which dictate that people should take reasonable care that others are not damaged by actions over which they have control, has yet to be clarified. It is likely that transnational human rights litigation involving corporations will eventually force courts across a number of jurisdictions to confront these issues.

---

[86] It was alleged that Bebidas conspired with paramilitary groups to murder Gil; those paramilitary groups in turn were apparently sanctioned by the Colombian government. Thus, State action was pleaded on the facts. See above, ch 2, pp 33–39, on the state action requirement in ATCA cases.
[87] *Sinaltrainal v Coca Cola* 256 F Supp 2d 1345 (SD Fla 2003) 1354.
[88] *Ibid*.
[89] ATCA and TVPA actions were permitted to proceed against Bebidas and its directors. On the other hand, the legal separation between a corporation and its subcontractors can facilitate action under RICO, as was the case in *Doe v The Gap* No CV–01–0031, 2001 WL 1842389 (DN Mar I Nov 6, CD Cal 2001). A RICO claim was dismissed in *Sinaltrainal*; see ch 3, n 102.

8
Conclusion

SUMMARY OF CURRENT LITIGATION

Human rights victims are increasingly seeking recompense against TNCs in the courts of those TNCs' home states. This increased litigation activity has not yet yielded any merits decisions. Hence, certain important issues, such as the extent to which courts will be prepared to pierce the corporate or contractual veil, or to accept arguments regarding direct parent corporation liability, are unresolved. The lack of merits decisions is because cases have been delayed or halted by preliminary litigation concerning various jurisdictional and procedural issues. If a plaintiff succeeds on these preliminary points, cases have tended to settle.[1] However, a number of cases have apparently made it through some important barricades, and, barring appeals and/or settlements, will proceed to trial. Below is a summary of the most important developments to date in transnational human rights litigation against corporations.

A number of ATCA cases have emerged since Paez J's seminal decision in *Doe v Unocal* (*Unocal 1997*). Subject matter jurisdiction under ATCA is available when the human rights abuse at issue is prohibited by the law of nations, which generally means that it is proscribed by customary international law. The courts have generally found that a law will breach the law of nations if it is definable, obligatory, and 'universally' (or rather, generally) condemned. Some courts however have taken a more flexible approach, and have recognised that, while a particular right may not, in all of its manifestations, have universal recognition, 'core' abuses of that right may nonetheless activate ATCA.

Though US courts have acknowledged that the 'law of nations' prohibits certain abuses in the absence of state action, most such breaches are not actionable without governmental involvement. Thus, plaintiffs usually have to establish the joint responsibility for a human rights abuse of a government (where the corporation directly commits the alleged abuse, as in *Abdullahi v Pfizer*) or the corporation (where the government directly commits the abuses, as in *Doe v*

---

[1] P Muchlinski, 'Holding Multinationals to Account: Recent Developments in English Litigation and the Company Law Review' 23(6) *The Company Lawyer* 168 (2002) commenting on the English cases. Uprendra Baxi has wryly suggested that TNCs opt for settlements to avert any 'precedent-creating effects'. See U Baxi, 'Geographies of Injustice: Human Rights at the Altar of Convenience' in C Scott (ed), *Torture as Tort* (Oxford, Hart Publishing, 2001) 197, 209, n 46.

Unocal). The notoriously unwieldy §1983 principles have been the main tool used by courts for the purposes of preliminary proceedings to establish such joint responsibility, though ordinary tort principles or international criminal law standards are arguably more appropriate tests. It is fair to say that the law regarding complicity under ATCA is in a state of flux.

As ATCA cases often involve the actions of foreign governments, certain principles of abstention associated with such litigation are often relevant, notably the doctrines of act of state, political question, and comity. Ordinarily, considering the seriousness of the abuses alleged in ATCA cases, the doctrines are not applicable. However, the recent objections by the US State Department to ATCA litigation in *Rio Tinto* and *Exxon* evince a new hostility by the current US government to such litigation, which increases the threat posed to plaintiffs by these abstention doctrines in the USA.

At the time of writing, a challenge was pending before the US Supreme Court regarding the interpretation of ATCA, and its constitutionality. It is possible that the Supreme Court could decide that ATCA is merely jurisdictional, and therefore of no modern-day effect, or that it is unconstitutional. Either decision would put a stop to ATCA litigation against companies. There was also a possibility of the US Congress repealing ATCA, or amending it so as to remove corporate liability thereunder. However, the removal or emasculation of ATCA will not stop human rights litigation against companies. Alternative causes of action also exist.

For example, the TVPA could likely provide an alternative basis for actions against TNCs regarding claims of torture and/or extra-judicial killings. RICO is another US statute that might prove very effective in combating certain corporate transnational human rights abuses, especially considering that the corporate veil could actually *facilitate* such liability, in light of the Supreme Court decision in *Cedric Kushner*. Alternative causes of action against TNCs for transnational human rights litigants have also been based on §1331 jurisdiction (as in *Bodner v Banque Paribas*), which might provide a wholesale replacement for ATCA if the latter should be 'struck down'.

Importantly, claims may be based on ordinary tort principles applied in an extraterritorial context (as in *Union Carbide*, *Aguinda v Texaco*, and *Martinez v Dow Chemicals*). These causes of action are particularly important as numerous 'human rights' causes of action fall outside the above-mentioned US statutes. In particular, tort claims can provide an action for human rights abuses that fall short of customary norms, and which are committed without the involvement of a government.

Common law tort principles have been the only source of the salient causes of action utilised outside the USA (eg *Connelly v RTZ*, *Lubbe v Cape Plc*, *Dagi v BHP*), where there are no ATCA equivalents. Other potential avenues for transnational litigation in those countries, such as common law claims based on customary human rights law in England and Canada, are unexplored apart from abortive attempts in *Bouzari v Islamic Republic of Iran* and (in a non-corporate context) *Al-Adsani v Government of Kuwait*.

Personal jurisdiction may be exercised over a corporation in common law jurisdictions if it is a national of or if it 'does business' within those forums. The issue of personal jurisdiction has arisen in a number of ATCA cases against non-US corporations, yielding results which are ambiguous, considering the differing results in *Doe v Unocal (Unocal 1998)* and *Wiwa v Royal Dutch Petroleum (Wiwa 2000)* (with the latter followed by *Presbyterian Church v Talisman*); such ambiguity is inherent in the vague 'doing business' requirement. The rules regarding extraterritorial jurisdiction in England, the Australian states, and possibly Canada seem more lenient than in the US, given the lack of strict constitutional due process requirements.

A formidable procedural hurdle for almost all transnational human rights litigants, unless their case has been dismissed for another reason, has been the doctrine of *forum non conveniens* (FNC). The earliest cases against Union Carbide, Texaco, and Dow Chemicals, were almost all dismissed for FNC. With the ATCA cases, the plaintiffs have been far more successful in staving off dismissal. The lesser vulnerability of ATCA cases to FNC may be explained by a number of factors. First, courts since *Bridgeway Corp v Citibank* have openly used State Department human rights reports in evaluating whether alternative forums are in fact adequate. As ATCA cases are more likely than ordinary tort cases to involve allegations of foreign government collusion in particularly egregious human rights abuses, courts are probably more likely to find the alternative forum to be either too corrupt to be adequate (eg *Eastman Kodak v Kavlin, Wiwa v Royal Dutch Petroleum (Wiwa 2002)*), or too dangerous for the plaintiff when balancing private interests (eg *Sarei v Rio Tinto*). Second, *Wiwa 2000* has realigned the public interests factors in all TVPA cases and at least some ATCA cases in favour of plaintiffs. *Bowoto v Chevron* (2000), in its reasoning that US States have a public interest in regulating their own companies, provides an as yet unreferenced precedent with an even broader potential impact.

Furthermore, *Martinez v Dow Chemicals*, the latest case in the DBCP saga, could herald a change in fortune for transnational human rights litigants in the USA pursuing ordinary tort claims, having recently survived an FNC challenge. Barbier J used State Department reports to find two of the alternative forums to be inadequate. All three putative alternative forums were in any case unavailable due to the existence of retaliatory legislation. Such legislation could have a profound effect on FNC arguments in the future.

FNC has also been a major issue in the relevant English cases. English courts have recently taken a more humanitarian stance in dismissing FNC applications in *Connelly* and *Lubbe*, on the grounds that the alternative forums were simply unable to offer a just resolution to the cases. An even greater revolution may ensue in England, if the European Court of Justice should declare the FNC doctrine to be contrary to EU law in all cases.

In the Australian case of *Dagi v BHP*, FNC was not even raised by the defendant, probably due to the narrow scope of FNC in Australia after *Voth v*

Manildra Flour Mill. Indeed, the *Renault* decision indicates that FNC may have been effectively abolished in cases where the defendant is an Australian, and has been substantially abridged in cases where the plaintiff is an Australian resident.

IS TRANSNATIONAL HUMAN RIGHTS LITIGATION AGAINST TNCS 'A GOOD THING'?

This book has been largely concerned with analyzing the legal consequences of the salient developments. In this section, I comment on the desirability of these developments.

Judicial imperialism in the form of developed nations passing judgment over actions within the proper jurisdiction of developing nations has been raised as a reason why transnational human rights litigation should be discouraged. For example, Keenan J stated that retention of jurisdiction in New York in *Union Carbide* would be imperialistic.[2] However, this comment is strange given that the defendant was a US corporation located down the road from the courthouse;[3] a state's exercise of jurisdiction over its own corporate nationals does not classify as undue interference with another state's sovereignty. Indeed, Ward has persuasively argued that home countries have a moral obligation to 'accept a role in promoting good behaviour on the part of "their" multinationals when they invest in other countries' because 'the profits of multinationals are taxed in home countries and form part of the home country's gross domestic product'.[4]

In any case, Keenan J's contention was ironic given that the Government of India as plaintiff argued before Keenan J *against* FNC dismissal.[5] Furthermore, the existence of retaliatory legislation in a number of Latin American countries, which has been designed to thwart FNC dismissals in cases such as the DBCP litigation, challenges the notion that developing nations do not approve of such cases being heard in the TNC's home country. Sometimes such countries believe it is incumbent upon Western courts to clean up the mess created by Western TNCs.

It has been argued that transnational human rights litigation retards the development and capacity of the legal systems of host countries, particularly

---

[2] 634 F Supp 842 (SDNY 1986) 867; see also Baxi, *ibid* at 205.
[3] See U Baxi, *Mass Torts, Multinational Enterprise Liability, and Private International Law*, 1999 Hague Academy Lectures, 276 *Recueil des Cours* 305 (The Hague, Martinus Nijhoff, 2000), cited in Baxi, *ibid* at 207.
[4] H Ward 'Towards a New Convention on Corporate Accountability? Some Lessons from the Thor Chemicals and Cape Plc cases' [2002] *Yearbook of International Environmental Law* 105, 140.
[5] See Baxi, above n 1, at 205, and also P Prince, 'Bhopal, Bougainville and Ok Tedi: Why Australia's Forum non Conveniens Approach is Better' (1998) 47 *International and Comparative Law Quarterly* 573, 576–77. Similarly, the government of South Africa argued in *Lubbe v Cape Plc* [2000] 4 All ER 268 (HL) that it preferred that the case be settled in the UK; see also Ward, *ibid* at 132, 140.

developing nations, to address rogue TNC activity.[6] This is an important consideration as local remedies are far more accessible to local human rights victims than transnational remedies. But there are too many instances where local remedies are simply not available, or are illusory. Human rights victims should not be denied redress simply because of their geographic location.

To be sure, there are undeniable human rights benefits in building up the capacities of all courts throughout the world to enforce the rule of law. However, transnational human rights litigation does not preclude the commencement of local litigation in the host country, particularly by a different plaintiff, even on similar facts.[7] Indeed, the existence of parallel local proceedings is a factor that can sway a court to dismiss a transnational case for FNC.[8] The conclusion of such 'local' proceedings in a manner in which justice is perceived to be done will also influence transnational courts in future relevant FNC applications, in that a 'just' result will provide evidence in future transnational litigation that the relevant forum is 'adequate'.[9]

Furthermore, enforcement of a local judgment against a TNC will often depend on the courts in the jurisdiction where their major assets are located, often the TNC's home state. For example, Keenan J's effective sending of the *Union Carbide* case to India may have put the Bhopal plaintiffs in a no-win situation. An appropriate award of compensation depended on a finding of liability against the US parent, UCC. Such a finding may have been likely in India given its endorsement of strict multinational enterprise liability if the case had not settled.[10] Baxi has cogently suggested that a judgment based on such a radical principle could have been deemed repugnant to US law, thus preventing enforcement against UCC of any Indian damages award in the US forum in which most of its assets were located.[11] In such a case, 'judicial imperialism' would have prevailed anyway; the Indian decision would only have been enforced had a standard of justice been applied to UCC that was acceptable to the USA.[12] Indeed, one may note that a US$489 million award against Shell Chemical, Dow Chemical, and Standard Fruit Company by a Nicaraguan court

---

[6] See F Schrage, 'Judging Corporate Accountability in the Global Economy' (2003) 42 *Columbia Journal of Transnational Law* 153, 165–66.

[7] The relevant cases almost always involve multiple potential plaintiff human rights victims.

[8] See ch 4, n 78, regarding the initial dismissal of the case in *Abdullahi v Pfizer* No 01 Civ 8118, 2002 US Dist LEXIS 17436 (SDNY 2002), where parallel proceedings had already commenced in Nigeria.

[9] Note that the Circuit Court in *Abdullahi v Pfizer* No 01 Civ 8118, 2002 US Dist LEXIS 17436 (SDNY 2002) has remitted the case to the District Court to investigate whether the concluded proceedings in Nigeria were indeed fair. See ch 4, n 57.

[10] See ch 7, pp 140–41 on the endorsement of enterprise liability, and at n 76 regarding the settlement.

[11] Baxi, above n 1, at 209; see also K Hofstetter, 'Multinational Enterprise Parent Liability: Efficient Legal Regimes in a World Market Environment' (1990) 15 *North Carolina Journal of International Law and Commercial Regulation* 299, 300; and P Muchlinski, *Multinational Enterprises and the Law*, 2nd edn (Oxford, Blackwell, 1999) 332. The broader issue regarding enforcement of foreign judgments is beyond the scope of this book.

[12] Baxi, above n 1, at 209.

in another chapter of the DBCP litigation was held to be unenforceable by a Californian federal court in October 2003.[13]

Of course, affected foreign governments do presumably disapprove of such proceedings on occasion, particularly in ATCA cases where governments, such as those in Myanmar, Indonesia, and Papua New Guinea, are accused of gross human rights abuses in collaboration with corporate partners. In response, one may note that states cannot themselves be exposed to liability due to the sovereign immunity doctrine. In those circumstances, judicial pronouncements are no more nor less 'imperialistic' than the criticisms frequently issued by the executive or the legislature of a foreign government's human rights practices. Human rights criticism per se is not imperialistic, but is in fact the main means by which international human rights law is actually enforced.[14]

Perhaps it is unfair to TNCs for them to be subjected to forum-shopping in the law of their home state, or a state in which they do business, rather than the laws of the country in which they are operating.[15] However, TNCs themselves have shopped around for the best investment conditions, simultaneously promoting a 'race to the bottom' in developing countries, for example, in terms of environmental and labor standards.[16] Forum-shopping is the flipside of the jurisdiction-shopping of TNCs; should not both TNCs and their apparent victims be able to play the game of globalisation? The orthodoxy which promotes the unique freedom from regulation for TNCs, in that their various components which usually operate as a single economic entity are not regulated by the laws of any single state, enabling the apportionment of legal responsibility according to least risk without any concern for humanitarian consequences, is unsatisfactory.[17] Economic globalisation, which generally confers huge benefits on TNCs, should be accompanied by the imposition of transnational responsibilities by a parallel globalisation of law.[18] In this respect, it is poignant to add that the putative forum-shoppers in the salient cases are innocent people who have been severely hurt by TNCs, and who are probably unable to receive appropriate recompense in the forum where the injury occurred.[19] The 'intolerable double

---

[13] 'Nicaragua: Pesticide Claim Dismissed', *New York Times* (New York, United States, 25 October 2003). The author is unable to clarify the reason for this decision, as the case is not reported.

[14] HJ Steiner and P Alston, *International Human Rights in Context: Law, Politics, Morals: Text and Materials*, 2nd edn (New York, Oxford University Press, 2000) 366.

[15] See, eg, DJ Doward, 'The Forum non Conveniens Doctrine and the Judicial Protection of Multinational Corporations from Forum Shopping Plaintiffs' (1998) 19 *University of Pennsylvania Journal of International Economic Law* 141.

[16] See MJ Rogge, 'Towards Transnational Corporate Liability in the Global Economy: Challenging the Doctrine of Forum non Conveniens in Re: Union Carbide, Alfaro, Sequihua, and Aguinda' (2001) 26 *Texas International Law Journal* 299, 314–17; see also Ward, above n 4, at 109.

[17] M Anderson, 'Transnational Corporations and Environmental Damage: Is Tort Law the Answer?' (2002) 41 *Washburn Law Journal* 399, 401–2.

[18] See also H Ward, 'Securing Transnational Corporate Accountability through National Courts: Implications and Policy Options' (2001) 24 *Hastings International and Comparative Law Review* 451, 454, characterising calls for foreign direct liability as 'the flip side of foreign direct investment'.

[19] See also Baxi, above n 1, at 204.

standard' that denies victims in the developing world but not the developed world relief from severe corporate maltreatment should not continue.[20]

Perhaps the most compelling argument against transnational human rights litigation against TNCs is that it may threaten foreign direct investment in the developing world, and therefore impact detrimentally on economic growth and consequent poverty alleviation in developing countries.[21] Transnational human rights litigation should not be used as a protectionist means of stunting legitimate comparative advantages that other nations might have.[22] For example, it is certainly acceptable for cheaper labor to be available in countries with lower costs of living. However, gross human rights and environmental abuses are *not necessary* in order to stoke economic development. Economic development does not legitimise the orchestration of or acquiescence in gross human rights abuses, or impunity for catastrophic acts of negligence.

LITIGATION PRESSURE WILL INCREASE

Regardless of the pros and cons of transnational human rights litigation, the truth is that it is unlikely to disappear.[23] Litigants have proven resilient, for example filing similar cases in the Texaco and DBCP sagas in successive US forums after dismissal in a previous forum. This tactic appears to have finally borne fruit in the *Martinez* DBCP case in a Louisiana District Court.

Moreover, the legal pressure is likely to increase. Legislation designed to impose extraterritorial human rights responsibilities on home corporations has been introduced in both the USA, UK and Australia.[24] Though none of these Bills have been passed, their proposal reflects a growing concern with the apparent impunity of TNCs regarding human rights, which will undoubtedly generate further attempts at legislative reform.

---

[20] See Ralph G Steinhardt, *Litigating Corporate Responsibility*, 1 June 2001, Global Dimensions Seminar, New York City, <http://www.lse.ac.uk/collections/globalDimensions/seminars/humanRightsAndCorporateResponsibility/steinhardtTranscript.htm> (20 October 2002). See also Baxi, above n 1, at 204, pointing out how a US court was eager to 'accomplish justice' for the US victims of Agent Orange, in a class action brought by Vietnam War veterans against the manufacturer of Agent Orange, even though the impugned events took place in Vietnam (North and South) and Cambodia. See *In Re: Agent Orange Product Liability Litigation* 580 F Supp 690 (EDNY 1984) 707–9 (though the discussion there concerned choice of law rather than forum non conveniens). Such eagerness was notably missing with regard to the Indian plaintiffs in the contemporaneous *Union Carbide* litigation. It will be instructive to see how US courts treat a new case filed by Vietnamese victims of Agent Orange against the manufacturers of the defoliant. See, 'More Vietnamese join Lawsuit against US Chemical Companies', *Vietnam News Briefs*, 29 March 2004.
[21] See GC Hufbauer and NK Mitrokostas, *Awakening the Monster: The Alien Tort Statute of 1789* (Washington DC, Institute of International Economics, 2003) 42–43.
[22] See S Joseph, 'Taming the Leviathans: Multinational Enterprises and Human Rights' (1999) 46 *Netherlands International Law Review* 171, 192–97.
[23] See also Schrage, above n 6, at 156 and 162–63.
[24] See *Corporate Code of Conduct Bill 2001* (US); *Corporate Code of Conduct Bill 2000* (Cth); *Corporate Responsibility Bill 2003* (UK). See, generally, A McBeth, 'A Look at Corporate Code of Conduct Legislation' (2004) *Common Law World Review*, forthcoming.

New avenues of transnational human rights litigation against TNCs will likely be forged, as has recently occurred in the *Nike* case. For example, cases could potentially be brought in civil law states against home corporations,[25] especially given that there is no doctrine of FNC in such nations.[26] France is currently investigating a complaint by Burmese refugees against TotalFinaElf regarding use of forced labor in Myanmar, which could potentially evolve into a criminal prosecution against that corporation for transnational human rights abuses.[27] Plaintiffs could start targeting company directors in their individual capacity, if issues such as the corporate veil or personal jurisdiction should prove insurmountable.[28] Though liability would then only attach to an individual, a TNC would be put under enormous 'pressure to assume responsibility and indemnify individuals', 'in order to recruit and retain its overseas executive force'.[29] Individual executive officers have in fact been sued along with their companies in *Unocal* and *Wiwa*. Numerous other potential tactics have been described in academic journals but may be on their way to court registration offices. These tactics may include: equitable claims of 'unjust enrichment' by, for example, dispossessed indigenous groups;[30] claims of unfair competition entailed by one corporation benefiting from unconscionable human rights abuse viz a competitor who does not;[31] and corporate law proceedings to dissolve a

---

[25] Civil law states rarely permit litigation against a foreign corporation simply on the basis that it is 'doing business' in the forum; B Stephens, 'Translating Filartiga: A Comparative and International Law Analysis of Domestic Remedies for International Human Rights Violations' (2002) 27 *Yale Journal of International Law* 1, 24.

[26] See, for discussion of the possibility of such cases in the Netherlands, G Betlem, 'Transnational Litigation against Multinational Corporations before Dutch Civil Courts' in M Kamminga and S Zia-Zarifi (eds), *Liability of Multinational Corporations under International Law* (The Hague, Kluwer Law International, 2000) 283–305. However, see ch 1, pp 15–16.

[27] See See H Ward, *Legal Issues in Corporate Citizenship*, Swedish Partnership for Global Responsibility, February 2003 <www.iied.org/docs/cred/legalissues_corporate.pdf> (29 December 2003) 17. A similar action in Belgium may have to be dropped as the relevant Belgian law, conferring universal jurisdiction over Belgian courts for universal crimes, has been amended so as to only apply to Belgian citizens. See 'Universal Incompetence' *The Economist* (New York, United States, 28 June 2003) 54.

[28] Tag jurisdiction, ie the service of a person within jurisdiction, is available in common law countries to establish personal jurisdiction over individuals.

[29] PI Blumberg, 'Accountability of Multinational Corporations: The Barriers Presented by Concepts of the Corporate Juridical Entity' (2001) 24 *Hastings International and Comparative Law Review* 297, 316–17. See also Ward, above n 4, at 141–42.

[30] See DN Fagan, 'Achieving Restitution: The Potential Unjust Enrichment Claims of Indigenous Peoples Against Multinational Corporations' (2001) 76 *New York University Law Review* 626. Indeed, a claim of unjust enrichment has been made against Unocal under Californian State law, see plaintiffs' complaint, available via <http://www.earthrights.org/unocal/index.shtml> (4 September 2003).

[31] Such a claim has been made in *Doe v Unocal* before the Superior Court of California. Chaney J in the Superior Court of California refused to dismiss this claim summarily, finding it 'viable': see 'Ruling on Defendants' Motion for Summary Judgment, or in the Alternative, Summary Adjudication on each of the Plaintiffs' Tort Claims' [Tort Ruling], Decision of the Superior Court of California, County of Los Angeles, 7 June 2003, available via <www.earthrights.org/unocal/index.shtml> (11 September 2003).

company on the basis that it has acted *ultra vires* or has abused the public trust by engaging in persistent breaches of international human rights law.[32]

THE LIMITS OF TRANSNATIONAL HUMAN RIGHTS LITIGATION AGAINST COMPANIES

Of course, transnational human rights litigation against corporations is no panacea to the human rights problems arising from TNC activity. Most notably, there have not yet been any relevant merits decisions. It is obvious that such litigation is time-consuming, and there is no guarantee of eventual success. Not all TNCs are vulnerable to such litigation; vulnerability depends on their nationality and places of operation. Most human rights victims, particularly in the developing world, are unable to access legal remedies abroad. Moreover, the human rights abuses caught within this litigation represent only the tip of an iceberg. Finally, litigation focuses on punishing the bad, rather than rewarding the good; litigation per se offers no incentive for companies to adopt 'best practices' with regard to human rights which are far better than those that can realistically be mandated by law. Therefore, transnational litigation should be only one of a number of strategies aimed at lessening the instances of TNC human rights abuses, or promoting good TNC behaviour. As mentioned in Chapter 1, alternative strategies include domestic litigation, NGO and consumer pressure, the promotion of socially responsible investment, and self-regulation.

AN INTERNATIONAL APPROACH?

The salient cases have one common theme: TNCs are accused of breaching internationally recognised human rights in developing nations. In the absence of strong international human rights law enforcement, domestic litigation in developed nations provides a powerful avenue for human rights vindication.

Ultimately, a preferable approach might be for all nations to agree on international minimum human rights standards for TNCs,[33] which could be incorporated into national legislation and enforced by domestic courts.[34] Proposed

[32] Steinhardt, above n 20. See also J Nolan, *Research Summary Report: prepared as part of the Monash Global Initiative's project on Corporate Social Responsibility* (copy on file with the author, December 2003) 17, suggesting that the fiduciary duty of directors to act in the best interests of a company may have evolved to incorporate duties to at least take account of human rights and environmental issues when making company decisions; see also ch 5, n 66.
[33] Hofstetter, above n 11, at 323–24.
[34] Perhaps a long term aim could be the creation of international tribunals to interpret and apply such standards. In the short term however, interpretation and application of such standards would preferably take place in domestic forums, which have far superior powers of enforcement. It is beyond the scope of this book to discuss the circumstances in which a domestic court should have jurisdiction (eg territorial jurisdiction, nationality jurisdiction) to enforce such standards against a TNC.

Conclusion

lists of international corporate human rights duties do exist, the most advanced being the UN Norms on Responsibilities of Transnational Corporations and Other Business Enterprises with Regard to Human Rights', adopted by the Sub-Commission on the Promotion and Protection of Human Rights in 2003.[35] Enforceable uniform standards would cure the unevenness which will result from transnational decisions binding certain corporations but not others (due to personal jurisdiction issues), and 'would presumably be more or appear more sensitive to legitimate cultural and economic differences'.[36] Currently, fear of competitive disadvantage is surely constraining the efforts of some companies to respect human rights standards. TNCs might hesitate for example to respect decent labour standards if such a practice enables a competitor to undercut their prices and gain market share by ignoring those standards. Uniform international principles would help to eliminate competitive advantages gained by unscrupulous TNCs over their more ethical competitors. TNCs would also benefit from greater clarity and consistency in their global responsibilities, and protection from the unilateral adoption in some forums of 'overly aggressive and idiosyncratic' approaches to TNCs' human rights duties.[37] Though states would be free to demand higher standards for corporate behaviour within their own territories, the existence of enforceable international minimums would provide a powerful moral argument against the application by domestic courts of higher standards in an extraterritorial context. Perhaps the proliferation of transnational human rights cases against TNCs is the catalyst needed to generate the political and commercial will to create new international human rights laws to govern commercial actors.

---

[35] United Nations, *United Nations Norms on the Responsibilities of Transnational Corporations and Other Enterprises with Regard to Human Rights*, UN doc E/CN/.4/Sub.2/2003/12/Rev.2 (2003). See ch 1, pp 10–11.
[36] Joseph, above n 22, at 185.
[37] Steinhardt, above n 20.

Appendix: Table of Selected Cases

Case name	Stage	Reference	Jurisdiction	Synopsis
Abdullahi v Pfizer	Motion to dismiss	No 01 Civ 8118, 2002 US Dist LEXIS 17436 (SDNY 2002)	US District Court for the Southern District of New York	Medical experimentation without informed consent held to be a violation of the law of nations which therefore activates ATCA. Case dismissed for FNC as Nigeria was a more appropriate forum.
Abdullahi v Pfizer	Appeal against dismissal	Nos 02-9223(L), 02-9303 (XAP) (2d Cir 2003)	US Court of Appeals for the Second Circuit	Case remitted back to the District Court on the question of whether recent dismissal of proceedings in Nigeria was evidence that Nigeria was a corrupt forum.
Abrams v Societe Nationale Des Chemins de fer Francais	Motion to Dismiss	175 F Supp 2d 423 (EDNY 2001)	US District Court for the Eastern District of New York	Holocaust survivors sued French rail co for violating ATCA in deporting French Jews to concentration camps. Case dismissed for sovereign immunity.
Abrams v Societe Nationale Des Chemins de fer Francais	Appeal against dismissal	332 F 3d 173 (2d Cir 2003)	US Court of Appeals for the Second Circuit	Case remitted back to the District Court, to decide if sovereign immunity statute has a constitutionally impermissible retroactive effect on plaintiffs' rights.
Abu-Zeineh v Federal Laboratories Inc	Motion to dismiss	975 F Supp 774 (WD Pa 1994)	US District Court for the Western District of Pennsylvania	Claim by Palestinians regarding the deaths of family members from CS gas sold to Israel by the defendants was dismissed, as the plaintiffs were stateless, and therefore did not have foreign citizenship for the purposes of diversity jurisdiction.
Aguinda v Texaco	Motion to dismiss	945 F Supp 625 (SDNY 1996)	US District Court for the Southern District of New York	Claims by Peruvian and Ecuadorian national against oil company dismissed for FNC.

Appendix: Table of Selected Cases

Case name	Stage	Reference	Jurisdiction	Synopsis
Aguinda v Texaco	Motion to dismiss (See also *Jota v Texaco* below)	142 F Supp 2d 534 (SDNY 2001)	US District Court for the Southern District of New York	Peruvian and Ecuadorian nationals sued oil company for property damage, personal injury and risk of disease from negligent pipeline management under ATCA and tort law. Cases dismissed on FNC grounds. Judge suggested claims of environmental damage were unlikely to activate ATCA.
Aguinda v Texaco	Appeal against dismissal	303 F 3d 470 (2d 2002)	US Court of Appeals for the Second Circuit	Affirmed decision of the District Court.
Al-Adsani v Government of Kuwait	Appeal against decision of immunity	[1996] TLR 192 (CA)	UK Court of Appeal	Case against government of Kuwait for breach of customary international law, entailed in alleged acts of torture; dismissed for sovereign immunity.
Al Odah v United States	Appeal against dismissal	321 F 3d 1134 (DC Cir 2003)	US Court of Appeals for the District of Columbia Circuit	Case concerning validity under, inter alia, ATCA of the detention of certain detainees by the US government in Guantanamo Bay, pursuant to the 'war on terror'. Case dismissed on various grounds. Randolph J rejected the broad *Filartiga* interpretation of ATCA.
Alomang v Freeport-McMoran	Appeal against dismissal	811 So 2d 98 (La App 2002)	Louisiana Court of Appeal	Indonesian nationals sued mining company for cultural genocide, environmental damage and human rights abuses under State equivalent of ATCA. Appeal denied because plaintiffs failed to prove defendant was the alter ego of Indonesian subsidiary.
Amlon Metals v FMC Corp	Appeal against dismissal	775 F Supp 668 (SDNY 1991)	US District Court for the Southern District of New York	Court found that transboundary environmental harms do not give rise to ATCA claims.

Appendix: Table of Selected Cases 157

Baker v Carr	Application for declaration	369 US 186 (SCt 1962)	US Supreme Court Seminal US case on the 'political question' doctrine.
Banco Nacional de Cuba v Sabbatino	Appeal against judgment	376 US 398 (SCt 1964)	US Supreme Court Seminal US case on the 'act of state' doctrine.
Bano v Union Carbide	Appeal against dismissal	273 F 3d 120 (2d Cir 2001)	US Court of Appeals for the Second Circuit	Claim for intrastate environmental harm held to come under diversity jurisdiction. Claims arising out of Bhopal disaster dismissed, due to settlement in India.
Bano v Union Carbide	Motion to dismiss	2003 WL 1344884 (SDNY 2003)	US District Court for the Southern District of New York	Case for intrastate environmental harm dismissed on statute of limitation grounds.
Bano v Union Carbide	Appeal against dismissal	2004 WL 516238 (2d cir, 2004)	US Court of Appeals for the Second Circuit	Claims relating to property damage reinstated and remitted to lower court
Beanal v Freeport-McMoran Inc	Motion to dismiss	969 F Supp 362 (ED La 1997)	US District Court for the Eastern District of Louisiana	Mining company sued under ATCA for cultural genocide and gross environmental abuse in Indonesia. Claims held not to activate ATCA. Held also that TVPA only binds individuals, not corporations.
Beanal v Freeport-McMoran Inc	Appeal against dismissal	197 F 3d 161 (5th Cir 1999)	US Court of Appeals for the Fifth Circuit	Court of Appeal upholds the district court decision, but makes no decision regarding the TVPA.

158 *Appendix: Table of Selected Cases*

Case name	Stage	Reference	Jurisdiction	Synopsis
Bigio v Coca-Cola	Appeal against dismissal	239 F 3d 440 (2d Cir 2000)	US Court of Appeals for the Second Circuit	Former Egyptian nationals sued Coke for role in nationalisation of property in 1960s. Act of state doctrine not applied. ATCA not activated as no evidence of corporate complicity with State actor. Case remitted to District Court regarding possible exercise of diversity jurisdiction.
Bodner v Banque Paribas	Motion to dismiss	114 F Supp 2d 117 (EDNY 2000)	US District Court for the Eastern District of New York	Holocaust survivors sued French bank for war crimes. Jurisdiction under ATCA and § 1331 affirmed; motion to dismiss denied. Case eventually settled.
Bouzari v Islamic Republic of Iran	Merits decision	[2002] Carswell Ont 1469	Ontario Superior Court of Justice	Iranian plaintiff sued Iran, including Iranian government company, for torture allegedly carried out by state agents in connection with operations of the state-owned oil company. State immunity held to apply as impugned actions were not commercial in nature. In obiter, the court suggested that jurisdiction and FNC threshold might be different for torture cases.
Bowoto v Chevron Texaco	Motion to dismiss	2004 US Dist LEXIS 4603 (ND, Cal 2004)		Motion to dismiss denied. Held that there was enough evidence for a jury to hold Chevron liable for the acts of its Nigerian subsidiary. ATCA and RICO claims allowed to proceed.
Bowoto v Chevron	Motion to dismiss	Case No 99-2506, unreported (ND Cal 2000)	US District Court for the Northern District of California	Chevron sued for gross human rights breaches in Nigeria under ATCA. Motion to dismiss on FNC grounds denied.
Bowoto et al v Chevron	Filed	Case No CGC-03-417580 (Cal 2003)	Superior Court of California	Case launched against Chevron for allegedly making false and misleading statements regarding its involvement in human rights abuses in Nigeria.

Appendix: Table of Selected Cases 159

Bridgeway Corp v Citibank	Appeal against refusal of summary judgment	201 F 3d 134 (2d Cir 2000)	US Court of Appeals for the Second Circuit	CA held courts may use US State Department human rights reports to determine whether an alternative forum is too corrupt to be adequate. Case concerned the enforcement of a judgment of the Supreme Court of Liberia.
Burger-Fischer v Degussa AG	Merits decision	65 F Supp 2d 248 (DNJ 1999)	US District Court for the District of New Jersey	Defendant charged with various war crimes in World War II. Case dismissed under 'political question' doctrine.
Burnett v Al Baraka Investment and Development Corporation	Motion to dismiss	274 F Supp 2d 86 (DDC 2003)	US District Court for the District of Columbia	Saudi bank sued for allegedly providing funds to 'September 11' hijackers. Motion to dismiss was granted for failure to state a claim against some defendants. For other defendants the court found other statements of plaintiffs' claims were needed before they would be required to answer the complaint or respond to discovery.
Buttes Gas v Hammer	Appeal against dismissal	[1981] 3 All ER 616 (HL)	House of Lords	Seminal British case on the doctrine of non-justiciability, the UK version of the 'political question' doctrine.
Carlson v Rio Tinto	Merits decision	[1999] CLC 551 (QB)	Queens Bench	Case followed *Connelly v RTZ* (see below).
Connelly v RTZ Corporation plc	Appeal against stay	[1996] QB 361 (CA)	UK Court of Appeal	English parent company sued regarding injuries in uranium mine operated by Namibian subsidiary. Court dismissed appeal on the grounds that provision of legal aid was not a factor to be taken into account when considering whether to stay proceedings on FNC grounds.
Connelly v RTZ Corporation plc	Appeal against stay	[1998] AC 854 (HL)	House of Lords	Appeal against grant of stay on FNC grounds allowed.
Connelly v RTZ Corporation plc	Motion to dismiss	(1998) Unreported; transcript available via LEXIS	Queens Bench	Case dismissed on statute of limitation grounds.

160 Appendix: Table of Selected Cases

Case name	Stage	Reference	Jurisdiction	Synopsis
CSR Ltd v Wren	Appeal against decision of negligence	(1997) 44 NSWLR 463 (CA NSW)	New South Wales Court of Appeal	Employee of CSR subsidiary sued CSR for asbestos-related injuries. CSR held liable for injuries. Held that, on the facts, CSR owed a duty to ensure subsidiary's operations were not dangerous.
Dagi v BHP	Preliminary hearing	[1995] 1 VR 428	Supreme Court of Victoria	BHP sued in tort for polluting Ok Tedi River and adjacent land, thus prejudicing the plaintiffs' enjoyment of that land and waters. Motion to dismiss denied. Parties settled.
Delgado v Shell Oil	Motion to dismiss	890 F Supp 1324 (SD Tex 1995)	US District Court for the Southern District of Texas	Tort claim by Latin American workers for exposure to DBCP. Case dismissed for FNC.
Deutsch v Turner Corp	Appeal against dismissal	324 F 3d 692 (9th Cir 2003)	US Court of Appeals for the Ninth Circuit	A California statute exceeded California's power to engage in foreign affairs because it intruded on the federal government's exclusive power to make and resolve war, including the procedure for resolving war claims.
Doe v Exxon Mobil	Filed	Docket No 01-1357 CIV (DDC 2002)	US District Court for the District of Columbia	Company sued for complicity in gross human rights abuses in Aceh, Indonesia. State Department has suggested that litigation prejudices US foreign policy interests. Decision pending.
Doe v The Gap et al	Motion to dismiss	No CV-01-0031, 2001 WL 1842389 (CD Cal 2001)	US District Court for the Central District of California	Claim against retailer and manufacturer for violation of labour rights. ATCA claim dismissed. RICO claims accepted for preliminary purposes. Case settled against all defendants except Levis.
Doe v Unocal (Unocal 1997)	Motion to dismiss	963 F Supp 880 (CD Cal 1997)	US District Court for the Central District of California	Myanmar nationals sued oil company for gross human rights violations. Jurisdiction under ATCA affirmed; motion to dismiss predominantly denied. First case to decide that ATCA can apply to corporations.

Appendix: Table of Selected Cases 161

Doe v Unocal (Unocal 1998)	Motion to dismiss re Total	27 F Supp 2d 1174 (CD Cal 1998) (aff'd 248 F 3d 915 2001)	US District Court for the Central District of California (aff'd US Court of Appeal)	Court denies personal jurisdiction over Unocal's partner, Total, so ATCA complaint against Total dismissed.
Doe v Unocal (Unocal 2000)	Motion to dismiss	110 F Supp 2d 1294 (CD Cal 2000)	US District Court for the Central District of California	ATCA claims against Unocal dismissed due to failure to plead sufficient complicity in alleged abuses by Unocal.
Doe v Unocal (Unocal 2002)	Appeal against dismissal of complaint re Unocal	2002 US App LEXIS 19263 (9th Cir 2002)	US Court of Appeals for the Ninth Circuit	Held that plaintiffs had sufficiently alleged corporate complicity by Unocal in breaches of the law of nations by the Myanmar government. Case overturned decision of Lew J in *Unocal 2000*. RICO claims dismissed.
Doe v Unocal	Application for re-hearing	2003 WL 359787 (9th Cir 14 Feb 2003)	US Court of Appeals for the Ninth Circuit	Unocal 2002 vacated, and appeal to banc panel now pending. Defendants have argued that the *Filartiga* interpretation of ATCA is too broad.
Doe v Unocal	Preliminary hearing	Unreported. Some decisions available via www.earthrights.org	Superior Court of California, County of Los Angeles	Tort claims proceeding against Unocal under State jurisdiction for alleged gross human rights abuses in Myanmar.
Dow Chemicals Co v Castro Alfaro	Motion to dismiss	786 SW 2d 674 (SCt Texas1990)	Texas Supreme Court	Early case in DBCP litigation. Costa Rican workers sued American chemical company for sterility and medical problems from exposure to pesticide banned in USA. Motion to dismiss denied on the basis that Texas had abolished FNC by statute. Case subsequently settled.

162 *Appendix: Table of Selected Cases*

Case name	Stage	Reference	Jurisdiction	Synopsis
Estate of Rodriguez v Drummond Co	Motion to dismiss	265 F Supp 2d 1250 (ND Al 2003)	USA district court for the Northern District of Alabama	Company accused under ATCA and TVPA of collusion in the killing of trade union leaders by paramilitaries at their mining facilities. ATCA claims permitted to proceed. Decided that TVPA claims could lie against corporations.
Eastman Kodak Co v Kavlin	Motion to dismiss	978 F Supp 1078 (SD Fla 1997)	US District Court for the Southern District of Florida	Plaintiff, an American company, sued Bolivian company regarding its business practices and also under ATCA for imprisoning its agent in alleged extortion scheme. Dismissal on FNC grounds denied because defendant failed to show alternative forum was adequate. Jurisdiction under ATCA affirmed; motion to dismiss denied.
Filartiga v Peña-Irala	Appeal against dismissal	630 F 2d 876 (2d Cir 1980)	US Court of Appeals for the Second Circuit	Seminal ATCA case. Paraguayan police inspector-general successfully sued for murder and torture of plaintiffs' relative.
Flores v Southern Peru Copper	Motion to dismiss	253 F Supp 2d 510 (SDNY 2002)	US District Court for the Southern District of New York	Peruvian nationals sued American mining company for violation of rights to life, health and sustainable development under ATCA. Claims found to fall outside the law of nations. Court also dismissed case for FNC.
Flores v Southern Peru Copper	Appeal against dismissal	343 F 3d 140 (2d Cir 2003)	US Court of Appeals for the Second Circuit	Upheld District Court decision.
Forti v Suarez-Mason	Motion to dismiss	672 F Supp 1531 (ND Cal 1987)	US District Court for the Northern District of California	Claim by Argentines against former General for human rights abuses by forces under his control. Court refused motion to dismiss. Source of three-pronged test for determining whether a human rights breach contravenes the law of nations.

Appendix: Table of Selected Cases 163

Case	Action	Citation	Court	Notes
Gagarimabu v The Broken Hill Proprietary Company Ltd	Application for anti-suit injunction	[2001] VSC 517 unreported) (SCt Vic)	Supreme Court of Victoria	The Ok Tedi issue returns to Victorian courts due to alleged reach by BHP of settlement reached in *Dagi* (see above).
Ge v Peng	Motion to dismiss	201 F Supp 2d 14 (DDC 2000) (aff'd in unreported decision)	US District Court for the District of Columbia (now aff'd US Court of Appeal)	ATCA case concerning forced labour in China. Case dismissed on the basis of insufficient evidence linking defendant company to the forced labour camps; other claims dismissed for sovereign immunity.
Gulf Oil v Gilbert	Motion to dismiss	330 US 501 (SCt 1947)	US Supreme Court	Seminal US case on *forum non conveniens*.
In re Holocaust Victim Assets Litigation	Application for settlement	105 F Supp 2d 139 (EDNY 2000)	US District Court for the Eastern District of New York	Case concerned several claims against Swiss banks regarding the assets of Holocaust victims. Court approved final settlement.
In re Union Carbide Corp Gas Plant Disaster at Bhopal	Motion to dismiss	634 F Supp 842	US District Court for the Southern District of New York (aff'd US Court of Appeals for the Second Circuit)	Seminal mass tort litigation arising out of the 1984 Bhopal industrial disaster. Case dismissed for FNC, as India found to be more appropriate forum.
In re Union Carbide Corp Gas Plant Disaster at Bhopal	Appeal against dismissal	809 F 2d 195 (2d Cir 1987)	US Court of Appeals for the Second Circuit	Affirmed District Court decision. However, appeal court did alleviate some of the conditions imposed by lower court on the defendant.
International Shoe Co v State of Washington	Appeal from judgment	326 US 310 (SCt 1945)	US Supreme Court	Seminal US case on personal jurisdiction.

164 *Appendix: Table of Selected Cases*

Case name	Stage	Reference	Jurisdiction	Synopsis
Iwanowa v Ford Motor Co	Motion to dismiss	67 F Supp 2d 424 (DNJ 1999)	US District Court for the District of New Jersey	ATCA case against company for collusion in forced labour during World War II dismissed for act of state.
Jota v Texaco Inc	Appeal against dismissal of complaint (see *Aguinda*)	157 F 3d 153 (2d Cir 1998)	US Court of Appeals for the Second Circuit	Appeal against dismissal on FNC grounds allowed because submission to alternative forum required. Remitted to district court.
Kadic v Karadzic	Appeal against dismissal	70 F 3d 232 (2d Cir 1995)	US Court of Appeals for the Second Circuit	Claim against de facto Bosnian Serb government officials for atrocities during Yugoslavian conflict. Held ATCA can apply to members of de facto but unrecognised governments, and to private bodies.
Kasky v Nike	Appeal against dismissal of complaint	24 Cal 4th 939 (SCt Cal 2002)	Supreme Court of California	Plaintiff sued Nike for making false and misleading claims regarding its labour practices. Court held Nike's claims were commercial speech and therefore could be regulated consistently with the US Constitution. Case eventually settled.
Kasky v Nike	Application for certiorari	123 SCt 2554 (SCt US 2003)	US Supreme Court	Majority in Supreme Court decided it did not have jurisdiction to hear an appeal at this preliminary stage of the litigation.
Khulumani et al v Barclays National Bank et al	Filed	Case CV 25952 (EDNY 2002)	US District Court of the Eastern District of New York	ATCA case launched against a number of companies for complicity in human rights abuses under the apartheid regime in South Africa.

Appendix: Table of Selected Cases 165

Case	Action	Citation	Court	Summary
Lubbe v Cape plc	Appeal against stay	[2000] 1 Lloyd's Rep 139 (CA)	UK Court of Appeal	South African nationals sued English parent of mining company for asbestos-related injuries. Appeal against FNC dismissed, South Africa was found by the court to be an appropriate forum for proceedings.
Lubbe v Cape plc	Appeal against refusal and grant of stay	[2000] 4 All ER 268 (HL)	House of Lords	Appeal against stay for FNC granted, as court found that justice could not be achieved in alternative forum.
MC Mehta v Union of India	Application for mandamus	AIR 1987 SC 975	Supreme Court of India	Court endorses principal of enterprise liability when the enterprise is involved in inherently dangerous activities.
Martinez v Dow Chemical Co	Motion to dismiss	219 F Supp 2d 719 (ED La 2002)	US District Court for the Eastern District of Louisiana	Costa Rican, Honduran and Filipino workers sued chemical company for producing chemical for banana farms causing sterility. No available, adequate alternative forum, so FNC motion denied.
Nat'l Coalition Gov't of the Union of Burma v Unocal, Inc	Motion to dismiss	176 FRD 329 (CD Cal 1997)	US District Court for the Central District of California	ATCA claims by a trade union and a government in exile dismissed for lack of standing. Some remaining claims dismissed for act of state.
Ngcobo v Thor and Sithole v Thor	Motion to dismiss	Unreported	Queens Bench	Case against company not dismissed for FNC. Court seemed to accept that the alleged tort arose in England, as the complaints targeted the decisions made at corporate headquarters regarding work practices by subsidiaries in Southern Africa.
Owusu v Jackson	Appeal against dismissal	[2002] IL Pr 45 (CA)	UK Court of Appeal	Case referred to ECJ to decide if the UK can dismiss cases for FNC when the alternative forum is a non-EU nation. ECJ decision pending.

166 Appendix: Table of Selected Cases

Case name	Stage	Reference	Jurisdiction	Synopsis
Propend Finance Pty v Alan Sing and the Commissioner of the Australian Federal Police	Appeal against dismissal	[1997] TLR 238	UK Court of Appeal	Case confirmed apparent broad scope of sovereign immunity in the UK.
Presbyerian Church of Sudan v Talisman Energy	Motion to dismiss	244 F Supp 2d 289 (SDNY 2003)	US District Court for the Southern District of New York	Oil company alleged to have collaborated in gross human rights abuses in Sudan. Defendant's motion to dismiss ATCA claim for FNC denied.
Prosecutor v Furundzija	Merits decision	(Case No IT-95-17/1-T), Judgment, 10 December 1998	International Criminal Tribunal for the former Yugoslavia	Source of test of 'aiding and abetting' used by the majority in *Unocal 2002*.
Regie Nationale des Usines Renault SA v Zhang	Appeal against stay	210 CLR 491 (HCA)	High Court of Australia	Medical treatment in NSW held to be sufficient connection for case to proceed against French defendant with no presence in jurisdiction. No stay for FNC granted. Also seemed to affirm that choice of law in Australia will always be that of the site of the tort.
Recherches Internationales Quebec v Cambior Inc	Merits decision	[1998] QJ No 2554, Quebec Super Ct, 14 August 1998	Quebec Superior Court	Tort case against Quebec company regarding alleged environmental harms in Guyana dismissed for FNC.
Roe v Unocal Corp	Motion to dismiss	70 F Supp 2d 14 (CD Cal 1999)	US District Court for the Central District of California	ATCA case in which forced conscript labour found not to breach the law of nations. Case also dismissed for act of state.

Appendix: Table of Selected Cases 167

Sarei v Rio Tinto Plc	Motion to dismiss	221 F Supp 2d 1116 (CD Cal 2002)	US District Court or the Central District of California	Defendant sued for collusion in gross human rights abuses in Bougainville, PNG. Motion to dismiss for lack of jurisdiction and FNC denied, but dismissed on the grounds of act of state, political question doctrine. US government submitted a brief arguing in favour of dismissal.
Sequihua v Texaco	Motion to dismiss	847 F Supp 61 (SD Texas 1994)	US District Court for the Southern District of Texas	Ecuadorians sued Texaco for contamination of oil, water and land. Dismissed for FNC because Ecuador deemed a more appropriate forum.
Sinaltrainal v Coca-Cola Co	Motion to dismiss	256 F Supp 2d 1345 (SD Fla 2003)	US District Court for the Southern District of Florida	Court lacked jurisdiction over claims against company under ATCA for acts of paramilitaries as well as its licensed bottlers because complicity could not be established. Actions against individuals in bottling plant permitted to continue.
Sosa v Alvarez-Machain	Application for certiorari	2003 US LEXIS 8572 (SCt 2003)	US Supreme Court	US Supreme Court agrees to hear a petition for certiorari, including arguments that ATCA is merely jurisdictional, or unconstitutional. Decision pending in mid-2004.
Tel-Oren v Libyan Arab Republic	Appeal against dismissal	726 F 2d 774 (DC Cir 1984)	US Court of Appeals for the District of Columbia	Early ATCA case, resulting in split DC Circuit Court. Bork J advocated a very narrow interpretation of ATCA. Terrorism found not to breach the 'law of nations'.
The Amoco Cadiz	Merits decision	[1984] 2 Lloyds Law Reports 304, (ND Ill 1984)	US District Court for the Northern District of Illinois	Case concerned an oil spill off French coast. Court held that parent company exercised such dominant control over subsidiaries that owned the ship that it was liable for its own negligence in failing to adequately maintain the vessel.

168 *Appendix: Table of Selected Cases*

Case name	Stage	Reference	Jurisdiction	Synopsis
The Paquete Habana	Appeal against judgement	175 US 677 (SCt 1900)	US Supreme Court	Case established that customary international law is incorporated into US law, unless overridden by statute.
Tolofson v Jensen	Appeal against lower court decision on 'choice of law'	[1994] 3 SCR 1022 (SCt Canada)	Supreme Court of Canada	Major Canadian case on choice of law, though it may not have effect in international conflicts of laws cases.
Torres v Southern Peru Copper	Motion to dismiss	965 F Supp 899 (SD Tex)	US District Court of the Southern District of Texas	Peruvian citizens sued Peruvian mine operators for air, water and ground pollution. Dismissed for FNC because Peru found to be a more appropriate forum.
Trendtex Trading Corp v Central Bank of Nigeria	Appeal against stay	[1977] 2 WLR 356 (CA)	UK Court of Appeal	Case confirms that customary international law is automatically incorporated into UK law.
Voth v Manildra Flour Mills	Appeal on application for stay	(1990) 171 CLR 538 (HCA)	High Court of Australia	Leading Australian FNC case; affirmed the 'clearly inappropriate' test, which is more liberal to plaintiffs than the tests in the USA and UK.
Wilson v Servier Canada	Motion for stay and certification application	50 OR (3d) 219 (SCJ Ont 2000)	Ontario Superior Court of Justice	Canadian case follows House of Lords decision in *Lubbe* on FNC. FNC motion denied in products liability case.
Wiwa v Royal Dutch Petroleum Co	Motion to dismiss	No 96 Civ 8386, 1998 US Dist LEXIS 23064 (SDNY 25 Sept 1998)	US District Court for the Southern District of New York	ATCA claim against oil company for complicity in gross human rights abuses. Case dismissed for FNC.

Wiwa v Royal Dutch Petroleum (Wiwa 2000)	Appeal against dismissal of complaint	226 F 3d 88 (2d Cir 2000)	US Court of Appeals for the Second Circuit	Appeal against FNC dismissal allowed. Plaintiff's choice of forum and US public interest in adjudicating on human rights abuse not given sufficient weight at first instance.
Wiwa v Royal Dutch Petroleum (Wiwa 2002)	Motion to dismiss	No 96 Civ 8386, 2002 US Dist LEXIS 3293 (SDNY 2002 unreported)	US District Court for the Southern District of New York	Claim against oil company for serious human rights abuses came within ATCA and RICO. Motion to dismiss largely denied.
Xuncax v Gramajo	Judgment in default	886 F Supp 162 (D Mass 1995)	US District Court for the District of Massachusetts	Guatemalan defence minister sued under ATCA for torture of plaintiff. Court held that cruel and inhuman treatment could come within ATCA. Held §1331 did not confer rights to sue.

Index

abduction, 28, 59
accountability:
  informal accountability, 6–7
  legal accountability, 8–13
  self-regulation, 7–8
acts of state, 40–4, 46, 121, 146
Adidas, 50
agency, 36, 69, 87, 114, 133
aiding and abetting, 38–9, 48–9, 51, 53, 71, 133
aircraft hijacking, 27, 48
Alien Tort Claims Act:
  and § 1331 claims, 78
  aiding and abetting, 38–9, 48–9, 51, 53
  Apartheid, 50–3
  appeals, 59
  and Australia, 89
  and Bush administration, 41, 55, 60, 146
  choice of law, 54–5
  and comity, 46–8, 146
  constitutional validity, 18, 21, 58, 59, 146
  corporate complicity, 50–3
  defusing, potential 61
  dynamic area, 48
  egregious human rights breaches, 21, 145
  Filigarta precedent, 21–2, 55–60
  and *forum non conveniens* 88, 92–4, 147
  future, 55–61
  history, 21–2
  international treaty requirement, 53–4
  justiciability, 44–7
  'law of nations,' 22–33, 52, 53, 145–6
  and ordinary tort litigation, 66
  perpetrators and commanders, 22
  political issues, 44–7, 146
  potential amendments, 60, 146
  private actor abuses, 22, 48–9, 50
  scope, 145–6
  state action requirement *see* state actions
  subject matter jurisdiction, 10, 18, 21, 22–33
  trade with dictatorships, 53
  and TVPA litigation 61–3
  universal crimes, 48–9
Allende, Salvador, 3
amnesty laws, 120
Apartheid, 50–3
Apparel Industry Partnership, 8
appeals, ATCA, 59
arbitrary arrest, 26
arbitrary detention, 25, 26, 59
Argentina, 62, 140

asbestos, 117, 134
assault and battery, 65
Australia:
  adequacy of forum, 89
  choice of law, 124–5
  corporate veil, 131
  extraterritorial human rights jurisdiction, 151
  Fairwear Campaign, 8
  forum non conveniens, 123–4, 147–8
  freedom of speech, 105–6
  Trade Practices Act 106
  transnational litigation, 19, 122–5

Barclays, 50–3
battery, tort of, 68
Belgium, universal jurisdiction, 13–14
Bhopal:
  cost cutting decisions, 75–6
  and *forum non conveniens,* 72, 90, 97, 148, 149
  and human rights issues, 76
  parent company liability, 134, 140–1
  scale of disaster, 2
  and US public interest, 92
Blumberg, PI, 98
Bolivia, 35
Bork, Robert, 58
BP, in Colombia, 4
bribery, 3
Brilmayer, L, 44–5
Brussels Convention on Jurisdiction, 119
Bush administration, 41, 55, 60, 146

Californian law:
  choice of law, 75
  Nike case, 19, 101–11
  personal jurisdiction, 85
  'private attorneys general,' 101
  proportionality, 108
Canada:
  and ATCA, 90
  adequacy of forum, 90
  choice of law, 127
  class actions, 90, 127
  extraterritorial jurisdiction, 125–6
  forum non conveniens, 126–7
  transnational litigation, 19, 125–7
Carter administration, 59
Chevron, in Nigeria, 3, 62, 92, 105, 132–3

Chile, 3, 53
China, 50
choice of law:
  ATCA litigation, 54–5
  Australia, 124–5
  Canada, 127
  England, 119–20
  US tort claims, 66, 74–6
civil actions:
  ATCA *see* Alien Tort Claims Act
  human rights litigation against TNCs, 14–15
  TVPA *see* Torture Victim Protection Act
civil law systems, 15–16, 96, 152
class actions, 17, 90, 98, 117, 127
Clinton administration, 59
Coca Cola:
  ATCA suit, 22
  NGO campaigns, 6
  operations in Columbia, 4, 142–3
  operations in Egypt, 50
  TVPA litigation, 61
codes of conduct, 6–8
collusion, 3, 5
Colombia, 4, 62, 142–3
comity, 46–8, 146
common law systems, 15–16
competition, and human rights, 12–13, 152
consumer boycotts, 6
consumer protection, 106, 107
contingency fees, 16, 90
Convention on Elimination of Discrimination against Women, 9
Convention on Rights of the Child, 25
conversion, 28
corporate veil, 5, 20, 129–32, 136, 138
corruption, 90, 91
Costa Rica, 97
costs, 16, 120
crimes against humanity:
  ATCA litigation, 26–7, 38–9, 40–1, 47
  acts of state, 40–1
  aiding and abetting, 38–9
  and comity, 47
  and TNC practices, 3
  universal crimes, 9, 48
criminal proceedings against TNCs, 13–14
cruel inhuman and degrading treatment, 25, 26, 30, 31, 48
customary international law:
  ATCA litigation, 25–33, 145
  Australian jurisdiction, 123, 146
  Canadian jurisdiction, 125, 127, 146
  English jurisdiction, 115, 146
  jus cogens, 23, 94, 126
  meaning, 23
  opinio juris, 23, 24, 31
  scope, 23–4

UNGA resolutions, 52
  and US federal jurisdiction, 77–8

damages, US levels, 17
degrading treatment, 25, 26, 30, 31, 48
Del Monte, in Guatemala, 4
developing nations:
  judicial imperialism, 12, 148
  lax regulation, 76
  legal aid, 5, 116–17, 118
  legal systems, 5, 11
  remedies, 5–6
  TNC abuses, 4–5, 153
  TNC race to the bottom, 150
dictatorships, 53
disappearances, 25, 26
discovery of documents, 5, 17
discrimination, freedom from, 27

Earthrights, 60
Eastman Kodak, 35, 91
economic globalisation, 150
Ecuador, 29, 72, 91, 95, 97, 98
Egypt, 41, 50
energy corporations, 3
England *see* United Kingdom
Enron, 4
environmental damage:
  ATCA litigation, 27, 28, 29, 30, 47, 48
  mining, 3, 124, 127
  parent company liability, 134, 135
  Shell *see* Shell
  transborder pollution, 29
Ethical Trading Initiative, 8
European Convention on Human Rights, 109, 118
European Union, 106, 119
exhaustion of domestic remedies, 62–3
exile, constructive exile, 28
expropriations, 28, 50
extra-judicial killings, 3, 61–3, 146
extraterritorial jurisdiction:
  ATCA, 57, 58
  Canada, 125–6
  crimes by nationals abroad, 11–12
  criminal liability, 13–14
  judicial imperialism, 12, 148, 150
  legislation, 151
  over English companies, 113–14
  over non-governmental entities, 12–13
  racketeering, 79
Exxon Mobil, 3, 22, 42–3, 46, 55–6, 62, 146

Fair Labor Association, 104–5
fair trial, and *forum non conveniens*, 118
Fairwear Campaign, 8
false imprisonment, 68

Index

false statements:
  Californian law, 101
  European Union, 106
  strict liability, 101, 105, 108
food, right to, 2
forced displacement, 26
forced exile, 26
forced labour, 4, 26, 45, 48, 49, 152
forced prison labour, 28
forced relocation, 26
Forcese, C, 3
forum non conveniens:
  ATCA litigation, 19, 88, 90–92, 147
  adequate alternative forum, 89–92, 98, 118
  Australia, 123–4, 147–8
  Bhopal action, 72, 90, 97, 148, 149
  and Brussels Convention on Jurisdiction, 119
  Canada, 126–7
  and civil law systems, 96
  conditional dismissals, 97–8
  deference to plaintiffs' choice, 88–9, 93
  England, 115–19, 147
  and legal aid, 116–17, 118
  parallel proceedings, 149
  and public interest, 92–4
  raising issue, 87
  retaliatory legislation, 96–7, 98
  and right to fair trial, 118
  Texas, 73
  TVPA litigation, 88, 90
  two-step test, 88
  US litigation, 66, 73, 87–99
  weighing respective private interests, 94–6
forum shopping, 150
France, 41, 109–10, 127, 152
franchise agreements, 143
fraud, 28
freedom of association, 27, 30, 48, 51
freedom of speech, 27, 30, 102–5, 107–9
freedom of thought, 27, 30
Freeport McMoran, 3–4, 22, 28, 34, 61, 87

genocide:
  ATCA litigation, 25, 26, 38, 47
  aiding and abetting, 38
  and comity, 47
  cultural genocide, 27
  Sudan, 44, 47, 91
  and TNC practices, 3, 13
  universal crime, 9, 48, 115
Germany, Nazi slave labour, 45
global ambulance chasing, 17
Global Reporting Initiative, 7
globalisation, 150
Guatemala, 4
Guyana, 126–7

hazardous products, marketing, 2
health and safety, 2, 116, 117
health, right to, 2, 27, 29
Honduras, 97
human rights:
  abuses as ordinary torts, 65
  artificial persons, 109
  and Bush administration, 41, 55, 60, 146
  international law *see* international human rights law
  international minimum standards, 153–4
  jurisdiction *see* extraterritorial jurisdiction; jurisdiction
  and 'law of nations,' 22–33, 52, 53, 78, 145–6
  litigation *see* transnational litigation
  social and economic rights, 32
  TNC abuses, 2–4
  treaties, 53–4, 76
  and US tort actions, 76–7

ILO, 10, 32
imperialism, judicial imperialism, 12, 148, 150
India:
  Bhopal disaster *see* Bhopal
  Enron practices, 4
  and *forum non conveniens,* 90, 97, 148, 149
  parent company liability, 141
Indonesia:
  Exxon Mobil operations, 3, 42–3, 46
  Freeport McMoran operations, 3–4, 28, 34
  human rights abuses, 150
  and TVPA litigation, 62
inhuman treatment, 25, 26, 30, 31, 48
Institute for Policy Studies, 1
International Covenant on Civil and Political Rights (ICCPR), 27, 54, 107, 109
International Covenant on Economic Social and Cultural Rights (ICESCR), 32
international human rights law:
  generally, 8–11
  treaties, 53–4, 76
  Universal Declaration of Human Rights, 8–9, 26
  US approach to sources, 57
investment:
  and ATCA, 56
  and Apartheid, 51–2
  badly governed countries, 52, 53
  socially responsible investment, 7, 107
  and transnational litigation, 151
Iran, torture, 126, 127
ITT, 3

joint ventures, 41
judicial imperialism, 12, 148, 150
jurisdiction:
  ATCA *see* Alien Tort Claims Act

174 Index

jurisdiction (*cont*):
   extraterritorial *see* extraterritorial jurisdiction
   forum non conveniens see forum non conveniens
   personal jurisdiction, 83–7, 147
   TVPA *see* Torture Victim Protection Act
   universal crimes, 9, 48–9
   US tort claims, 19, 65–77, 146
jus cogens, 23, 94, 126

killings, extra-judicial killings, 3, 61–3, 146

labour rights, 2, 32, 101
Latin America, *forum non conveniens*, 96
'law of nations,' 22–33, 52, 53, 78, 145–6
Lawyers' Committee for Human Rights, 60
legal aid, 5, 116–17, 118
legal costs, 16, 120
legal globalisation, 150
legal personality, TNCs, 79
legislation, municipal legislation, 11–12
liberty, right to, 27
life, right to, 2, 27, 29
limitation of actions, 62, 97
limited liability doctrine, 131, 138–9
litigation *see* transnational litigation

marketing policies, 2, 3
McCorquodale, R, 7
McDonalds, 6
Meeran, Richard, 139–40
Mercedes-Benz, 62
militarised commerce, 3, 4, 5, 13
mining, 3, 51, 116, 124, 127
minority rights, 2
multinationals *see* transnational corporations
municipal legislation, 11–12
murder, 13, 25, 49
Myanmar:
   energy companies in, 4
   forced labour, 4, 49, 152
   human rights abuses, 150
   Total, 4, 14, 69, 85, 152
   trade with dictatorship, 53
   and TVPA litigation, 62
   Unocal operations, 22, 35–8, 48–9, 50, 68–71, 80, 85, 137–8
   Yadana pipeline, 22, 35–8, 69, 80, 85

Namibia:
   English mining, 116
national legislation, and TNCs, 11–12
negligence, 28, 65, 67–8, 70
Nestlé, 2n12, 6
NGOs, 6, 10
Nicaragua, 149–50
Nigeria:
   acts of state, 41
   Chevron operations, 62, 92, 105, 132–3
   collusion in human rights abuses, 3
   and *forum non conveniens*, 89, 95
   Pfizer operations, 35
   Shell *see* Shell
Nike case:
   assessment, 106–11
   Californian law, 19, 101
   corporate freedom of expression, 102–4, 107–9
   and corporate information, 109–11
   description, 101–5
   false statements, 101
   generally, 19, 101–11
   improving human rights debate, 111
   labour practices, 101
   multinational economic network, 142
   NGO campaigns, 6
   proportionality, 108
Nuremberg Tribunal, 48

opinio juris, 23, 24, 31

Papua New Guinea:
   Australian mining, 124
   civil war, 95
   human rights abuses, 150
   Rio Tinto operations *see* Rio Tinto
paramilitary forces, 3
parent company liability:
   agency, 133
   aiding and abetting, 133
   contractual relationships, 142–3
   corporate veil, 5, 20, 129–32, 136, 138, 139
   direct parent liability, 134–8
   English extraterritorial jurisdiction, 114
   enterprise liability, 139–42
   for subsidiaries, 67, 69, 72, 129–43
   generally, 20
   joint liability, 132–3
   limited liability doctrine, 131, 138–9
   multinational economic networks, 142–3
   multinational group liability, 138–42
   and personal jurisdiction, 84–6
   ratification, 133
personal jurisdiction:
   agency, 87
   parent companies and subsidiaries, 84–6
   substantial business dealings, 83–4
   United States, 83–7, 147
Peru, 94
pesticide cases, 72–3, 76, 88, 97, 98, 151
Pfizer, 22, 35
Philippines, 97
Pinochet, Augusto, 53
piracy, 9, 48
political question doctrine, 44–7

product liability, 73–4, 127
proportionality, 108
protectionism, 12–13
protests, informal accountability, 6–7
public interest, and *forum non conveniens*, 92–4
public opinion, mobilising, 6–7

race discrimination, 25, 27, 47, 48, 51
Racketeer Influenced and Corrupt Organisations litigation, 18–19, 78–81, 146
rape, 48, 49
Reagan administration, 59
recklessness, 67, 71, 138
Rio Tinto:
  and ATCA, 55–6, 146
  and *forum non conveniens*, 89, 94, 95, 98
  Papua New Guinea operations, 4, 28–9, 35, 40–1, 41–2, 43, 44, 45–6, 47, 124
  parent company liability, 135–6
  TVPA litigation, 62
Rwanda tribunal, 9, 48

Seattle, Battle of, 6
security forces, TNC use of, 3
security, right to personal security, 27, 29
self-determination, right to, 2
self-regulation, 6, 7–8
separation of powers, 40
sexual assault, 26
shareholder revolts, 6
Shell:
  ATCA suits, 22, 30
  and *forum non conveniens*, 91, 92–5, 98, 99
  NGO campaigns, 6
  Nigerian operations, 2, 3, 30, 62, 79–80, 85, 92–3
  and personal jurisdiction, 85–7
  pesticide cases, 72–3, 97
  RICO litigation, 79–80
slave labour, Nazi Germany, 45
slavery, 13, 25, 26, 48
social and economic rights, 32
soft law, 10–11
South Africa, 50–3, 110, 117
sovereign immunity, 39–40, 121, 128, 150
state actions:
  ATCA requirement, 18, 33–44
  acts of state, 40–4, 46, 121, 146
  aiding and abetting, 38–9, 48–9, 51
  corporate complicity, 50–3
  English jurisdiction, 115
  and *forum non conveniens*, 90–92
  government authority to private crimes, 33
  international precedents, 37–9
  joint liability, 35–7, 49, 145–6
  joint ventures, 41
  justiciability, 44–7
  political issues, 44–7
  public function liability, 33
  and sovereign immunity, 39–40, 121, 128, 150
  state compulsion, 33–4
  TVPA litigation, 62
state sovereignty, 28
states, actors of international law, 9
subsidiaries *see* parent company liability
  liability of parent companies, 20, 67, 69, 72, 129–43
  and personal jurisdiction, 84–6
Sudan:
  adequacy of forum, 90, 91
  genocide, 44, 47, 91
  human rights abuses, 44, 91
  Talisman operations, 3, 38, 43–4, 46, 47, 90–1
  and TVPA litigation, 62
summary executions, 48
sustainable development, 27

Talisman:
  and *forum non conveniens*, 90, 94, 96
  and personal jurisdiction in US, 86
  Sudan operations, 3, 38, 43–4, 46, 47, 90–1
  and TVPA litigation, 62
terrorism, 27, 43, 44, 55–6
Texaco, 29, 72, 91, 97, 98, 134
tobacco marketing, 3
Tokyo Tribunal, 48
torts:
  acting in concert, 67, 69
  aiding and abetting, 71
  alien torts *see* Alien Torts Claims Act
  assault and battery, 65, 68
  or ATCA litigation, 66, 146
  choice of law, 66, 74–6
  commercial torts, 28
  Doe v Unocal, 68–71
  false imprisonment, 68
  forum non conveniens, 66, 73
  human rights abuses, 65
  joint liability, 67
  negligence, 65, 67, 68
  pesticide use, 72–3
  principles, 67–8
  private defenders and human rights issues, 76–7
  product liability, 73–4
  recklessness, 67, 71, 138
  Union Carbide, 72
  US case law, 72–4
  US jurisdiction, 19, 65–77, 146
  vicarious liability, 67, 69–70
  wrongful death, 65, 68, 73

torture:
　ATCA litigation, 21, 48
　English extraterritorial jurisdiction, 114
　and *forum non conveniens*, 98
　Iran, 126, 127
　meaning, 62
　Sudan, 91
　TNC practices, 3, 13
　TVPA litigation, 61–3, 146
Torture Victim Protection Act:
　and ATCA litigation, 61–3
　exhaustion of domestic remedies, 62–3
　and *forum non conveniens*, 88, 93
　limitation clause, 62
　litigation, 61–3
　state action requirements, 62
　use, 18, 22, 146
Total, 4, 13–14, 69, 85, 152
trade with dictatorships, 53
transnational corporations:
　human rights abuses, 2–4
　informal accountability, 6–7
　international minimum human rights standards, 153–4
　legal accountability, 8–13
　legal personality, 79
　litigation against *see* transnational litigation
　power, 1, 4–5
　racketeering *see* Racketeer Influenced and Corrupt Organisations
　self-regulation, 7–8
　torts *see* Alien Tort Claims Act
　UN Norms, 10, 154
transnational litigation:
　ATCA *see* Alien Tort Claims Act
　Australia, 19, 122–5
　Canada, 19, 125–7
　civil actions, 14–15
　common and civil law systems, 15–16
　criminal actions, 13–14
　forum non conveniens see forum non conveniens
　forum shopping, 150
　generally, 13–20
　increasing trend, 151–3
　or international minimum standards, 153–4
　judicial imperialism, 12, 148, 150
　limits, 153
　new tactics, 152
　personal jurisdiction in US, 83–7
　preliminary issues, 145
　pros and cons, 148–51
　RICO statute, 18–19, 78–81, 146
　TVPA *see* Torture Victims Protection Act
　United Kingdom, 19, 113–22
　United States, 16–19
treaties:
　and ATCA litigation, 53–4

human rights, 76
and sources of US law, 57

UN:
　arms embargo on South Africa, 52
　Code of Conduct on Transnational Corporations, 10
　GA resolutions, 52
　Global Compact, 10
　Norms on Responsibilities of Transnational Corporations, 10, 154
UNCLOS, 25, 30, 47, 48
unfair competition, 152
Union Carbide:
　Bhopal disaster, 2
　cost-cutting, 75–6
　and *forum non conveniens*, 90, 97, 148, 149
　human rights issues, 76
　parent liability, 134, 140–1
　and US public interest, 92
　US tort action against, 72
United Kingdom:
　choice of law, 119–20
　corporate veil, 130, 131
　Ethical Trading Initiative, 8
　extraterritorial human rights jurisdiction, 113–14, 151
　forum non conveniens, 115–19, 147
　legal costs, 120
　pros and cons of transnational litigation, 120–2
　sovereign immunity, 121
　subject matter jurisdiction, 115
　transnational litigation, 19, 113–22
United States:
　28 USC § 1331 jurisdiction, 77–8, 146
　ATCA *see* Alien Tort Claims Act
　Apparel Industry Partnership, 8
　California *see* Californian law
　class actions, 17
　contingency actions, 16
　corporate veil, 130, 131–2
　extraterritorial human rights jurisdiction, 151
　federal law jurisdiction, 77–8
　Foreign Sovereign Immunities Act, 39–40
　forum non conveniens, 87–99
　legal costs, 16
　level of damages, 17
　litigiousness, 17
　National Foreign Trade Council, 60
　personal jurisdiction, 83–7
　plaintiff-friendly forum, 16–20, 90
　procedural hurdles, 19
　Racketeer Influenced and Corrupt Organisations statute, 18–19, 78–81
　tort claims *see* torts
　Torture Victim Protection Act, 18, 22, 61–3

transnational litigation, 16–19
TVPA *see* Torture Victim Protection Act
universal crimes, 9, 48–9
Universal Declaration of Human Rights, 8–9, 26
unjust enrichment, 152
Unocal:
   and ATCA, 56, 59
   California State claim 68–71
   Myanmar operations, 4, 22, 35–8, 48–9, 50, 68–71, 137–8
   personal jurisdiction, 85
   RICO Litigation, 80
   TVPA litigation, 62
USA-Engage, 60

vicarious liability, 67, 69–70

war crimes:
   ATCA litigation, 26, 38, 40–1, 47
   acts of state, 40–1
   aiding and abetting, 38
   and comity, 47
   federal jurisdiction, 78
   Sudan, 91
   and TNC practices, 3
   universal crimes, 9, 48
war on terrorism, 43, 55–6
wrongful death, 65, 68, 73

Yugoslavia tribunal, 9, 38, 48, 49

Zia-Zarifi, S, 85